Everything Worth Preserving

MELISSA K. NORRIS

Legal Disclaimer:

The information provided within this book is for general informational purposes only. While we try to keep the information up-to-date and correct, there are no representations or warranties, express or implied, about the completeness, accuracy, reliability, suitability or availability with respect to the information, products, services, or related graphics contained in this book for any purpose. Any use of the methods described within this book are based on the most recent canning and preservation resources and authorities available at the time of authorship. They are not intended to be a definitive set of instructions for this project. You may discover there are other methods and materials to accomplish the same end result. Should you rely on the information, instructions, methods, or materials contained within this book, you do so at your own risk.

Homestead Living Publishing
126. N. 3rd St. Suite 200
Minneapolis, MN, 55401

© Homestead Living Publishing

Cover Design and layout by Allan Nygren of Mosaic Productions
Cover photo and interior photography by Cheryl Constable
Editing and Review by Georgia Varozza and Kat Ruth-Leigh
Assistant editor - Michelle Hedgcock

All rights reserved. No part of this publication may be reproduced, stored in a retrieval system, or transmitted in any form or by any means—electronic, digital, mechanical, photocopying, recording, or otherwise—except for brief quotes in printed reviews, without prior permission of the publisher.

For more information about our other products, please visit:
www.homesteadliving.com

ISBN:979-8-9868229-0-7

To my husband, for embracing this way of life (and eating) though it's not one you came from. For building me pantries, planting gardens, and building a life together that truly is everything worth preserving.

To my grandmother Revonda, for teaching my mother, who taught me, how to make blackberry jam without any outside pectin sources. Though you've been gone for over twenty years, I always think of you each time I make it.

To my father-in-law, your love of mustard pickles resurrected a long-lost family recipe, but your love for me as a daughter-in-law will be remembered with every jar. You left a legacy.

To Michelle Hedgcock, this book wouldn't have happened without your organizational skills (and pep talks). Thank you for all the years of friendship and work and reigning me in when it's for my own good.

To Rachel Costenbader, my homesteading sister. Thank you for the laughter, packing up almost your entire kitchen for photos, and the delicious foods.
Also, thank you for sharing your Jewish mother with me; you're both a joy.

To Darrell Vesterfelt, who saw the potential in me before I could see it myself.

To Carolyn Thomas, there aren't pages to fill the words, so I'll keep it short; for the kinship, the prayers, the tears, and the laughter; you're a true blessing.

Contents

Introduction ix

PART 1: BEFORE YOU BEGIN 1

   1. Getting Started 3
      How to Use this Book 3
      Food Preservation Safety 4
      General Equipment for Food Preservation 11
      Jar Size and Use Chart 14
      Method Overview 17
      Home Food-Preservation Methods 23

PART 2: PRESERVATION METHODS AND TUTORIALS 27

   2. Canning 29
   3. Dehydrating 59
   4. Freezing 77
   5. Fermenting 101
   6. Root Cellaring 119
   7. Freeze-Drying 141
   8. Infusion 147
   9. Salting and Smoking 153

PART 3: RECIPES 159

   10. How to Preserve Vegetables 161
   11. How to Preserve Fruits 267
   12. How to Preserve Meat 375
   13. How to Preserve Soups and Stew 407

Conclusion 423
Index 425
Resources 432
Notes 433
About the Author 435

Introduction

Preserving food fills the heart as much as it fills the stomach. You will find yourself gazing at your jars and shelves of preserved foods like an artist at their art show, admiring the colors of each individual jar and the body of work as a whole.

Less than a hundred years ago, the majority of households grew and preserved some of their own food, if not the majority. The rise of the supermarket, including produce grown and shipped from all climates and countries, coupled with convenience foods, resulted in just two generations' time an almost extinction of home food-preservation skill sets in modern society.

With the advent of easily accessible processed foods (or more accurately, food-like items), we've witnessed a rise in health problems, a loss of connection with our food, loss of sustainability, and a greater loss of family ties.

As a generational homesteader (we didn't even use that term growing up; we simply lived as country folk have lived for centuries), there has never been a point in my life when we didn't produce and preserve some of our own food. During my childhood we used a canner and deep freezer.

Those carried over into my own household as a newlywed, but it was for meat, a few jars of jam, and a year's worth of green beans. By no means was this enough food to fully feed us for every meal.

As a young working wife and mother, I found myself relying on store-bought versions and boxed mixes of this and that. A biopsy of my upper stomach and esophagus in my late twenties showed erosion and cellular change, but thankfully no cancer.

In order to afford and find foods with ingredients that wouldn't trigger my acid reflux, I turned back to our garden. Living in a northern climate, our growing season is rather short. This means, preserving the harvest so we can eat from it year-round is a necessity.

Not only did I find restored health but also a tangible connection to the past. My grandmother's technique of not using store-bought pectin to make jam and jelly makes her memory come alive in my kitchen every time I use her recipe.

Each year we strive to preserve at least one or two more items for a year's worth. Quickly we went from only doing beef and green beans to over 70 percent of our food being preserved (and most of it grown ourselves).

As my children have grown, their help in the height of harvest and preserving season means time spent together while teaching them skill sets that I hope will be carried to their own children someday.

The more food we preserved, the more I wanted to preserve. I also wanted to make sure I was using safe methods. The whole point of this was to improve my health, and the last thing I wanted to do was use unsafe techniques and make myself, or worse, my family, sick. As a result, I have spent years learning, reading, and researching in order to fully understand how to can food safely for the best flavor and texture, as well as for long-term storage.

With a growing homestead, business, and family, I find time is a premium asset, especially during the busyness of harvest season. When I have ten pounds of asparagus sitting on the counter, I want a book that tells me which methods of home food preservation are safe for asparagus, and then gives me the recipes and tutorials for those methods.

Most home food-preservation books focus largely on one singular method. I didn't want to pull out five different books and hunt and peck all over the internet (and worry about triple-checking the safety of said internet recipes) when I already have little time. No such book existed (many alluded to it but when I had the book in my hands, it fell short). Thus, this book was born.

This book is an accumulation of those who have gone before me, modern science, family and friends, and my own decades of gleaned knowledge and experience. It is the very resource I wish I'd had and many of you have asked for.

While this very much is a resource with practical recipes and tutorials, it is more than that. We are preserving true health, ownership of our food, connections with our families, and food that tastes amazing. Isn't that everything worth preserving?

May your jars be filled!

PART 1
Before You Begin

CHAPTER 1
Getting Started

How to Use this Book

This book is broken into two main parts. The first part is a description of how to safely preserve all varieties of food with the different types of preservation methods, how each preservation method works, and step-by-step tutorials. The second part has each fruit, vegetable, and meat in alphabetical order with recipes utilizing the methods from the first half along with a quick reference chart of which methods may be used for that specific food.

Unless you're a master food preserver, I *highly recommend* you read the chapter on safe preservation and understand these concepts. Once you're comfortable, you can pick and choose which methods you want to learn and take them in any order you like. If you reference a recipe that calls for a certain preservation method, be sure to read the chapter on that method so you can accurately and *safely* prepare the recipe.

1. True beginners—read the first part of this book through so you fully understand each mechanism and method.
2. People with experience—you may be tempted to skip straight to the recipes and foods listed by alphabetical order but there are many tips to be found in each method as well as handy charts, so be sure to reference them.

Why Preserve Food at Home?

My family and I raise 99 percent of our own meat and over 70 percent of our own fruits and vegetables for our family of four. Living in a northern climate we have a short growing season, so knowing how to preserve food for long-term storage is a must if we want to enjoy it for the full year.

Growing your own food is wonderful, but knowing how to preserve food at home for year-round sustainability is priceless. From May to October, the hiss and jiggle of my pressure canner, the hum of the dehydrator, trays in and out of the freeze-dryer, and a plethora of Mason jars with ferment tops litter the counter in an almost constant rhythm.

It's likely if you're reading this book that you're already convinced of the benefits of food preservation, but with decades of experience under my belt, I realize it's not just about having food in the off-season or building up your larder.

It's preserving wisdom that in a few generations has been lost by many families—a connection to those who have gone before us and to the children and future generations yet to come.

Many people think of canned vegetables as blah, and if all they have to compare is metal cans of vegetables from the grocery store, they'd be right. True story, neither I nor my kids can eat canned store-bought green beans due to the lack of flavor.

Preserved food at home in most cases is taken straight from the garden and preserved—if not the same day then within a short time of being picked. The result is increased nutrients and flavor!

There are so many wonderful fermented and flavor variations you'll never find on store shelves. If your only experience is store-bought ferments, oh my friend, you're about to awaken your taste buds.

These are the main ways we preserve most of our own food at our homestead, and you can too!

Food Preservation Safety

One can't (or shouldn't) have a food preservation book without discussing safety. Humans have been preserving food for thousands of years, so why do we have all of this "safety"

information now? A good portion of our home food preservation is based on studies and work done during the 1940s and World War II when food was needed for the Allies, and victory gardens and canning were encouraged. In order to make sure the food was safe, the government funded studies, which resulted in many of the procedures we still use today.

With canning, there have been updates to safety and procedures. Canning recipes and books older than the mid '90s should not be used because of this. (Though much of the information from the 1940s is still the same, there are a lot of people who didn't learn it back then and therefore didn't pass it down as they were teaching others.)

One of the biggest arguments I see as a home food-preservation educator when sharing why it's not safe to use a particular method is "my (insert name of relative or friend) has been doing it this way for decades and never got sick."

Well, thank the good Lord, because even though it wasn't their intention to use an unsafe method, they were. Just because my mother as an infant had a lead-based painted crib and is fine doesn't mean I'm going to use a lead-based crib with the updated science we now have on the dangers.

You'll find within these pages a multitude of ways to preserve food at home and do so safely. You're not limiting yourself by following updated food-safety methods, other than limiting becoming sick, or worse, if you ate food tainted with botulism.

Once you understand the mechanisms we have to preserve food and why specific methods are chosen, you'll gain confidence and realize the importance of each step.

Many people are extremely hesitant to can food because of botulism fear (and botulism isn't limited to canning). My goal with this book isn't to reinforce that fear but to have you understand how to avoid it so you can experience food security and freedom!

Why Following Proper Procedure Is Important

There are many different methods for food preservation. Not all forms of food preservation are appropriate for every food, so it's important to have a good understanding of what is happening during the food preservation process in order to know which method to use.

It's also my strong recommendation to *always* follow a tested recipe when preserving food, especially in regard to canning. All of the canning methods and recipes in this book are from tested sources such as the National Center of Home Food Preservation, Ball Corporation, university extension offices, or similar.

Why Does Food Spoil?

Food goes bad because of enzyme activity and the growth of microorganisms. The enzymes are not necessarily bad for us but will break down the food until it is inedible. The microorganisms can be bacterial (such as botulism) or fungal (such as yeast), and these can multiply, depending upon the microorganism, causing us to get very sick or even possibly die.

Botulism is a neurotoxin that can kill you, so please be careful! It is caused by toxins that grow in an anaerobic environment (without oxygen), like a sealed canning jar. The good news is that botulism and other forms of food-borne bacteria are actually very rare, and if you follow the proper procedure, it's completely avoidable! Read that again, *completely avoidable*.

How Is Food Preserved?

Food can be safely preserved by reducing the enzyme activity and growth of microorganisms when we manipulate conditions such as pH levels, moisture, and temperature. Some methods will slow down this activity, while others will halt and even destroy it.

What Are the Basic Mechanisms Used in These Methods?

These are the basic mechanisms, though many of the preservation methods use multiple mechanisms:

- Acidity (pH levels)
- Moisture
- Temperature
- Oxygen

If you're unfamiliar with any of these, I'll give you a general idea of what each method does.

Acidity (pH Levels)—Microorganisms, such as botulism, cannot grow at a pH of 4.6 or lower. Changing the acidity of food (as in fermentation) or via pickling vegetables with appropriate brine ratios will halt the growth of microorganisms.

Moisture—Microorganisms need moisture to grow. Depending on how much moisture is removed (as in dehydration or curing), the growth of microorganisms is drastically reduced or halted.

Temperature—Temperature can either be increased (as in pressure canning) or decreased (as in freezing) to affect the growth of microorganisms. When raised high enough, the temperature can destroy the microorganisms, and when lowered it will halt the growth.

Oxygen—Microbial growth can be slowed down when placed in an anaerobic state (removal of oxygen) in methods such as canning and submersion in oil (botulism is an exception; it grows in an anaerobic state, which is why we use carefully tested methods when canning or using anaerobic techniques).

Methods of Preserving

Curing—You can stop microorganism growth by drawing out water with salt. Not only can you preserve meats at home, like salt-cured ham and dry-cured meat, but you can also preserve fresh herbs in salt as well.

Freezing—Freezing can reduce the water content by turning the water into a crystallized state. Additionally, it lowers the temperature of the food to a state where the bacteria can no longer multiply and grow. However, it doesn't actually kill the bacteria; it just puts it into a dormant state, so when the food is thawed, the bacteria will become active and can multiply again.

This is why freezing does not kill the bacteria on raw meat—you still need to cook it. The heat from the cooking process kills the harmful bacteria in the meat. It is optimal whenever more than one mechanism for food preservation is in play.

For example, it is recommended that some fruits and vegetables that have continued enzyme activity after harvesting need to be blanched before freezing.

Blanching will destroy the enzyme activity, which can otherwise continue even at the frozen temperature. I learned this the hard way one year by skipping the blanching step on my butternut squash. The result was that no matter how long I cooked it, the texture never quite tasted done, and it had an odd flavor.

When blanching foods for freezing, you are using three mechanisms. The first is using heat to kill the enzymes, the second is lowering the temperature so the microorganisms cannot multiply, and the third is removing the water so that the microorganisms cannot multiply.

Canning—Canning relies on proper pH levels, heat, and the removal of oxygen to preserve food. If the pH level of the food is not acidic enough, those foods need to be pressure canned in order to use heat to destroy the microorganisms present.

If your jars are simply sitting in a pot of boiling water, the temperature cannot rise above 212°F/100°C no matter how long they sit there. Microorganisms such as botulism will not die unless they have reached a temperature of 248°F/120°C.

Pressure canning is unique in that it allows you to bring the internal temperature of the food up to 248°F/120°C for a specified amount of time.

Sugar comes into play in the canning process by absorbing water and making it less available. You cannot use sugar as a preservative by packing food in sugar as you do with salt, but sugar does play a role in extending the shelf life of canned goods after the jar has been opened.

The canning process itself relies on acid and pH levels to preserve the food. We know that botulism cannot grow at a pH of 4.6 or lower, and many fruits and berries are acidic, naturally falling under this pH level, so the need to add sugar isn't necessary but does help retain color and flavor.

However, sugar helps to absorb water, so the more sugar in the recipe, the longer the shelf life will be after the jar is opened because the reduction in water will reduce the ability for mold to grow after the seal is broken. With the health consequences of sugar in mind, I use low-sugar recipes in my strawberry, cherry, blackberry, blueberry, peach, and apple pie jams, and I process them in the smallest jars possible. That way, we have the ability to go through the product before it has a chance to go bad once opened in the fridge.

Pasteurization—Most people don't use pasteurization (heating foods with mild heat for a short period of time to kill pathogens and extend the shelf life) as a home-preservation method, but like canning, it brings the temperature of the food up to a specified temperature for a specified period of time in order to kill the microorganisms present. Depending on the product you are pasteurizing, these temperatures and times will vary.

Oil Immersion—You must be very careful when using oil to preserve food—read that again. Because, yes, oil does create an anaerobic environment (without oxygen), but this method also relies on acidity. Botulism can still grow in an anaerobic environment if the acidity level is not 4.6 or below. Especially if using root vegetables like garlic.

Fermentation—This method uses three mechanisms. The first is drawing out the water by either salting the vegetable (as in sauerkraut) or using saltwater brine.

Second, the vegetable is fully submerged under the liquid level to cause an anaerobic state.

Last, the salt also acts to keep the good and bad bacteria balanced so that the bad bacteria are kept at bay until the lactic acid is formed. This acid works to change the pH level to an acidity where food is preserved.

Alcohol Fermentation—This method initially follows the fermentation process but is allowed to continue to ferment until the yeast that is consuming the sugars in the food then begins to excrete alcohol.

Dehydration—Although heat is used in dehydration, it is not high enough to kill the microorganisms. Dehydration relies on the removal of water only.

Cold Storage—It is recommended that a root cellar temperature is in the range of 32–40°F/0–5°C in order to slow microbial growth, though some vegetables will store fine at higher temperatures. Not everyone is able to use a root cellar, but we'll discuss using your garden to store your vegetables over the winter and which vegetables can be successfully stored closer to room temperature.

General Equipment for Food Preservation

We'll go over specific gear for each type of food preservation technique, but the list below includes items you'll likely use for many of the methods. The good news is that you probably already have some of these on hand.

Measuring Spoons and Cups—Both standard measuring spoons and cups (for dry as well as wet ingredients), as well as larger measuring bowls such as 1 cup, 4 cups (1 quart), and 8 cups (2 quarts/half gallon).

Food Processor—When doing large batches of sauerkraut, salsa, relishes, jams, or sliced pickles, nothing is faster than a food processor (an 8 cup is best, but smaller ones will work; you'll just have to do more batches). It also comes in handy when dicing food to freeze-dry, or when powdering freeze-dried food for long-term storage.

High-Powered Blender—If you don't have a food mill, a blender can be used to puree your skinned and seeded tomatoes for sauce. I use it for jam because the glass attachment shows exactly how many cups of crushed berries I have for easy recipe calculations. It's also handy for pureeing fruit for dehydrating fruit leather.

Mandoline—These slicers are extremely sharp (use the guard!) but they make slicing vegetables for ferments, pickles, or dehydrating very efficient and fast as well as uniform.

Glass Jars—Obviously you need them for canning, but they're also used for ferments, storing dehydrated and freeze-dried foods, oil immersion, and alcohol. Pretty much any form of food preservation will use a glass jar either in the preparation or the storage.

Jar Lids and Bands—You'll need new metal lids for canning each time (used ones are fine for ferments, dehydrated, freeze-dried, and dry goods storage but not canning). Reusable canning lids such as Tattler or Harvest Guard are a two-piece system and can be reused many times for canning. Screw-down one-piece lids are fine for ferments and dry-goods storage.

Funnel—I use a jar funnel for canning, fermenting, and jarring dehydrated and freeze-dried food. I always have two on hand, but one will suffice to start with.

Food Scale—Not necessary but can be helpful for certain recipes.

Utensils—Spatula, slotted spoon, ladle, knives, vegetable peeler, cutting board, colander, an assortment of medium and large bowls.

Cherry Pitter—If you're not preserving cherries, then no need for this, but if you've ever done cherries, having a pitter that will pit multiple cherries at once is a must. Dehydrated cherries are one of my must-have favorite fruits (my husband likes the cherry pie filling more) and one of these beauties saves a lot of time. These will pit olives as well (depending on the size of the olives).

Sieve/Food Mill—Not necessary, but if you're making sauces or jellies, they're extremely helpful and time-saving for separating out skins and seeds.

Jar Size and Use Chart

Regular-Mouth Mason Jar Size	Ounces	Cups	Canning Safe	Freezer Safe	General Use
Jelly jar	4 oz	½	yes	yes	jam, jelly, condiments, small portions
Half-pint	8 oz	1	yes	yes	jam, jelly, conserves, chutney, preserves, fruit syrup, and pizza sauce
Three-quarter pint	12 oz	1½	yes	yes	jam, jelly, marmalade
Pint	16 oz	2	yes	no	salsa, sauce, relish, pie filling, large portion jam, jelly, fruit syrup, soup, stew
Quart	32 oz	4	yes	no	sliced fruits/vegetables, ferments, sliced pickles, tomato sauce and juice, soup, stew

Wide-Mouth Mason Jar Size	Ounces	Cups	Canning Safe	Freezer Safe	General Use
Half-pint	8 oz	1	yes	yes	jam, jelly
Pint	16 oz	2	yes	yes	small batch ferments, small batch pickles, salsa, sauces, relishes, fruit butter, soup, stew
Pint-and-a-half	24 oz	2½	yes	yes	asparagus, pickles, sauces
Quart	32 oz	4	yes	yes	ferments, tomato, whole/halved fruit and vegetables, pie filling, soup, stew
Half-gallon	64 oz	8	yes*	no	ferments, juice, freeze-dried, dehydrated, dry goods
Gallon	128 oz	16	no	no	large batch ferments, freeze-dried, dehydrated, dry goods

*Only safe for canning apple and grape juice

Which Food Preservation Method Is Best?

We are fortunate to have so many methods of food preservation to build a proper food-security and food storage system. I highly recommend using multiple methods of preservation.

We need a good variety of food for a healthy diet, and since not all methods are appropriate for every food, learning the different methods ensures variety.

There is no one best method. They all have their place, though you may develop a preference for one over another. Some methods have a lower barrier to entry because they don't require specific types of equipment, like a pressure canner or freeze-dryer.

Pick a method and get started—the best one is the one you're actually putting into practice.

Method Overview

Here is a brief overview of each method and which foods it can be used for where safety is concerned. Some of these may be new to you and will give you an idea of which methods you'd like to jump into first or learn more about.

Methods of Preserving Food at Home

1. Water-bath and Steam Canning
2. Pressure Canning
3. Dehydrating
4. Cold Storage or Root Cellar
5. Freezing
6. Freeze-drying
7. Salt Curing and Smoking
8. Fermenting
9. Infusion

1. Water-bath and Steam Canning

Water-bath or steam canning is safe for acidic foods that are 4.6 pH or lower, as botulism can't grow in acidic environments of 4.6 pH or lower.

There are two ways to can your food. The first is a water-bath or steam canning method—both are used for acidic fruits, jams, jellies, syrups, and pickling. Water-bath canning is immersing canning jars filled with food in a bath of boiling water or in a steam canner and processing for a set amount of time per the recipe.

Foods that can be safely water-bathed are most fruits, jams, jellies, fruit butters, fruit syrups, chutneys, marmalade, pickled vegetables, tomato sauce, and salsas. To be done properly and safely, tomato sauce must have added acid, and salsas must be tested in canning recipes to ensure the overall pH level is 4.6 or lower to avoid botulism.

Water-bath canning is a great entry point for home canning because all you need are Mason jars, lids, bands, and a large pot with some type of rack to keep the jars up off the bottom of the pot.

Steam canners must be purchased but have some great advantages (see Steam Canning section on page 40).

2. Pressure Canning

Pressure canning is the only safe way to can non-acidic food such as certain vegetables, meat, soups, and combination recipes. The pressure canner allows the jars to reach a higher temperature than just boiling water, which is crucial to ensuring all bacteria (especially botulism, a fatal form of food poisoning) are killed.

When done correctly, pressure canning is a very safe way to preserve food at home.

One advantage of canning is the food is fully cooked and ready to serve—you merely have to open the jar. This makes getting food on the table when life is hectic easy. Home-canned food is a must during emergencies and power outages because it doesn't rely on electricity to keep it from perishing. Because it's fully cooked, you don't have to have water in order to prepare it, making it a truly open-and-eat food source.

3. Dehydrating

Dehydrated food takes very little storage space, and it's lightweight enough to take with you on the go, which makes it an ideal way to preserve food at home.

To prolong the shelf life of dried food, store it in a cool, dark, dry area. We air-dry herbs and beans the old-fashioned way, but we use an electric dehydrator for our fruits and vegetables.

Dehydrated food is shelf-stable, and some forms (dehydrated fruit, for instance) are eaten from the dried state. Other items, like dehydrated carrots, zucchini noodles, and such, should be rehydrated before using in cooking and eating.

All fruits, vegetables, and herbs are candidates for dehydrating. You can dehydrate some forms of cooked meat and eggs, but you need to make sure you're following proper safety and storage procedures.

4. Cold Storage or Root Cellar

Most people who grow large amounts of root veggies and some fruit might plan to store their food in a root cellar or cold storage as these kinds of food do really well.

This simply requires a cool, damp, and dark area for root crops such as potatoes, carrots, beets, parsnips, cabbage, and apples. (Winter squash and pumpkins prefer it a bit warmer and drier.)

I think this is my favorite way to preserve food at home because it honestly requires very little work on my part.

In many parts of the world where the soil doesn't freeze too hard, you can mulch your carrots and potatoes and leave them in the ground to harvest straight from the garden.

When using root cellar techniques, you must cure your crops before putting them into storage.

5. Freezing

Freezing food allows it to keep for many months and sometimes years if packaged properly. We use a deep freezer for our beef, chicken, and some fruits and vegetables.

Many foods can be frozen that people don't typically consider. You can freeze butter, milk, cheese, and even eggs.

Yep, you read that right. In the summer when the hens are laying like crazy, you can put some of the eggs into the freezer to use later.

The drawback to the freezer is space and the cost to operate, and during power outages, you can stand to lose a lot of costly food.

6. Freeze-drying

Freeze-drying requires a home freeze-dryer (and they're definitely an investment piece), but I have quickly come to love using this form of food preservation. In full disclosure, Harvest Right (the only other freeze-dryer for home use is from 4Patriots, but it's brand new and I have not tested it) sent me my freeze-dryer to review for free.

Freeze-drying works by freezing the food (raw or cooked) to negative temperatures. A vacuum pump sucks out the vaporized water. Then the food is dehydrated. The result is a very light and crispy shelf-stable product.

Freeze-drying allows you to safely preserve raw meat, dairy, eggs, casseroles, soups, and products not safe for canning. Freeze-dried food stored in proper conditions can be safe to eat for 20+ years and retain almost all of the nutrition.

7. Salt Curing and Smoking

Salt curing and smoking are used to draw out moisture and inhibit bacterial growth, both with meat, cheese, vegetables, and herbs. Many items still need to be kept in a controlled cold environment.

While you can dehydrate herbs, not all herbs keep their flavor once dried, especially basil. Once you know how to make herb salt, you'll likely never dehydrate basil again. It tastes fresh and keeps for months—all winter and into the next spring.

8. Fermenting

Fermentation is a long-practiced form of food preservation that actually enhances the health benefits of the food where other methods can degrade it.

Fermenting food uses a culture of good bacteria to preserve the food at home and contains many health benefits along with its preservation benefits. Fermenting vegetables (think sauerkraut, pickles, kimchi) is done by using a saltwater brine and time.

After the food has been fermented, it does need to be kept in a cooler environment to slow the fermentation process down and for long-term storage.

9. Infusion

Many foods can be immersed in liquids to preserve them. Herbs and fruits are immersed in alcohol, vinegar, oil, and honey to create a melody of items.

We make our own mint, vanilla, and lemon extracts this way. It's one of the most special ways to preserve food at home. *Now if only I could grow my own vanilla beans!*

Your summer fruit can also be preserved in alcohol for winter baking.

Home Food-Preservation Methods
(Picking Your Preservation Method)

When picking your food-preservation method and creating your plan, there are three things to consider:

1. What foods does your family enjoy eating?
2. When are those foods in season?
3. What method are you going to preserve them with?

For example, cucumbers and blueberries come on at the same time. The majority of our cucumbers get preserved into pickles. In order to have crunchy pickles, they need to be processed as soon as possible once harvested. Our blueberries get made into jam and syrup.

I can make jam and syrup from frozen blueberries later (and enjoy having some frozen blueberries throughout the year). This means that when the harvest is on, blueberries get put in the freezer so I can focus on the cucumbers.

I make sure I have enough salt, spices, and vinegar for pickle making beforehand.

Make Your Plan to Avoid Overwhelm

You can see why it's really helpful to know how you're going to preserve and eat each of these crops, because it's going to determine how you'll deal with that produce when it comes into your kitchen. This allows you to make sure you have the supplies needed based on the preservation method.

What if you don't have a huge garden or maybe are not growing all of that fruit yet? It's helpful to know what is going to be in season right now so that you can plan to go to a you-pick farm near where you live.

If you don't have you-pick farms, then farmers' markets are the next best thing, or the grocery store. I love focusing on raising it yourself or supporting a CSA program, you-pick farms, and farmers' markets, but sometimes that might not be an option for a crop. It's okay to get some of this at the grocery store. The great thing about knowing when things are in season though is that you usually will get the best price and the best quality of that produce if you're getting it when it is in its natural season and not being shipped from a different country in a different hemisphere during the off season.

See individual fruit and vegetables to determine which methods are advised per item, and from those, which ones you'll be using this year.

Below is the Seasonal Harvest Chart to help you create your plan.

Seasonal Harvest Chart

Season	Fruits	Veggies 1	Veggies 2
January/February	Citrus Orange Lemon Grapefruit Tangerines Papaya	Broccoli Brussels sprouts Cabbage Cauliflower	Kale Parsnips Turnips Potatoes
March/April	Mango Pineapple Rhubarb	Artichoke Asparagus New potatoes	Radishes Spring peas Snow peas
May/June	Apricots Rhubarb Strawberries	Lettuce New potatoes Spring onion Swiss chard	Zucchini – southern states Broccoli Spinach Radish
July/August	Blackberries Blueberries Boysenberries Cherries Melons Peaches Plums Raspberries	Corn Cucumbers Eggplant Garlic Green beans Lettuce	Okra Onions Peppers (sweet and hot) Summer squash/ zucchini Tomatillos Tomatoes

Season	Fruits	Veggies 1	Veggies 2
September/October	Apples Dates Figs Grapes Pears Pomegranates	Winter squash (butternut, pumpkin, spaghetti, acorn, etc.) Carrots Garlic	Kale Onions Potatoes Broccoli Spinach Tomatoes
November/December	Apples Cranberries Dates Pears	Beets Brussels sprouts Cauliflower Parsnips Potatoes Winter squash (butternut, pumpkin, spaghetti, acorn, etc.)	Rutabaga Sweet potato Swiss chard Turnips Carrots Celery Leeks

PART 2

Preservation Methods and Tutorials

CHAPTER 2

Canning

Canning food (or jarring may be a more accurate description) is what comes to most people's minds when you mention food preservation. There are more safety protocols with canning than other forms of food preservation, but if you follow them, canning is a rewarding and safe way to preserve food.

It is the ultimate in batch cooking and means homemade healthy "convenience" food on the shelf. We'll start with equipment and terms and then break down each method.

Canning Equipment

Must-Have Items for Canning	Recipe Dependent BUT Must Have for Those Recipes
Canning jars	Salt (canning friendly)
Canning lids	Bottled lemon juice, vinegar, or citric acid
Canning bands/rings	
Large pot, water-bath or steam canner for acidic foods	
Canning rack or homemade version	

Must-Have Items for Canning	Recommended Items for Canning (they make life easier)
Pressure canner for all non-acidic foods	Jar lifter
Pot holder and towels	Canning rack
	Headspace measurer and air bubble tool
	Canning funnel
	Candy thermometer for jams, jellies, and syrups

Canning Terms

Acidic. Acidic foods may be safely processed via the water-bath method when they have a pH level of 4.6 or lower. Most fruits, pickles, jams, jellies, chutneys, marmalades, preserves, relishes, and tomatoes with added acid fall into this category.

Botulism. A neurotoxin that can be deadly, it is caused by toxins that grow in an anaerobic environment (without oxygen), like a sealed canning jar.

Headspace. The amount of space between the top of the food in the canning jar and the top of the jar. Essential to have this correct for safe sealing of your food.

Hot-pack method. Heating the food and then filling your jars with the hot food; water in the canner should be 180°F/82°C.

Raw-pack method. Placing uncooked food in the jars (sometimes hot liquid is added over the raw food, but not always); water in canner should be 140°F/60°C.

Water-bath. In canning, this means processing your jars in boiling water for a specified amount of time. Only acidic foods can be safely processed with this method.

Low-acid foods. Foods that don't have a natural pH level of 4.6 or lower. This is all vegetables, meats, and combination recipes. You must use a pressure canner to can these items safely.

Run. Processing a full set of food in the canner, from start to finish, example: "I'm canning a run of tomatoes today."

Swell. When the lid on your jar of canned food swells, this usually breaks the seal and is a sign you have some sort of food poisoning or spoilage going on. The food should be thrown out and not consumed.

Exhaust. Removing air from the canning jar and/or the steam/pressure canner. Very important for a proper seal.

Vacuum. This means the exhausting of the air out of the jar and creating a proper seal. The pressure is lower inside the jar than outside. We want a good vacuum to ensure a good seal on our jars.

Which Canning Method to Use for Processing

In order to avoid botulism, you must use the appropriate method of canning for each food type. Because botulism doesn't grow in acidic conditions, you can safely water-bath or steam can foods that are 4.6 pH or lower.

Non-acidic foods MUST be pressure canned—they cannot reach hot enough temperatures in boiling water to sufficiently kill botulism spores.

Acidic Foods to Process via Water-Bath or Steam Canning	Non-Acidic Foods to Process via Pressure Canning
Fruit, with the exception of bananas, melons, and Asian pears—they can't be safely water-bath canned by themselves. Some recipes exist for using them in a combination recipe with other acidic fruits in jellies and jams, but only use a recipe from an approved and tested source like the *Ball Book of Canning* or USDA website, etc.	Beef
Other fruit and fruit sauces	Lamb
Fruit jams, jellies, conserves, preserves, marmalades	Poultry (with and without the bones)
Pickles, relishes	Pork (including pork chops and ham, but not bacon by itself)
Pie fillings	Rabbit
Tomatoes and tomatillos (steam-canning processing time cannot exceed 45 minutes)	Seafood
Salsa (only with recipes specific for canning)	Soup and soup stocks (aka broth)
	Vegetables (including vegetable sauces like spaghetti sauce and combination recipes like soup, stews, and chili)

This often comes as a surprise to canners (and not just folks new to canning) but you cannot safely can at home everything you see canned on store shelves. Commercial pressure canners reach MUCH higher temperatures than home pressure canners. You may see the below items canned on store shelves but they're NOT to be canned at home.

The Do-NOT-Can-at-Home List:

1. Dairy products
2. Grain and wheat products (including pasta and noodles)
3. Fats (no canning bacon or oil, except a small amount in approved pressure-canning recipes) or butter (despite what someone on Pinterest says)
4. Eggs—even pickled (these are for your fridge and cold storage only)
5. Mashed or pureed* vegetables (no pumpkin butter or pumpkin pie filling canned at home)
6. Sage (it turns bitter when canned)
7. Thickeners such as flour, cornstarch, tapioca, or arrowroot. Either use approved canning products like Clear Jel or add your thickener when cooking or baking.
8. Dry beans that have not been prepared properly for canning

*There is a split pea soup recipe approved for canning that has you puree the cooked peas. This is one of the few exceptions.

Canning Jar and Recipe Prep

Regardless of method, your jar prep is the same.

Prep ahead: Ensure all jars are free of cracks or chips. Wash lids in hot soapy water and set aside (newer manufacturing and guidelines do NOT have you heat them on the stove beforehand). If processing time is 10 minutes or longer, you do not need to sterilize jars (almost all updated recipes are 10 minutes or longer). Jars must be kept warm to avoid thermal shock or may crack if hot contents are poured into room-temperature glass. Keep bands at room temperature to avoid burnt fingertips.

Ways to Keep Jars Warm

- Dishwasher can be used to wash and keep warm.
- Place jars in heated canning water (fill jars with water from canner to keep from tipping).
- Leave jars in hot soapy water and rinse with hot water immediately prior to filling.

Read through the recipe to ensure you know all the steps and headspace before starting. Prepare each canner type as indicated in the step-by-step tutorials.

Always refer to the specific recipe you're using for headspace, but the below chart shows general headspace for recipe types.

Food	Jar Size	Headspace
Jams, jellies, syrups	jelly jars, half-pint, pint	¼ inch (½ cm)
Fruits, tomatoes, tomato sauce in water-bath, pickles, relishes, chutneys, condiments	pint, half-pint, quart	½ inch (1 cm)
Vegetables, soup, broth, meat, tomato sauce in pressure canner	pint, half-pint, quart	1 inch to 1¼ inch (2 to 3 cm)

Water-Bath Canning Tutorial

Water-bath canning is what many folks remember their grandparents or parents doing. It's an excellent starting place for acidic foods because you can use any pot that's deep enough to cover the top of the jars with at least one inch of water. Your large pot of boiling water is what we're referencing as a canner in this tutorial, whether it's a large pot you own or if you purchased a specific water-bath canning pot.

1. Place the canning rack in the bottom of the canner. Add enough water to ensure there are 1 to 2 inches of water over the top of the filled jars. Heat the water to 140°F (60°C) for raw-pack/180°F (82°C) for hot-pack.

2. While the canner is heating up, begin preparing the food to go in the jars. One at a time fill your hot jars using a funnel to indicated headspace.

3. Measure using either a ruler or headspace tool to appropriate headspace.

4. Remove air bubbles by inserting a spatula or bubble remover between the food and jar. Slide up and down around the inside circumference of the jar two to three times. Add more food if needed to maintain headspace.

5. Wipe the rim and thread of the jar clean with a damp cloth to remove any food particles (these can impede a seal).

6. Place lid on jar, then the band, and screw the band down to fingertip tight.

7. Take filled jar of food and put into prepared canner. Repeat until all jars are filled and in canner. Make sure water covers jars by one to two inches of water. Two inches are recommended for processing times over 30 minutes.

8. With the lid on, bring the water to a full boil. Start processing time only once a full boil is reached. Keep the lid on during the processing time. Process at a full boil for complete recipe time, then turn off heat. Remove the lid and wait 5 minutes before removing jars.

9. Remove jars from the canner and place upright onto a folded towel. Leave jars to cool for 12 to 24 hours before checking the seal; do not retighten or touch bands.

10. Remove bands and check seals. Lids should be concave. To fully test, pick the jar up by just the lid; it should hold. Wipe off the outside of the jar and lid, dry, and label. Store in a cool, dark, and dry place.

Steam Canning Tutorial

Only recipes that have been approved by trusted authorities (National Center for Home Food Preservation, state extension agencies, see resource section for full list) for water-bath canning with a processing time of less than 45 minutes may be used with a steam canner (including any additional time for altitude).

It is recommended to use a steam canner with a temperature gauge in the knob so you know the internal temperature is correct for starting and maintaining processing times.

Follow jar prep instructions on page 34.

1. Place the recommended amount of water in the canner and heat to the correct temperature (listed below); put jars in and then the cover on.

    Raw-Pack: The water in the steam canner needs to be preheated to 140°F (60°C).

    Hot-Pack: Water temperature in the steam canner needs to be heated to 180°F (82°C).

2. Turn up the heat to high, until it vents. When there's a solid, unbroken column of steam 6 to 8 inches (15 to 20 cm) tall coming out the vent and the temperature gauge needle reaches your zone, start your processing time. Do NOT remove the lid during the processing time. You should see steam venting during the entire processing time; it should remain constant (not a broken stream). Adjust if boiling too hard, as it can boil dry in 20 minutes. Regulate the heat to maintain temperature. When the processing time is done, turn off the heat. Leave the lid on for five minutes. This is REQUIRED.

3. Remove the lid and let sit for an additional five minutes before removing the jars from the canner and transferring to a towel. Once moved to the counter, cool for 24 hours. Check lids to ensure they seal. Remove the bands, wipe down the jars and lid, label, and put away.

Reference Charts and Information

Canning

Altitude Adjustment Chart for Steam and Water-Bath Canner

Feet	Meters	Increase Processing Time
1,001-3,000	306-915	5 minutes
3,001-6,000	916-1,830	10 minutes
6,001-8,000	1,831-2,440	15 minutes
8,001-10,000	2,441-3,050	20 minutes

Pickling

Say "pickle" and many people immediately think cucumber. There are many vegetables you can safely pickle at home, both with water-bath or steam canning and fermenting. The advantage to canning pickles is that they're shelf stable for at least 18 months. Fermented pickles need to be stored in a cool environment (usually a fridge) but will last there for up to a year and have increased nutritional benefits.

You'll want to follow the specific canning recipe for each vegetable type (see the vegetable section on page 161) as brine ratios change based on the vegetable. But the tips below will serve you well for creating crunchy pickles!

When canning, use a 5% or higher vinegar. Some specialty vinegars are only 4% and shouldn't be used for safety reasons. Always use a tested recipe—some vegetables require a higher amount of vinegar to water. If a recipe calls for LESS vinegar than water, it's likely outdated and shouldn't be used.

Pickling Spices

While you can purchase premade blends of pickling spices, I prefer to stock my own spices to make my own blends depending on the vegetable and flavor profile I like.

These are my must-have spices:

- allspice, whole berries
- black peppercorn, whole
- celery seed
- cinnamon sticks
- cloves, whole (only if you must, personal bias)
- mustard seed
- red pepper flakes (for those who like some heat)

Universal Tips for Crisp Pickles

Use fresh, just-picked vegetables that aren't overripe. Harvest in the morning, before the heat of day. Don't throw those larger or slightly overripe cucumbers out, instead make relish.

When pickling cucumbers, remove a 1/16 to 1/4 inch of the blossom end; this eliminates an enzyme that can cause soft pickles.

Add a leaf with tannin to the jar. Sources of tannins for pickles are grape leaves, oak leaves, or black tea. Use one fresh grape or oak leaf per jar or one teaspoon of loose-leaf black tea per quart of pickles (or one bag of tea). You can either put the loose tea directly in the jar of pickles or let it simmer in the brine and strain out. I prefer straining.

Pressure Canning

Pressure canning opens up a whole new world to the foods you can safely can at home—from ready-to-eat meals, shelf-stable proteins (aka meat and bone broth), and a plethora of vegetables.

Many people are nervous about pressure canning. You've probably heard cautionary tales of great aunt-so-and-so exploding her canner (my grandmother did have one blow up). Older models (pre-1980s) did not have the built-in safety features newer models do with over-pressure relief plugs and multiple safety mechanisms. While they do sound a bit scary, they're incredibly safe to use IF you follow the instructions and never skip a step.

There are two types of pressure canners on the market; one is dial gauge and the other a weighted gauge. A few models, like the All American, have both the dial and weighted gauge. The weighted gauge has selections of 5, 10, and 15 pounds.

The dial gauge must be tested and calibrated when new and each subsequent year for accuracy. Most county extension offices in the United States will perform this service. I prefer a weighted gauge to avoid this.

There are different sizes of canners. Before getting a large pressure canner (they allow you to double-stack pints and do a larger amount at once), make sure you have adequate clearance above your stove according to the pressure canner manufacturer. Your pressure canner should be large enough to hold a minimum of four one-quart jars in the upright position of the canner to ensure it reaches and maintains accurate pressure.

You may not use a pressure cooker (including electric pressure cookers EVEN if they have a canning button or instructions in the manual; as of this writing ALL have failed third-party testing for safe pressure canning) for pressure canning—it must be a pressure canner. Unless you purchase an All American canner, your pressure canner will have a rubber gasket on the lid to help it seal. Inspect it for cracks or wear and have a backup gasket on hand. The All American is a metal-to-metal seal and doesn't use a gasket.

Pressure Canning
Step-by-Step Tutorial

Pressure canning is how we safely can non-acidic items at home. Each step is important to follow for safety.

1. Place rack in the pressure canner and fill with 2 to 3 inches of water (or according to manufacturer guidelines); over medium heat (smoked fish requires more water due to a longer processing time and no preheating), bring water to 140°F/60°C for raw-pack and 180°F/82°C for hot-pack.

2. Fill hot jars with broth, vegetables, or meat to the appropriate headspace following raw/hot-pack instructions per recipe one jar at a time. Raw-pack is uncooked fruit, vegetables, or meat with hot liquid poured over top (some meats are raw-packed without additional liquid). A hot-pack is where the ingredients are all heated to a simmer and then ladled into the jar.

3. Measure headspace with a tool or ruler (most low-acid foods are an inch but some meats or beans may require more).

4. Remove air bubbles on vegetables and meat. Add more content if needed to maintain headspace.

5. Wipe the rim clean to avoid food particles inhibiting the seal.

6. Place just-washed and rinsed lid and band on jar; tighten to finger-tip tight.

7. Place jar inside the prepared canner using a jar lifter, and repeat until all jars are filled and in canner.

8. Place lid on canner and lock into place. Turn heat to high until a steady stream of steam is present from the vent pipe. Set timer for 10 minutes. After 10 minutes of a steady stream, place the weighted gauge or counterweight on appropriate pounds of pressure for recipe and altitude (do not skip this step or trapped air may lower temperature). Start processing time ONLY after the canner has reached selected pounds of pressure.

9. After processing time, turn off the heat and let the canner reduce pressure naturally. Once pressure is reduced to zero, wait 5 minutes. Remove the gauge and wait 10 minutes, then carefully remove the lid with it facing away from you to protect you from any steam. Let jars sit in the open canner for 10 minutes to reduce siphoning.

10. Carefully remove jars with a jar lifter (or oven mitt) from the canner onto a towel folded over. Let jars cool undisturbed (and away from drafts) for 12 to 24 hours. Do not adjust or touch bands during this time.

11. Remove bands and check seals. Lids should be concave. To fully test, pick the jar up by just the lid; it should hold. Wipe off the outside of the jar and lid, dry, and label. Store in a cool, dark, and dry place.

Altitude Adjustments for Pressure Canning

Instead of increasing processing times for higher altitudes like with water-bath/steam canning, for pressure canning you need to increase the amount of pressure. The chart below is based on the National Center for Home Food Preservation recommendations for non-acidic foods.

Feet	Meters	Weighted Gauge PSI	Dial Gauge PSI
0–1,000	0–305	10 lbs	11
1,001–2,000	306–609	15 lbs	11
2,001–4,000	610–1,219	15 lbs	12
4,001–6,000	1,220–1,828	15 lbs	13
6,001–8,000	1,829–2,438	15 lbs	14
8,001–10,000	2,439–3,048	15 lbs	15

Canning Problems and Troubleshooting

Even when following a recipe and correct procedure, you can experience unexpected results. I've listed the most common and how to avoid them here.

Siphoning

Siphoning is when you have a jar of food with proper headspace at jarring time but when processing is finished you notice the liquid level inside the jar is low. Occasionally you'll see bits of the contents on the outside of the jar too. This is more frequent with sauces or fruits that have a lot of oxygen in them.

Make sure you remove air bubbles before putting on the lid and bands. Siphoning is increased with extreme temperature differences. Preheat canning jars before you fill them with hot food.

Remove as much oxygen as possible by blanching fruit and using a hot-pack. This helps push the oxygen out of the fruit. The hidden air in fruit or air bubbles trapped inside the jar rise to the top of the jar. This makes it appear as if liquid has disappeared when in reality it's been redistributed because the air rose to the top.

Jars removed too fast from a canner may siphon. In a water-bath canner, once your processing time is up, turn off the heat and remove the lid. Then let the whole batch sit for five minutes before you remove the jars onto a folded towel on your counter.

When pressure canning, turn off the burner as soon as processing is complete but leave the lid on. A pressure canner has to cool naturally—never pour cold water over the canner to force this. Once pressure is fully reduced and it is safe for you to remove the lid, do so, then let jars sit for 10 minutes inside the pressure canner before you remove them to a folded towel.

In both instances, leaving jars in the canner to rest helps to reduce siphoning. However, you *don't* want to let your jars sit inside a pressure canner and cool all the way down without removing them.

The jars need to come out while they are still hot because the lids vacuum seal when the temperature difference is significant as they cool down. If you leave the jars inside the canner where the temperature reduces slowly, they could have a weaker seal because they missed the more dramatic change in temperature.

Any temperature changes during your processing time should be done gradually. If you need to reduce your heat because the pressure is too high, do so in small increments if possible. Try to minimize getting the pressure too high in the first place.

In water-bath canning, liquid loss occurs if the jars aren't sufficiently covered with one to two inches of water during the processing time.

If you're reusing lids (which you shouldn't do because they aren't guaranteed to maintain a seal), you may experience liquid loss. The lid gasket isn't as strong as it is when a brand-new lid is used.

Missing the step of wiping the jar rim before placing the lid and band on can cause food particles to be trapped and prevent the lid from sealing. This in turn leads to the potential of liquid loss.

Tighten the band to fingertip tight. If the band is too loose, it can vent too much.

Despite doing all of these steps correctly, sometimes you still will experience a small amount of siphoning. If a jar has lost more than half of its liquid, it's not considered safe for the shelf. You can put that in the fridge to eat within the next few days or you can put it in the freezer, but it's not something you're going to store at room temperature.

Buckled Lids

Lid buckling is usually caused by tightening the band too tightly. Very rarely is it a defective lid.

You only want to tighten it fingertip tight. Don't crank it down. While a buckled lid may appear to be sealed, it's not safe to put on the shelf. Either freeze or refrigerate it.

Bubbles

You may see bubbles in something thick, like apple pie filling. Those bubbles don't move and are trapped air.

Bubbles that we're concerned about are ones that move when the jar is stationary. A jar that is sitting on a shelf that has active bubbles is one that has gone bad. That is a sign of spoilage and you do not consume that food even if it's still sealed.

White Crystals

You may see white grainy crystals on your jams, jellies, syrups, or juice. These sugar crystals could be caused by the following:

- If the jar has been opened and is in the fridge, it's because the liquid has evaporated.
- If you see it in the jars sitting on the shelf, it's because the sugar wasn't completely mixed in and dissolved.
- The jam or jelly got too hot and was cooked too long. You'll see the crystals on the side of the pot.
- Be sure you're scraping down the sides of your pot using a spatula or spoon to capture all the sugar crystals when cooking.
- Grape products will often have this happen because grapes contain tartrate crystals. The way to reduce that from happening is to refrigerate the juice for your jelly for 24 to 48 hours and then make the jelly.

Reprocessing When a Jar Doesn't Seal

If you have a jar or jars that didn't seal, there are certain times when you can or cannot reprocess them. Then there are times when it's not advisable, not because of safety, but because of texture issues.

- Reprocessing, according to the National Center for Home Food Preservation, should be done within 24 hours (with the exception of fish; do NOT reprocess unsealed jars of fish). Use new lids, clean jars, and reheat food before jarring (jams/sauces back to a simmer, etc.).
- Don't reprocess if it's going to be a texture issue. For example, green beans can be reprocessed but they'll be really mushy and very overcooked. Put the jar in the freezer instead to use in a casserole or in the fridge to use right away.
- Something like pumpkin or winter squash I do not reprocess. We already know that they cannot be canned as a puree because it causes it to be too dense. Reprocessing with the density of the product could be unsafe. Use immediately, or put it in the fridge or the freezer to use later.

- Sauces, like tomato sauce or apple sauce, lend themselves great for reprocessing because there's no texture issue.
- Pickles would turn mushy, so it's not recommended to reprocess them.

How to Store Home-Canned Food Safely

Stacking jars of home-canned food on top of one another or storing with the bands on is surprisingly a hot debate in home food-preservation circles. There are a ton of myths or incorrect advice swirling around out there.

I'm a huge stickler for safety when it comes to canning and only use advice or recipes from tested sources, but the tested sources' advice on these two subjects may surprise you.

With canning jars, the band is the part that you screw down after you put your lids on top of your jars before processing them in a pressure canner or a water-bath canner.

Here is where the controversy comes in. When it comes to your canning bands, you should actually remove the bands after they've gone through that minimum 12-to-24-hour period where you don't touch them.

Why You Should Remove Canning Rings from Home-Canned Food

The main reasons I remove my canning rings (or canning bands) after processing are these:

1. They will rust. Once the bands rust, they don't screw down easily and can get to the point they're unusable. No one wants to purchase things again if they don't have to, especially the canning bands.
2. Storage. I can around 600 jars of food a year and do NOT have the storage space for 600 canning bands/rings. By removing the bands after processing, I only need to keep 50 bands of wide-mouth and 50 bands of regular. My All American 21.5-quart pressure canner will hold up to 20 pint jars, so as long as I have 50 bands, I can reuse them each time I can (and have enough to do another run while the first batch is cooling), making it much easier to store.
3. Easier to see if a seal is broken. If you store with the bands on, it's much harder to see if a jar has lost a seal.

4. Hiding food and bacteria growth. When canning, liquid or contents often siphon out before the jar seals, leaving some food trapped between the band and the glass. If you don't remove the band, you could have food and bacteria growing between the band and jar, even if the jar is sealed.

If you decide to leave the bands on for storage (which I don't recommend), make sure you remove the band/ring after the jar is cooled from processing, and then wash and dry thoroughly before placing the band back on. Always check your seal when taking out a jar before consuming it.

Is It Safe to Stack Your Home-Canned Jars?

The National Center for Home Food Preservation says to not stack jars too high, no more than two jars. Personally, I only stack at the end of the season if I'm totally out of room, and I only stack a smaller size jar on top of a larger jar.

Make sure your shelf can support the extra weight. Never stack jars on the front of the shelf. I only stack in the back, against the wall. Some people like to line cardboard between the rows to help distribute the weight.

Make sure you check the seals when stacking (especially the lower jar) to make sure you haven't disrupted the seal or compromised it.

How Long Is Home-Canned Food Good For?

Most sources say to use it within 12 months, as longer it slowly begins to drop in increments on the nutritional value. But as long as you follow proper canning procedure, updated recipes, and times, newer lids will hold up to 18 months. Honestly, home-canned food is safe for longer than 18 months, but we do try to use ours within two years.

Practice proper rotation with any of your food but especially your canned goods so that you're eating the oldest stuff first.

CHAPTER 3
Dehydrating

Dehydrating is one of the oldest forms of food preservation. It works by removing the moisture or liquid from a food so bacteria can't grow in it. This is done with air and/or heat.

Dehydrated food has a very long shelf life if kept at 70°F/21°C or cooler without oxygen (aka sealed up tight). It will last for approximately 8 to 10 years. Dehydrated food is very lightweight and small, ideal for travel and storage with limited space.

Dehydrating Equipment

Must-Have Items for Dehydrating	Recommended Items (they make life easier)
Canning jars, lids and bands. I store most of my dehydrated items in jars.	**Mandoline.** Helpful to cut produce into even slices.
Knife and cutting board. Try to keep food as uniform as possible so it dries evenly.	**Parchment paper or silicone mats.** Helpful when working with sticky items/fruit leather.
Vegetable peeler. Much faster than using a paring knife.	**Kitchen scale.** You can weigh items before dehydrating and after to determine exact moisture loss.

Must-Have Items for Dehydrating	Recommended Items (they make life easier)
Twine or string. Used for air-drying herb bundles, leafy greens, or strings of vegetables.	**Vacuum sealer with Mason jar attachment.** This allows you to remove oxygen from jars to increase shelf life and create a strong seal. You can also use it for bags.
Dehydrator. You can dehydrate without one, but I consider them a must-have for vegetables, fruit, and meat.	**Food processor.** Grind your dried food into powders, or fast grating for shredded vegetables.
	Mylar bags. Mylar bags are great for long-term food storage of dehydrated goods.
	Oxygen absorbers. Removes oxygen, prolonging quality and shelf life. Best used with products that are low in moisture and oil content, such as freeze-dried food. Moisture content above 10% in reduced oxygen packaging could result in botulism poisoning.

Dehydrator Options

There are many different models of dehydrators. I prefer rectangular/square tray designs. Inexpensive units have a fan that blows from the top, and when using these, it's recommended to rotate the trays for even drying (this is preferred for small herbs or flowers). More expensive units have a fan that blows from the back of the unit, and this helps with cross-contamination of flavors and eliminates having to rotate trays. Some units allow you to add more trays. I personally like this flexibility so I can do as little or as much as I need.

There are also solar dehydrators. They're harder to maintain exact temperatures and require the sun to be out but are great as a backup or in an off-grid situation.

Ways to Dehydrate

1. Air-drying. This is best done with a small bunch of herbs/greens tied together where air can circulate, either a covered porch or even near (but not where it can cause a fire hazard) a wood stove. You can put small flowers or leaves in a paper bag to keep dust/bugs off to dry, but make sure they're not packed tightly.

2. The oven. If your regular oven temperature will go down to 150°F/66°C, you can prop open the oven door for ventilation (make sure children and animals cannot get inside) and use your oven as a dehydrator.

3. Solar oven. Use a solar oven and the power of the sun to dehydrate your food. Some people will place trays of food in their car in summertime. I haven't personally tried this, but you can see how you can get creative.

4. Dehydrator. Most people are familiar with these. I prefer a square-tray dehydrator (I feel like I can fit more food on it) and one that allows me to select the temperature.

Temperatures for Dehydrating Food	Food Type
95°F/35°C	Herbs and Spices
105°F/41°C	Nuts and Seeds
135°F/57°C	Fruits and Vegetables
160°F/71°C	Fish, Jerky, and Meats

Vegetables, unless specified, should be blanched or cooked before dehydrating for optimal color, flavor, and end result. Follow blanching times listed under the Freezing section on page 80. Vegetables should be washed thoroughly to remove any dirt and debris.

You can eat your dehydrated foods in their dehydrated form but you can also reconstitute them to prepare in recipes. Most people enjoy their fruit in the dehydrated form and prefer to rehydrate vegetables (see Rehydrating Food notes at the end of this section for further info).

Vegetable Dehydrating Chart

Vegetable	Preparation	Drying Time in a Dehydrator (hours)**
Artichoke, globe	Cut into ⅛-inch strips. Heat in a boiling solution of ¾ cup water and 1 tablespoon lemon juice.	4-6
Asparagus	Cut large tips in half.	4-6
Beans, green	Cut in short pieces or lengthwise.	8-14
Beets	Cook fully. Cool and peel. Cut into shoestring strips ⅛-inch thick.	10-12
Broccoli	Trim, cut as for serving. Quarter stalks lengthwise.	12-15
Brussels sprouts	Cut in half lengthwise through stem.	12-18
Cabbage	Remove outer leaves, quarter, and core. Cut into strips ⅛-inch thick.	10-12

Dehydrating | 63

Vegetable	Preparation	Drying Time in a Dehydrator (hours)**
Carrots	Use only crisp, tender carrots. Cut off roots and tops. Peel, cut into slices or strips ⅛-inch thick.	10-12
Cauliflower	Prepare as for serving.	12-15
Celery	Trim stalks and then slice.	10-16
Corn, cut	Husk, trim, and blanch. Cut corn from the cob after blanching.	6-10
Eggplant	Cut into ¼-inch slices.	12-14
Garlic	Peel and finely chop. No blanching needed.	6-8
Horseradish	Remove small rootlets and stubs. Peel or scrape roots. Grate. No blanching needed.	4-10
Leafy Greens – chard, kale, turnip, beet, collard	Use only young tender leaves.	8-10
Mushrooms	Scrub thoroughly. Discard any tough, woody stalks. Cut into short sections. Do not peel small or button mushrooms. Peel large mushrooms. Slice. No blanching needed.	8-10
Okra	Slice crosswise in ⅛- to ¼-inch disks. No blanching needed.	8-10

Vegetable	Preparation	Drying Time in a Dehydrator (hours)**
Onions	Remove outer papery shells. Remove tops and root ends. Cut into ⅛- to ¼-inch slices. No blanching needed.	3-9
Parsley	Separate clusters. Discard tough stems. No blanching needed.	1-2
Peas, green	Shell.	8-10
Peppers and Pimientos	Remove the core and "partitions." Cut into disks about ⅜-by-⅜ inch.	8-12
Potatoes	Peel. Cut into strips ¼-inch thick or slices ⅛-inch thick.	8-12
Spinach	Use only young tender leaves.	8-10
Squash, winter	Cut into pieces and remove seeds and cavity pulp. Cut into 1-inch strips. Peel rind. Then cut strips into pieces about ⅛-inch thick.	10-16
Squash, summer	Cut into ¼-inch slices or shred (shredded does fine without blanching).	10-12
Tomatoes	Remove skins. Cut into slices ¾-inch thick. Pear and plum tomatoes cut in half.	10-18

**Drying times in a conventional oven could be up to twice as long, depending on air circulation.*

WARNING: *Toxins in poisonous varieties of mushroom are not destroyed by cooking or dehydrating.*

Pretreating Fruit

The purpose of pretreating fruits prior to drying is threefold. It keeps light-colored fruit from browning and darkening, both during drying and storing (dehydrated food doesn't always look appealing and this can help with picky eaters). For fruit with tough skins, pretreating speeds up drying. Research studies show using an acidic solution or sodium metabisulfite dip helps kill potentially harmful bacteria during drying, including *Escherichia coli* O157:H7[1], *Salmonella*[2] species, and *Listeria monocytogenes*[3].

Pretreatment Methods

Citric Acid Pretreatment: Prepare by stirring 1 teaspoon of citric acid into one quart of cold water. Allow fruit to soak for 10 minutes, then remove with a slotted spoon, drain well, and dehydrate.

Lemon Juice Solution: Mix equal parts lemon juice and cold water. Allow fruit to soak for 10 minutes, then remove with a slotted spoon, drain well, and dehydrate.

Ascorbic Acid Pretreatment: Mix 1 teaspoon of ascorbic acid into one gallon of water. Allow fruit to soak for 5 minutes, then remove with a slotted spoon, drain well, and dehydrate.

Fruits with skin take an extremely long time to dehydrate if you don't use a procedure called checking. Checking is piercing the skin. This can be done by blanching OR by freezing and then thawing the fruit. Alternatively, you can sit and prick each piece of fruit with a needle, but I find freezing to be the least amount of hands-on time and my preferred method.

Fruit	Preparation	Drying Time in a Dehydrator (hours)
Apple	Peel and core, cut into ⅛- to ¼-inch thick rings or slices. Dip in pretreatment to prevent browning.	6-12
Apricot	Cut in half and remove the pit. Dip in pretreatment to prevent browning.	24-36

Fruit	Preparation	Drying Time in a Dehydrator (hours)
Aronia Berry (aka chokeberry)	Rinse and drain.	24-72
Banana	Use solid yellow or slightly brown-flecked bananas. Avoid any bruised or overripe bananas. Peel and slice ¼- to ⅜-inch thick pieces (either crosswise or lengthwise).	8-10
Blackberry	Wash and drain.	24-36
Blueberry	Wash and drain berries. Plunge into boiling water for 15 to 30 seconds to check skin. Then place the berries into ice water. Drain on paper towels. Alternatively, freeze berries, then thaw to check skin, and dehydrate.	24-36
Cantaloupe	Halve cantaloupe and remove seeds. Slice into ¼-inch thick semicircles and remove the rind.	18-20
Cherry	Stem, wash, drain, and pit fully ripe cherries. Cut in half, chop, or leave whole. If you choose to do it whole, dip in boiling water 30 seconds or more to check skins.	24-36
Cranberry	Wash and drain berries. Plunge into boiling water for 15 to 30 seconds to check skin. Then place berries into ice water. Drain on paper towels. Alternatively, freeze berries, then thaw to check skin, and dehydrate.	24-36

Fruit	Preparation	Drying Time in a Dehydrator (hours)
Currant	Wash and drain currants. Plunge into boiling water for 15 to 30 seconds to check skin. Then place currants into ice water. Drain on paper towels. Alternatively, freeze berries, then thaw to check skin, and dehydrate.	24-36
Dewberry	Wash and drain.	24-36
Fig	Select fully ripe fruit. Immature fruit may sour before drying. Wash or clean the whole fruit with a damp cloth. Leave small fruit whole, otherwise cut in half. Dip whole figs in boiling water 30 seconds or more to check skins. Plunge in ice water. Drain on paper towels. Alternatively, freeze figs, then thaw to check skin, and dehydrate.	6-12
Gooseberry	Wash and drain berries. Plunge into boiling water for 15 to 30 seconds to check skin. Then place berries into ice water. Drain on paper towels. Alternatively, freeze berries, then thaw to check skin, and dehydrate.	24-36
Grape	Seedless: Leave whole. Dip in boiling water 30 seconds or more to check skin. Plunge into ice water. Drain on a paper towel. Alternatively, freeze grapes, then thaw to check skin, and dehydrate. With seeds: Cut in half and remove seeds.	
Grapefruit	Wash fruit. Leave peels intact. Slice into ⅛- to ¼-inch slices.	7-15

Fruit	Preparation	Drying Time in a Dehydrator (hours)
Huckleberry	Wash and drain berries. Plunge into boiling water for 15 to 30 seconds to check skin. Then place berries into ice water. Drain on paper towels. Alternatively, freeze berries, then thaw to check skin, and dehydrate.	24-36
Kiwi	Wash and peel kiwi. Slice ⅛- to ¼-inch thick.	10-18
Kumquat	Wash fruit. Leave peels intact. Slice into ⅛- to ¼-inch slices.	7-15
Lemon	Wash fruit. Leave peels intact. Slice into ⅛- to ¼-inch slices.	7-15
Loganberry	Wash and drain.	24-36
Lime	Wash fruit. Leave peels intact. Slice into ⅛- to ¼-inch slices.	7-15
Mango	Wash and peel. Slice ¼-inch thick.	8-12
Melon	Halve melon and remove seeds. Slice into ¼-inch thick semicircles and remove the rind.	18-20
Nectarine	Wash thoroughly. Cut away any bruises and slice into ¼-inch slices. Dip in pretreatment to prevent browning.	8-16

Fruit	Preparation	Drying Time in a Dehydrator (hours)
Orange	Wash fruit. Leave peels intact. Slice into ⅛- to ¼-inch slices.	7-15
Papaya	Wash well. Thinly peel, cut in half, and remove the black seeds. Cut lengthwise into ¼-inch-thick strips. If you want, for trail mix or granola, cut the strips into 1-inch-wide pieces.	7-15
Peach	Wash thoroughly. Cut away any bruises and slice into ¼-inch slices. Dip in pretreatment to prevent browning.	8-16
Pear	Cut in half and core. Peeling is preferred. May also slice or quarter. Dip in pretreatment to prevent browning.	24-36
Persimmons	Use firm fruit of long, soft varieties and fully ripe fruit of round varieties. Peel and slice using a stainless-steel knife.	12-15
Pineapple	Use fully ripe, fresh pineapple. Wash, peel, and remove thorny eyes. Slice lengthwise and remove the core. Cut into ½-inch slices, crosswise.	10-18
Plum	Rinse plums, cut into halves, remove pit (slice all the way around the pit and gently twist to separate), and place on trays.	24-36
Raspberry	Wash and drain.	24-36

Fruit	Preparation	Drying Time in a Dehydrator (hours)
Rhubarb	Pick non-woody stalks (smaller) of rhubarb and clean. Chop into ¼- to ½-inch pieces.	8-12
Saskatoon (aka Juneberry, Serviceberry)	Rinse and drain.	24-72
Strawberry	Wash and drain. Remove stem, hull, and halve or slice.	24-36
Watermelon	Cut watermelon into 1-inch-thick slices. Discard ends and remove rinds. After removing the rind, cut slices into about ¼-inch-thick strips. (Optional step: lightly salt watermelon strips.)	18-20

Dehydrating Step-by-Step Tutorial

Process product as outlined in the above charts. Arrange in a single layer on trays. The pieces should not touch or overlap. Dry for the recommended time; however, drying times may vary due to local humidity, variations in air circulation, type of cut (drying times are shorter for sliced/shredded as opposed to whole and halves), and dehydrator being used. Watch closely as food dries much faster at the end of the drying period.

For fruit, you may want to spray the drying trays with nonstick cooking spray before placing the fruit on the trays or use parchment paper/silicone liner. Fruits contain sugar and are sticky, so spraying the trays will help them not stick. After the fruit dries for one to two hours, turn each piece over using a spatula. Fruit should be dehydrated at 135-140°F/57°C.

Dried fruits should be leathery and pliable; they also benefit from being conditioned. Conditioning is a process used to equalize the moisture across all pieces and reduce the risk of mold growth. To condition fruit, take the cooled dried fruit and pack it loosely in plastic or glass jars. Seal the container and let them stand for seven to ten days. The excess moisture in some pieces will be absorbed by the drier pieces. Shake these containers daily to separate the pieces and check the moisture condensation. If condensation develops, return the fruit to the dehydrator to dry more. After conditioning, package and store the fruit.[4]

A quick test that has never failed me is to take the still-warm fruit and place it in a jar or plastic bag (take a small sample of the largest pieces) and close immediately; if moisture beads within 30 to 40 minutes, dehydrate longer.

When food is fully dry, place in an airtight container. Glass jars with metal lids or a wire bale lid with a gasket work well. Using the Mason jar attachment with a vacuum sealer provides additional shelf life. Plastic or Mylar bags can also be used. If using a Ziplock type bag; try to get out as much of the air as possible. Store out of direct sunlight, in a dry, dark place, preferably below 70°F/21°C or cooler environment for up to a year. Cooler temperatures will prolong the shelf life.

Vegetables should be brittle or crisp. Vegetables do not need to be conditioned like fruit does.

Dried fruit can be eaten as is or reconstituted. They're great used in cobblers, breads, pies, puddings, smoothies, shakes, and cooked cereals.

Dehydrated vegetables are best used in soups, casseroles, sauces, and stews.

Rehydrating Dried Foods

Reconstitution Ratio: 1 cup fresh fruit or vegetable = ⅓ to ¼ cup dried = 1 tablespoon powdered.

Rehydrating is done by soaking or cooking (or a combination of both) the dehydrated food in water until volume is restored. Don't rehydrate food until you're ready to use them. Don't try storing rehydrated food, as drying temperatures aren't high enough to destroy microbes. Spoilage can occur quickly after rehydration.

Vegetables rehydrate best when you use boiling hot water, and fruits do best with room-temperature water. When rehydrating fruit, don't add any sugar to it until the fruit is tender, because the sugar will toughen the product.

The general rule of thumb for rehydrating is two parts water to one part food. Any excess water left over after the product is fully rehydrated can be tossed or used during cooking. Let the food soak for 20 minutes to 2 hours. The food will swell to around four times its dehydrated size. It will never look the same as it did when it was fresh, so if it still looks wrinkled and a little shriveled, don't worry.

CHAPTER 4

Freezing

Instead of ice houses or spring houses where either frozen blocks of ice or cold water helped to maintain the temperature, most of us have used a freezer for preserving food. Chest or upright freezers (not attached to a refrigerator) are best, as they maintain colder temperatures.

Your freezer is an excellent way to preserve food, but when it comes to vegetables, one should always blanch the food first when it's recommended. The first time I froze butternut squash, I thought blanching was a waste of time. The result was frozen squash with an odd texture and off taste that I had to throw out. Blanching slows or stops enzymatic activity and should never be skipped if you want to enjoy and actually eat the vegetables.

One of the drawbacks to using a freezer for preservation is that in the event of a power outage that is longer than 24 hours, you'll need to use a generator or risk losing your food.

Freezing Equipment

Must-Have Items for Freezing	Recommended Items (they make life easier)
Freezer. I prefer a chest freezer for maximum freezer space. But a stand-up freezer is preferred over the freezer/fridge combo as the temperature is colder and more consistent.	**Vacuum Packer.** Go for the model with rolls of plastic rather than pre-cut/sized bags. These extend the freezer life of vegetables, fruit, and meats in the freezer. If meat is being frozen to use within the next 6 months, we don't use butcher paper.

Must-Have Items for Freezing	Recommended Items (they make life easier)
Steamer. Either a pot with a colander, Instant Pot, or steamer can be used to blanch vegetables.	**Butcher Paper.** Meat wrapped in plastic and then butcher paper will last much longer than plastic alone; place shiny side against the food, dull facing out.
Large Bowl. Fill with ice and cold water to stop cooking after blanching foods.	**Tape.** To secure the butcher paper.
Containers and Lids. I prefer glass containers; wide-mouth Mason jars work well too (wide-mouth allows for liquid expansion without breaking).	**Chest-Freezer Dividers.** To avoid digging through piles of food, we use plywood dividers to easily stack ground meat, roasts, seafood, and chicken in their own compartments.
Freezer Bags. Yes, they're plastic, but I reuse my gallon bags for fruit year after year. They allow me to stack gallons of fruit efficiently, maximizing space.	**Permanent Marker.** Mark the outside of the package with content name and date (it will wash off glass and paper/plastic will be recycled or thrown out).
Baking Trays. A must for flash-freezing berries, vegetables, dough balls, etc., before transferring to a freezer container for long-term storage.	
Sharpie and Masking Tape. I write the year straight on plastic bags, but for containers, place a piece of tape and then record contents and date.	

Vegetables

Blanching Directions

1. Wash, drain, trim, and cut vegetables.
2. Use 1 gallon of water per pound of vegetables. Or use 2 gallons of water per pound of leafy vegetables.
3. Put vegetables into a blancher (for example, a wire basket or metal strainer) and place into boiling water. If steaming, boil 2 inches of water in a pot and then put a single layer of vegetables in a blancher.
4. Cover, and start the timer as soon as water returns to a boil. If steam blanching, start the timer immediately.
5. Cool in ice or cold water (60°F/15°C or below) immediately for the same time used in the blanching. The exception is corn on the cob, which requires twice as much time.
6. Drain thoroughly. Freeze either by dry-pack or tray-pack (aka flash freezing).
7. Dry-pack: Pack vegetables tightly into container or freezer bags. Press out the air and seal tightly.
8. Tray-pack: Place vegetables in a shallow pan or cookie sheet in a single layer. Place the pan/sheet into the freezer. Once vegetables are frozen, remove them from the pan/sheet and put them into a freezer bag or container. Press out the air and seal tightly.
9. Frozen vegetables are best used within 8 to 12 months when stored at 0°F/32°C or lower.

Vegetable	Boiling Water Blanching (minutes)	Steam Blanching (minutes)
Artichoke, globe, cut into ⅛-inch strips	6-8	-
Asparagus, small stalk	2	3
Asparagus, medium stalk	3	5

Vegetable	Boiling Water Blanching (minutes)	Steam Blanching (minutes)
Asparagus, large stalk	4	6
Beans, snap, green, or wax	3	5
Beans, small – lima, butter, or pinto	2	3
Beans, medium – lima, butter, or pinto	3	5
Beans, large – lima, butter, or pinto	4	6
Beets	Cook	-
Broccoli, 1½ inches across	3	5
Brussels sprouts, small heads	3	5
Brussels sprouts, medium heads	4	6
Brussels sprouts, large heads	5	7
Cabbage or Chinese cabbage, shredded	1½	2½
Carrots, small, whole	5	8
Carrots, diced, sliced, or strips	2	3
Cauliflower, 1 inch	3	5

Vegetable	Boiling Water Blanching (minutes)	Steam Blanching (minutes)
Celery	3	-
Corn – on the cob, small ears	7	10
Corn – on the cob, medium ears	9	13
Corn – on the cob, large ears	11	16
Corn – whole kernel – ears blanched before cutting corn from the cob	4	6
Eggplant	4	6
Greens, all other	2	3
Kohlrabi, whole	3	-
Kohlrabi, cubes	1	-
Leafy greens, collards	3	5
Leafy greens, all other (Swiss chard, beet greens, mustard greens, turnip greens)	2	3
Mushrooms, whole*	-	9
Mushrooms, buttons or quarters*	-	9

Vegetable	Boiling Water Blanching (minutes)	Steam Blanching (minutes)
Mushrooms, slices*	-	5
Okra, small pods	3	5
Okra, large pods	5	8
Onions – blanch until center heated	3-7	-
Onions, rings	10-15 seconds	-
Peas, edible pods	2-3	4-5
Peas, green	1½ - 2½	3-5
Peppers, sweet – halves	3	5
Peppers, sweet – strips or rings	2	3
Potatoes, Irish (new)	3-5	5-8
Rutabagas	3	5
Soybeans, green	5	-
Spinach	2	3
Sweet potatoes	Cook	-

Vegetable	Boiling Water Blanching (minutes)	Steam Blanching (minutes)
Squash, summer (zucchini)	3	5
Squash, winter (including pumpkin)	Cook	-
Tomatoes	2	4
Turnips, ½-inch cubes	3	5

Vegetables That Must Be Fully Cooked Before Freezing

- Beets
- Pumpkin
- Sweet potatoes
- Winter squash

*Pretreat by soaking 5 minutes in an anti-darkening solution: 1 teaspoon of lemon juice or 1½ teaspoons of citric acid to a pint of water.

WARNING: Toxins in poisonous varieties of mushroom are not destroyed by cooking or dehydrating.

Fruits

Freezing fruits retains much of their fresh flavor and nutrition; however, the texture may be somewhat softer than that of fresh fruit.

Recommended Freezer Containers: Plastic freezer containers, freezer bags, or glass canning/freezing jars. If canning jars are used, use wide-mouth jars for fruits packed in liquid with 1 inch of headspace. Headspace for dry pack is ½ inch.

Types of Packs

The type of pack depends on the intended use. There are several types of packs for freezing fruit:

- Syrup Pack – Ideal for uncooked dessert use, such as pouring over ice cream
- Sugar Pack – Good for most cooking purposes
- Dry Pack – Best for most cooking purposes and general use; this is what I use for all berries.
- Unsweetened Pack – Best for most cooking purposes

Syrup Pack: A 40% syrup is recommended for most fruits. Lighter syrups are best for mild-flavored fruits to prevent masking of the fruit flavor. Conversely, if the fruit is very sour, you may want to use a heavier syrup.

Sugar Pack: Sprinkle sugar over the fruit and mix gently until the juice is drawn out and the sugar has dissolved. Soft sliced fruits such as peaches, strawberries, figs, deseeded grapes, plums, and cherries will yield sufficient syrup for covering if the fruit mixed with sugar is allowed to stand for 15 minutes. Some small whole fruits may be coated with sugar and frozen. Artificial sweeteners give a sweet flavor but do not furnish the beneficial effects of sugar, such as color protection and thickness of syrup.

Dry Pack: Good for small whole fruits such as berries. Flash freeze the fruit on a tray, then pack into a container after frozen. Flash freezing prevents the fruit from sticking together and forming a large clump. I've always had good success by freezing blueberries directly in the container—no flash freezing. If they do stick, I can break them up easily with a spoon or measuring cup.

Unsweetened Pack: Unsweetened fruit can be packed in water or unsweetened juice. The fruit generally doesn't have the plump texture and good color of those packed with sugar. The fruit freezes harder and takes longer to thaw. Fruits such as raspberries, blueberries, steamed apples, gooseberries, currants, cranberries, rhubarb, and figs give a good product without sugar.

Preventing Discoloration

Fruits such as peaches, apples, pears, and apricots darken when exposed to air and during freezing. They may also lose flavor when thawed. To prevent darkening and flavor loss, use a pretreatment of citric acid or lemon juice dip (instructions listed under dehydrating fruits on page 68). Steaming may also be used for fruits that will be cooked before use. Steam the fruit just until hot according to the directions for each fruit.

How to Flash Freeze

Fruits such as berries, chunks of banana, watermelon, and pineapple are best to be flash frozen. What does it mean to flash freeze? In food industry terms it means to freeze the food in a "flash" at extremely low temperatures; however, in home-cook terms it means freezing individual pieces of food separately. The benefit of flash freezing is that the food freezes faster and keeps the pieces from clumping together. Come January when you want to make that smoothie, you'll really appreciate that you took that extra step.

1. Prepare the fruit (wash, core, hull, slice, etc.).
2. Dry the fruit by getting as much water off as possible. A salad spinner works great for things like blueberries and strawberries, although it might not be the best for softer berries like raspberries and blackberries.
3. Line a tray(s) with parchment paper or silicone mat.
4. Place the fruit in a single layer on the lined tray. Fruit should not touch. Place the tray in the freezer.
5. Once frozen, transfer to a labeled freezer container (fine if they touch) and place in the freezer.

Fruit	Preparation	Type of Pack (Choose One)
Apple	Wash, peel, core, and slice. Medium apples should be sliced into twelfths, large ones into sixteenths. Pretreat if desired.	Syrup pack in a 40% syrup. Sugar pack using ½ cup per quart of fruit, after steaming or boiling for 1½ to 2 minutes to prevent darkening. Cool fruit in cold water and drain before mixing fruit and sugar. Dry pack using the instructions for sugar pack, but omit the sugar.
Apricot	Wash, halve, and pit. Peel and slice if desired. If apricots are not peeled, heat in boiling water for ½ minute to keep skins from toughening during freezing. Cool in cold water, drain. Pretreat if desired.	Syrup pack in 40% syrup. Pretreat if desired. Sugar pack using ½ cup sugar per quart of fruit. Mix until all sugar is dissolved.
Ariona Berry (aka chokeberry)	Sort ripe berries, removing any leaves, stems, and defective berries.	Use dry pack. Do not wash the berries until just before serving.
Banana	Select firm, ripe bananas. Peel. Slice or cube the bananas. Can also be frozen in their skin in a freezer container.	Dry pack.
Blackberry	Wash and sort ripe, firm berries.	Syrup pack in 40 or 50% syrup. Sugar pack using ¾ cup sugar per quart of berries. Use dry pack.

Fruit	Preparation	Type of Pack (Choose One)
Blueberry	Sort ripe berries, removing any leaves, stems, and defective berries.	Use dry pack. Do not wash the berries until just before serving. Crush or puree the berries and mix with 1 to 1⅛ cups sugar per quart of crushed or pureed berries.
Cantaloupe	Select firm-fleshed, well-colored ripe melons. Remove seeds and peel. Cut into slices, cubes, or balls.	Syrup pack in 30% syrup.
Cherry	Sour: Wash, stem, and pit bright red, tree-ripened cherries. Sweet: Wash, stem, and pit bright, fully ripe cherries of dark-colored varieties. Pretreat if desired.	Sour: Syrup pack in 60 to 65% syrup. Sour: Sugar pack using ¾ cups sugar per quart of fruit. Mix until sugar is dissolved. Sweet: Syrup pack in 40% syrup.
Cranberry	Wash and drain firm, deep-red berries with glossy skins.	Use dry pack. Syrup pack in 50% syrup.
Currant	Select fully ripe, bright red fruit. Wash and stem.	Syrup pack in 50% syrup. Sugar pack Use dry pack.

Fruit	Preparation	Type of Pack (Choose One)
Dewberry	Wash and sort ripe, firm berries.	Syrup pack in 40 or 50% syrup. Sugar pack using ¾ cup sugar per quart of berries. Use dry pack.
Fig	Wash fully ripe fruit. Peel if desired. Use a pretreatment if desired.	Syrup pack in 35% syrup. Use dry pack.
Gooseberry	Select fully ripe (for pie) or slightly underripe (for jelly) berries. Wash and remove stems and blossom ends.	Use dry pack.
Grape	Sort, stem, and wash fully ripe, firm sweet grapes. Leave seedless grapes whole; cut table grapes with seeds in half and remove seeds.	Syrup pack in 40% syrup. Juice: Crush grapes. Add 1 cup water per gallon crushed grapes. Simmer 10 minutes. Strain juice through a jelly bag. Let juice stand overnight in refrigerator or other cool place so tartrate crystals will settle. Pour off clear juice and freeze. If freezing juice for jelly-making, use some slightly underripe fruit.

Fruit	Preparation	Type of Pack (Choose One)
Grapefruit	Wash and peel firm fruit. Divide fruit into sections, removing membrane and seeds.	Syrup pack in 40% syrup made from excess juice or water. Juice: Squeeze juice from the fruit, being careful not to press any oil from the rind. Freeze as is or add 2 tablespoons sugar per quart of juice.
Huckleberry	Wash and sort ripe berries, removing any leaves, stems, and defective berries.	Use dry pack. Do not wash the berries until just before serving. Crush or puree the berries and mix with 1 to 1⅛ cups sugar per quart of crushed or pureed berries.
Kiwi	Peel and slice or dice the fruit.	Dry pack. Syrup pack in 30% syrup.
Kumquat	Wash and peel firm fruit. Divide fruit into sections, removing membrane and seeds.	Syrup pack in 40% syrup made from excess juice or water. Juice: Squeeze juice from the fruit, being careful not to press any oil from the rind. Freeze as is or add 2 tablespoons sugar per quart of juice.

Fruit	Preparation	Type of Pack (Choose One)
Lemon	Wash and peel firm fruit. Divide fruit into sections, removing membrane and seeds.	Syrup pack in 40% syrup made from excess juice or water. Juice: Squeeze juice from the fruit, being careful not to press any oil from the rind. Freeze as is or add 2 tablespoons sugar per quart of juice.
Loganberry	Wash and sort ripe, firm berries.	Syrup pack in 40 or 50% syrup. Sugar pack using ¾ cup sugar per quart of berries. Use dry pack.
Lime	Wash and peel firm fruit. Divide fruit into sections, removing membrane and seeds.	Syrup pack in 40% syrup made from excess juice or water. Juice: Squeeze juice from the fruit, being careful not to press any oil from the rind. Freeze as is or add 2 tablespoons sugar per quart of juice.
Melon	Select, firm-fleshed, well-colored, ripe melons. Remove seeds and peel. Cut into slices, cubes, or balls.	Syrup pack in 30% syrup.
Mulberry	Wash and sort ripe, firm berries.	Syrup pack in 40 or 50% syrup. Sugar pack using ¾ cup sugar per quart of berries. Use dry pack.

Fruit	Preparation	Type of Pack (Choose One)
Nectarine	Sort, wash, and peel. Pretreat if desired.	Syrup pack in 40% syrup. Sugar pack using ⅔ cup sugar per quart of fruit. Mix until sugar dissolves. Crush or puree peeled and pitted nectarines and mix with 1 cup sugar per quart of prepared fruit. Heating the pitted nectarines for 4 minutes in just enough water to prevent scorching makes them easier to puree.
Orange	Wash and peel firm fruit. Divide fruit into sections, removing membrane and seeds.	Syrup pack in 40% syrup made from excess juice or water. Juice: Squeeze juice from the fruit, being careful not to press any oil from the rind. Freeze as is or add 2 tablespoons sugar per quart of juice.
Papaya	Choose ripe fruit. Wash, cut in half, remove the seeds. Quarter the papaya and remove the skin. Cut into cubes.	Dry pack. Syrup pack in 30% syrup.

Fruit	Preparation	Type of Pack (Choose One)
Peach	Sort, wash, and peel. Pretreat if desired.	Syrup pack in 40% syrup. Sugar pack using ⅔ cup sugar per quart of fruit. Mix until sugar dissolves. Crush or puree peeled and pitted peaches and mix with 1 cup sugar per quart with prepared fruit. Heating the pitted peaches for 4 minutes in just enough water to prevent scorching makes them easier to puree.
Pear	Wash, peel, core, and slice. Pretreat if desired.	Syrup pack: heat pears in boiling 40% syrup for 1 to 2 minutes. Drain and cool. Pack pears in cold 40% syrup.
Pineapple	Choose ripe pineapple. Remove the skin and core. Slice or chunk the fruit. Optional: Put in a strainer to remove some excess juice before placing it on a tray.	Dry pack.
Plum	Sort and wash ripe fruit that is soft enough to yield to gentle pressure. Leave whole or cut in halves or quarters and pit. Pretreat if desired.	Syrup pack in 40 to 50% syrup.

Fruit	Preparation	Type of Pack (Choose One)
Raspberry	Wash and drain fully ripe, well-colored berries.	Sugar pack using ¾ cup sugar for each quart of berries. Mix carefully to avoid crushing. Syrup pack in 40% syrup. Use dry pack.
Rhubarb	Select firm, well-colored stalks with few fibers. Wash, trim, and cut into ½-inch pieces. Blanch rhubarb in boiling water for 1 minute and cool promptly in ice water. Can also be frozen raw.	Syrup pack in 50% syrup. Dry pack.
Saskatoon (aka Juneberry, Serviceberry)	Sort ripe berries, removing any leaves, stems, and defective berries.	Use dry pack. Do not wash the berries until just before serving.
Strawberry	Wash and remove caps from fully ripe, firm berries with a deep-red color.	Syrup pack whole berries using 50% syrup. Sugar pack whole, sliced, or crushed berries using ¾ cup sugar per quart of fruit. Dry pack.
Watermelon	Select firm-fleshed, well-colored, ripe melons. Remove seeds and peel. Cut into slices, cubes, or balls.	Syrup pack in 30% syrup.

Syrup for Freezing Fruit

Type	Percent Sugar*	Cups of Sugar	Cups of Water	Yield of Syrup in Cups
Very Light	10%	½	4	4½
Light	20%	1	4	4¾
Medium	30%	1¾	4	5
Heavy	40%	2¾	4	5⅓
Very Heavy	50%	4	4	6

*Approximate

Headspace to Allow Between Packed Food and Closure

Type of Pack	Container with Wide Opening		Container with Narrow Opening	
	Pint	Quart	Pint	Quart
Liquid Pack: Fruits packed with juice, sugar, syrup, or water. Crushed or pureed fruit.	½ inch	1 inch	¾ inch	1½ inches
Dry Pack: Fruits or vegetables packed without added sugar or liquid.	½ inch	½ inch	½ inch	½ inch
Juices	½ inch	1 inch	1½ inches	1½ inches

Freezing Meat

Freezer Space Guide for Meat

When freezing meat, you want to ensure it's not exposed to air, nor does it form large ice crystals that can lead to freezer burn.

Wrapping smaller portions of meat is easier than huge portions. Ideally, package it in the size your family will eat for a meal.

A deep freezer is best for the long-term storing of meat, with temperatures at 0°F (-18°C). Freezers attached to refrigerators don't stay as cold and have more temperature fluctuations.

For the longest shelf life in the freezer, wrap the meat in plastic wrap and then butcher paper (shiny side against the meat), making sure it's sealed up tight. Label and date the outside of the package. This is how our beef comes from the butcher (we raise our own but have it processed at a local butcher shop) and we've had roasts that were three years old turn out as tender and delicious as roasts that were frozen for a few months.

Vacuum sealing is another excellent route because it sucks the oxygen out and helps prevent freezer burn.

We butcher our own chickens and use the same technique with a large thick plastic bag and a hot pot of water. Again, I've had birds be in the freezer for two years and roast up as tender and juicy as can be.

I don't recommend purposely going that long, but sometimes freezer Tetris gets the best of you.

Yes, I know, you've seen freezer-life charts of meat say it's only good for a few months. While that may indicate absolute best quality, we've never had any issues personally going longer. Of course, use sound judgment. If it looks off, smells off, etc., then don't use it.

How Much Space Does Your Bulk Purchase Use?

Beef	
Whole Cow	16-17 cubic feet
½ Cow	8 cubic feet

¼ Cow	4 cubic feet

Pork

Whole Pig	5-6 cubic feet
½ Pig	3-4 cubic feet

Chicken and Rabbit

1 Chicken	¼-½ cubic foot
12 Chickens	3-5 cubic feet
1 Rabbit	⅓ cubic foot

Turkey, Duck, and Goose

1 Turkey	2-3 cubic feet
1 Duck	¼-½ cubic foot
1 Goose	2-3 cubic feet

Lamb and Deer

Whole Lamb	1 cubic foot
Whole Deer	2 cubic feet

All freezer space sizes listed are averages.

CHAPTER 5
Fermenting

Fermentation dates back thousands of years and has been a way of preservation in households for generations. It's much easier than you might expect and creates a delicious and healthy probiotic-rich food, snack, or condiment. Here's everything you need to know about fermented vegetables.

Fermented vegetables (and other fermented foods) can seem off-putting if you've never tried them before. Many people are a little reluctant at first, but once they realize the depth of flavor and health benefits, they're hooked!

I never had fermented food growing up, and honestly, it was the last form of food preservation I learned here on the homestead. This is amazing as it's honestly one of the *easiest* forms there is.

Some of the most recognizable ferments today are items like sauerkraut, kombucha, milk kefir, or maybe you've seen that jar of Bubbies pickles at the grocery store?

What most don't realize is just how easy it is to make those fermented pickles at home, or that sauerkraut can take on so many different flavors depending on what you add into it. You can even turn your condiments into fermented foods (like ketchup, mayonnaise, and mustard) in just a few hours!

In the fall, one of my favorite ferments to make is my homemade apple cider vinegar with the apple scraps, cores, and peels left over after preserving our apples. In winter, there's nothing easier than doing fermented lemons to have lemon juice on hand for savory meals throughout the entire year.

Fermented vegetables are probably one of the easiest forms of fermentation (and food preservation) you can start with. It's as simple as mixing some vegetables with salt, either in a dry or water brine, and letting them sit at room temperature anywhere from 3 days to up to 2 or more weeks.

How long a specific ferment takes to finish is dependent on your taste preference and room temperature. The hotter it is, the faster it ferments.

Something like sauerkraut can ferment for 2-4 weeks, the flavors will change throughout the entire process, and many times people will then move it to cold storage to sit for 6+ months for the flavors to further develop. Others only take a few days.

The best thing you can do is to experiment and find what you and your family like best. After all, that's the point of from-scratch and homemade: to make things you and your family like.

There are three kinds of fermentation.

Lactic Acid

Lactic acid fermentation happens when naturally occurring yeast and bacteria convert sugars into lactic acid. This naturally preserves the food for long-term storage (as long as proper temperatures are maintained) and is the typical form used for fermented vegetables.

Examples of this type of fermentation are fermented pickles, sauerkraut, tomatoes, yogurt, buttermilk, cheese, sourdough bread, and even miso and some soy sauces.

Ethyl Alcohol

The most common forms of ethyl alcohol fermentation are beer, wine, hard cider, and other alcoholic beverages. These ferments use yeast to break down starches and sugars and transform them into carbon dioxide, which gives your ferment that nice bubbly effect we all love so much.

Acetic Acid

Acetic acid fermentation occurs when starch from grains and sugars from fruit ferment. This is the case for foods like apple cider vinegar, fruit vinegar, kombucha, water kefir, and milk kefir.

Fermenting Equipment

Must-Have Items for Fermenting	Recommended Items (they make life easier)
Canning jars, wide-mouth: wide-mouth allow for easier packing and allow room for weights.	Fermenting lid: I also like using something like a pickle piper lid, or a fermentation lid specifically designed to fit on a Mason jar. I have much less mold contamination when I use an airlock system.
Lids and bands: If you don't have a fermenting lid, you can use a band and metal lid, but you'll need to "burp" the jar to release built-up pressure. Simply unscrew the band to let the gasses release. Once the item is ready for cold storage, metal bands and lids work best as they're airtight (plastic lids are not).	Digital scale: If you want to get nerdy and ensure exact percentages on brines, this is the way to go.
Pure sea salt: Avoid salt that has iodine, sugar, or anti-caking agents as this will negatively affect the ferment. Sea salts and Redmond's Real Salt are excellent picks.	Food processor: Helpful for large batches of shredded vegetables.
Knife and cutting board: Try to keep food as uniform as possible so it dries evenly.	Fermentation weight (or even an empty, clean baby food jar): Can come in handy for helping the veggies stay below the brine. If you're checking your ferment daily, you can simply press any food that pushes its way above the brine back down, then screw the lid back on, but a weight cuts back on mold contamination.

Must-Have Items for Fermenting	Recommended Items (they make life easier)
Filtered water: When making fermented vegetables, it's important to try to use as pure water as possible. Any chlorine, fluoride, or other mysterious items found in tap water need to be avoided at all costs. Our well water works great.	Kraut pounder: Long-handled wooden utensil that fits inside jars with a wider base on one end to push down on cabbage-based ferments to help release more liquid.

How to Ferment Vegetables Step-by-Step Tutorial

This tutorial is written for sauerkraut but can be used with any of the vegetables listed and their appropriate brine percentage. The key part is making sure the vegetables are submerged beneath the brine liquid.

Clean your vessels and utensils with hot soapy water. Start with fresh vegetables; rinse and remove any bruised or discolored parts.

1. Rinse and prep vegetables per recipe instructions. Reserve two large whole cabbage leaves. Quarter and core cabbage; either slice thinly or use a food processor to shred.

2. Combine ingredients in a large bowl and sprinkle salt over top. Use hands to massage salt into ingredients and encourage water release. Cover bowl with towel and let sit at room temperature for 45 to 60 minutes, until liquid releases.

3. Add in herbs. Squeeze cabbage as you mix herbs in to release more liquid.

4. Pack contents into clean jars (wide-mouth works best) with hands. Pack tightly, pushing to release more liquid as you go, to a ½- to 2-inch headspace.

5. Use a kraut pounder or the knuckles of your hand to push down on the contents until liquid covers the top of the contents.

6. Tuck whole reserved cabbage leaf on top to help secure contents beneath brine level. Place weight on top of cabbage leaf; press down until liquid completely covers all of the recipe.

7. Secure lid on jar. Place jars on a shallow platter or tray to catch any overflow. Check after 24 hours to make sure the brine level is still covering the contents. Add additional 2% brine if not. If not using a special fermenting lid, make sure to burp jar daily to avoid pressure buildup.

8. You should see small bubbles form and the colors become more muted as contents ferment; brine will become cloudy. If any scum or mold forms on the top, scrape it off, wipe the rim clean, and allow it to continue fermenting.

9. Taste-test recipe after 7 days. The longer it ferments the stronger the flavor (I prefer mine at 21 days, but you can go up to 6 weeks). When desired flavor is reached, place a lid on the jar and store in the fridge or cool environment.

Types of Brines

Dry brines, like kimchi and sauerkraut, create their own brine by adding salt to the vegetables. The salt pulls out moisture from the vegetables to create enough liquid.

Wet brine, used for things like cucumbers, beets, and carrots, mixes water with salt to create a brine that the vegetables are submerged in.

The salt to liquid ratio is important; too little salt, you'll have mold growth; too much, and you run the risk of inhibiting fermentation. Most vegetables require a 2 to 5% brine solution. Items that are more prone to mold growth typically have a higher salinity.

Starter Cultures

You do not need to purchase starter cultures for vegetables or fruits. For vegetables the salt and liquid (either dry or wet brine) is all you need to ferment. You can use a ¼ cup of brine from a previous ferment if you wish but it's not necessary.

Fermenting Brine Percentage Chart

Food	Brine Percentage
Beets	2%
Bell Peppers	5%
Broccoli	2%
Cabbage	2%
Carrots	2%
Cauliflower	2%
Celery	2%

Food	Brine Percentage
Cucumbers	3.5% to 5%
Garlic	2% to 3%
Green Beans	2%
Kohlrabi	3.5%
Onion	5%
Peas, Sugar Snap	2%
Peppers, Hot	5%
Pepper Mash	10%
Lemons	3%
Potatoes	2%
Radish	5%
Tomatoes (crushed or whole)	2%
Turnips	2% to 3.5%

Combination Recipes	Brine Percentage
Beet Kvass	2%
Coleslaw	2%
Curtido*	3.5%
Hot Sauce	5%
Kimchi	2%
Salsa	2%
Sauerkraut	2%
Tomato Sauce	1%

Brine Solutions by Percentage Chart

Brine %	250 ml water	500 ml water	750 ml water	1,000 ml water	2,000 ml water	3,000 ml water	4,000 ml water
2%	5 grams salt	10 grams salt	15 grams salt	20 grams salt	40 grams salt	60 grams salt	80 grams salt
3.5%	9 grams salt	18 grams salt	26 grams salt	35 grams salt	70 grams salt	105 grams salt	140 grams salt
5%	13 grams salt	25 grams salt	38 grams salt	50 grams salt	100 grams salt	150 grams salt	200 grams salt
10%	25 grams salt	50 grams salt	75 grams salt	100 grams salt	200 grams salt	300 grams salt	400 grams salt

Brine %	1 cup water (½ pint)	2 cups water (1 pint)	3 cups water (1½ pints)	4 cups water (1 quart)	8 cups water (2 quarts)	12 cups water (3 quarts)	16 cups water (4 quarts or 1 gallon)
2%	5 grams salt	9 grams salt	14 grams salt	19 grams salt	38 grams salt	57 grams salt	76 grams salt
3.5%	8 grams salt	17 grams salt	25 grams salt	33 grams salt	66 grams salt	99 grams salt	132 grams salt
5%	12 grams salt	24 grams salt	35 grams salt	47 grams salt	95 grams salt	142 grams salt	189 grams salt
10%	24 grams salt	47 grams salt	71 grams salt	95 grams salt	189 grams salt	284 grams salt	379 grams salt
Dry Brine	1 pound vegetable	2 pounds vegetable	3 pounds vegetable	4 pounds vegetable	5 pounds vegetable	6 pounds vegetable	7 pounds vegetable
Clean prepared vegetables for combo recipes	5 to 6 grams salt	10 to 12 grams salt	15 to 18 grams salt	20 to 24 grams salt	25 to 30 grams salt	30 to 36 grams salt	35 to 42 grams salt

(Metric is easiest to convert if you have a different liquid amount. Simply multiply the mls by the brine percentage to get the amount of salt needed in grams): mls x brine percentage = grams of salt.

Example: 300mls x 2% = 6 grams of salt

Different types of salt weigh different amounts, which is why it's best to use a scale when making brines. However, humans have been fermenting for centuries and I doubt many used a scale. Below are approximates on converting weight of salt in grams to volume.

Each gram is approximately ¼ teaspoon of fine salt. If using a coarser mineral salt (which I recommend), you'll need to use less volume to reach the correct grams. The weights for coarse salt below were done with Redmond's Real Fine Salt.

Salt Gram to Volume Fermenting Chart

Grams	Volume - Fine Salt	Volume - Mineral Salt
5 grams	1¼ teaspoons	scant 1 teaspoon
10 grams	2½ teaspoons	1¾ teaspoons
12 grams	1 tablespoon	2 teaspoons
18 grams	1½ tablespoons	1 tablespoon
24 grams	2 tablespoons	1 tablespoon + 1 teaspoon
36 grams	3 tablespoons	2 tablespoons

*When making curtido or sauerkraut, I've always had excellent outcomes by combining 1½ tablespoons of mineral salt to 1 medium head of cabbage.

Best Fermenting Practices

Initial Fermenting Rules

Make sure your solid food pieces stay underneath the brine at all times.

Keep vegetable ferments away from other ferment types, like dairy, kombucha, kefir, and sourdough, by at least four feet so they don't cross. (Kimchi, kraut, and fermented pickles can be next to one another.)

Keep ferments on a plate, cookie sheet, or container during the initial first days of fermenting so if they overflow you don't have a mess on your counter or in your cupboard.

Your ferment is done when you like the flavor profile, but remember, the coolness of the fridge slows it down but doesn't stop it completely—it will continue to ferment in the fridge.

Adjusting Flavors

It's fine to add less fish sauce, peppers, or spices. You can leave out ingredients like ginger or stronger-flavored vegetables. Adjust it to your tastes.

Best Temperatures

If you're new to fermenting, keep ferments between 70–75°F/21–24°C and only let them ferment for 2 to 3 days before moving to the fridge. If your home isn't that warm during the winter, move ferments close to your heat source (like a woodstove).

Storing Your Ferments

The fridge is optimal because it's a controlled cool temperature, but if you have a room in your home that's closed off in the winter that stays between 30–50°F/-1–10°C, you can store your ferments there.

Don't Cross-Contaminate

Do not taste it from the spoon and dip it back in there. Always use a new spoon or don't put it in your mouth. Just scoop it into your plate as you go.

Even once food is in the fridge, keep it under the brine. Usually this means leaving the weight in, unless you have enough liquid that the food stays beneath without it.

Troubleshooting

If you see mold growing on the surface of your ferment, you likely had pieces above the brine level and exposed to air. Unlike other forms of food preservation, as long as you're using a 2% brine solution or higher, your ferment is safe to eat.

Simply scrape off the mold (including any solid pieces of fruit/vegetables exposed), wipe the rim of the jar clean, and allow it to continue fermenting. Air-lock lid systems greatly reduce the appearance of mold. You'll know when a vegetable ferment goes bad because it will smell putrid and taste horrible.

If you're experiencing a high percentage of mold contamination or fermenting an item for more than a few days, try sterilizing your fermenting jar and weight in boiling water for 10 minutes.

Sometimes a film forms on the surface of your ferment, usually white, and is mistaken for mold. However, it is often Kahm yeast. Kahm yeast doesn't get fuzzy like mold; it isn't harmful but can affect the flavor and is best to skim off immediately.

Kahm yeast develops often in the beginning before the acidity level has been reached, room temperature is too warm, and/or not enough salt was used. Ferments should never smell or taste unpleasant; they will taste tangy and strong, but if it tastes off or rotten, toss it in the compost.

Fruit Vinegar

While many ferments are done with vegetables, you can easily create homemade vinegar from fruits. Fruit vinegar is delicious and relatively easy to make, though it does take several months to reach completion. This method was first shared with me by Autumn Keim from atraditionallife.com.

Time: three months minimum
Yield: 1 quart

INGREDIENT

4 c. fruit juice of choice

1. **Stage One**: Alcohol phase. Pour juice into a quart-sized glass jar.
2. Cover the container with a breathable cloth (coffee filters or butter muslin work well; loose-weave cheesecloth must be doubled over multiple times so fruit flies can't enter). As the juice ferments, it releases carbon dioxide. If it's sealed, pressure can build up and explode the container.
3. Keep your juice temperature between 60 to 80° F (16 to 27° C). This temperature range allows natural yeast, which is found on the skin of the fruit as well as airborne in the home, to come in and start consuming the natural sugars and converting it to alcohol.
4. A half-gallon jar of juice, depending on the sugar content, takes three to six weeks to turn into vinegar. You'll see bubbles on the sides of the container during this time. When it smells like alcohol, you're likely ready to enter stage two.
5. **Stage Two**: Acetic acid phase. Once the yeast dies back, a different group of bacteria take over. Acetobacter bacteria are a natural airborne bacterium that take alcohol and transform it into acetic acid (aka vinegar). To ensure you have colonization of acetic acid bacteria, you may add a couple of tablespoons of raw vinegar.
6. It takes three to six times (a minimum of three months) longer than stage one to transform all the alcohol to acetic acid. Do not use an airtight lid; they are aerobic bacteria and require oxygen.

Test Before Storing

To test your vinegar to make sure it's completed the phases, take a cup of the vinegar and seal it in an airtight bottle or Mason jar with a metal lid and band.

Put the bottle on the back of your kitchen counter for a day. The next day, break the seal (or pop the top). If there was a release of carbon dioxide (or you audibly hear a "pop"), then it's not ready to be sealed up yet and should remain on the counter for another week or so.

Do this test again in another week; once there is no pressure in your container, you can bottle it up and stash it away.

Troubleshooting

If your vinegar is molding, check the following:

- Are there particles on the surface of your liquid? It should be straight juice.
- Is there airflow? Don't stuff it in the back of your pantry or the back of a cupboard.

Why Is My Fruit Vinegar Foamy or White?

Sometimes the combination of fruit juice that has a higher sugar content and warmer temperatures can get a layer of bubbly scum on the surface of your vinegar.

If this happens, skim it off. It's harmless, but it can affect the flavor, so remove it as soon as it appears (which means you should be checking on your ferment daily).

CHAPTER 6
Root Cellaring

This is my favorite method because it's simple and, in some cases, requires almost no work on my part. You do not have to have a root cellar or basement to successfully preserve and store specific vegetables using the root cellar methods (though they can be used).

Traditional root cellars were dug into a hill or underground. Other methods include burying a garbage can or gutted-out chest freezer into the ground or creating a clamp. Some vegetables store very well by digging a trench in the garden and "burying" the produce to store through the winter.

Root Cellar Options

No matter which option you choose, you want to ensure ventilation (this is the biggest mistake most people make), humidity levels, cool temperatures, and limited light exposure. Routinely check your crops and immediately dispose of any pieces that show rot (discoloration usually turns to rot quickly; consume first).

In the garden—Many root crops (and cabbage) will overwinter in the ground. Soil needs to be well-draining and either mild temps OR thick enough mulch so that the crop won't freeze. I cover potatoes, carrots, and beets with four to six inches of straw in fall. We've had temps as low as 5°F/-15°C without any loss. Snow will act as an insulator but makes digging out the food to use harder. Brussels sprouts and kale are extremely hardy and will last for months in the garden (plus flavors are enhanced by frosts) as is (for extremely cold winter temps, a cold frame or frost fabric may be necessary).

My friend harvests cabbage in the fall, digs a trench in the ground, and sticks the cabbage in head first, with just the roots sticking out. When they want cabbage, they pull it out by the roots, rinse, and remove the outer layers. Check crops frequently and if they're beginning to rot, pull the rest to preserve them in another manner.

Cold rooms/spaces—While a traditional root cellar is a thing of beauty, any insulated room that is unheated (but kept above freezing) can work well. This may be a corner of a basement, unused back room away from a heat source, a camper trailer, or even a crawl space.

Box—Spread an inch-thick layer of damp sawdust, sand, or leaves in a carton or box. Place root vegetables side by side on top of the bedding in a single layer. Place another layer of bedding on top and repeat until the carton or box is full. Store in a cool area according to temperatures for specific root vegetables.

Clamp—This is digging a hole into the ground several feet down (up to six feet deep), placing root vegetables inside on top of one another, covering with a few inches of soil, and then providing another thick layer of straw on top. I find leaving them in the ground and just covering them with straw to be much easier personally, but if you live in an area where the top of your ground stays frozen during the winter several inches thick, this may be a better option.

Repurposing—Use an old chest freezer, fridge, tote, or bucket by placing drain holes in the bottom. Laurie Neverman from *CommonSenseHome.com* recommends using a large barrel with a smaller barrel inside, punching holes in the bottom of both. You'll need to dig a hole wider and deeper than your largest barrel/container and fill it with small rock to provide a drain. Place the prepared container (with drain holes and vent holes on top covered with wire mesh to keep rodents out) into the hole lined with rocks. If using the larger and smaller barrel, place some rock in the bottom of the large barrel and place the smaller barrel on top (your food will go into the smaller barrel). Cover the top with a bale of hay or straw.

The most important aspect is to mimic the temperature and humidity for each specific crop and keep crops out of direct sunlight. Humidity is important so the item doesn't dry out too fast in storage. If you've ever discovered your potatoes shriveled up or your apples were no longer crisp but wrinkly, you've dealt with humidity levels that were too low.

Temperature is how we slow the process of decay. Some crops require colder temperatures than others.

For success, you want to make sure you're selecting long-term storage varieties of fruits and vegetables. This is especially true for apples, garlic, onions, pears, and potatoes. If you ever tried to cure and store Walla Walla onions, you likely had them go bad within a few months, if not faster, whereas a Patterson onion will store for up to a year.

Before you can put your produce into root cellar storage, they must be prepared properly. In most cases, this requires proper curing. When cured properly, specific vegetables will last for months, even if you don't have a root cellar or basement.

For fruit or vegetables that have stems, always leave the stem on; this will prolong shelf life.

Curing allows the outer skin to dry out and harden, making it harder for pathogens or decay to set in. If you're not planning on storing the vegetables and you want to eat them immediately, you can skip the curing process. If possible, harvest on a dry day at the beginning of a sunny stretch.

Do not wash your vegetables when curing. Brush off any large dirt clumps and lay them out in a single layer with good ventilation.

Allow crops to cure as outlined below. The chart and info below are shared from my book *The Family Garden Plan: Grow a Year's Worth of Sustainable and Healthy Food*.

The below crops need to be cured so they don't rot in storage. Curing is needed to remove excess moisture.

Crop	Temperature	Humidity	Curing Time	Signs Curing Is Finished
Garlic and Onion	68–85°F (20–29°C) (don't exceed 85°F/29°C)	70%	Up to 2 weeks	Outer skins are dry and papery; stems have shrunk and are hard (no green shows when you cut the stems near the neck).
Potato	45–60°F (7–15°C)	85–95%	2 weeks	Small nicks and cuts are hardened.

Crop	Temperature	Humidity	Curing Time	Signs Curing Is Finished
Sweet Potato	80–85°F (27–29°C)	80%	2 weeks	Small nicks and cuts are hardened.
Winter Squash	80°F (27°C)	80–85%	10–14 days	Stem is dry and skin is tougher.

What If My Temps Aren't Quite Warm Enough?

We rarely have a full two weeks of exactly correct temps for onions and garlic in the fall. Erring on the cooler side simply increases the curing time to three to four weeks.

If you don't have those types of temperatures (come harvest time in September and October, we're never this warm), you can cure winter squash in a corner of your house at cooler temps; optimal is around 50°F/10°C, making sure you turn them over and no rot sets in.

Proper conditions, as listed in the Root Cellar Storage Chart, will give you produce for the longest period of time.

Curing for Long-Term Storage

Not all crops have specific long-term storage varieties (up to a year), but for those that do, I've listed my favorites below.

Garlic and Onion

Onion and garlic curing temps should not exceed 85°F/30°C, with optimal temps between 68–85°F/20–30°C and 70% relative humidity. Temperatures over 90°F/32°C and direct sunlight can cause sun scald; avoid this.

The curing process can take up to two weeks (or longer if temps are cooler and higher humidity). You know your onions and garlic are cured when the outer skins are dry and papery and the stems have shrunk and are hard (no green shows when you cut the stems near the neck).

I braid mine and store them in our back pantry with an average of 60–65°F/16–19°C, and my garlic lasts a full year.

Long-term garlic storage varieties (softneck store longer than hardneck in most cases):

- Chesnok Red
- Creole
- German Red
- Inchelium Red (my personal favorite)
- Romanian Red
- Silverskins
- Thermadrone

Long-term onion storage varieties:

- Blush - pink onion
- Copra – yellow onion
- Newberg – yellow onion
- Patterson – yellow onion
- Red Wing – red onion

Potatoes

Potatoes, both sweet and regular, require curing. To help toughen the skins, stop watering a few weeks before harvest. Don't wash, but brush off dirt before curing. If you must wash your potatoes, make sure they dry thoroughly before laying them out to cure.

All varieties of potatoes, except sweet potatoes, are best cured at 45-60°F/7-16°C with 85-95% humidity for two weeks. You'll notice that small nicks and cuts will harden up. Potatoes should be stored in the dark (or they'll turn green due to chlorophyll, which can mean the presence of solanine, a toxic alkaloid in large amounts) at 40–45°F/4–7°C with 90% humidity. They'll shrivel up in drier conditions and sprout in warmer conditions.

We tried storing ours in our unheated camper trailer, but the fluctuating temperatures and lower humidity resulted in shriveled and sprouted potatoes after three months, with several turned bad.

My favorite way to store potatoes is by leaving them in the ground. The key is making sure they're deep enough that they don't freeze. I put six inches of straw on top. We've had temperatures down to 5°F with no ill effects to the potatoes. Snow is insulating but makes it difficult to harvest.

They store beautifully until soil temperatures reach 60°F consistently, then they'll begin to sprout. Ours keep from summer clear through until mid-April.

Long-term potato storage varieties:

- German Butterball
- Fingerling
- Russet
- Russian Blu

Below is a list of all crops that can be successfully stored using root cellar techniques. You'll see there are many that don't require curing, but do follow the tips for success.

Root Cellar Storage Chart

Food	Temperature	Humidity	How Long It Will Last	Tips
Apples	32–40°F (0–4°C)	80–90% humidity	4–6 months	Late-maturing apples are best for root cellar storage. Leave the stems on for longest shelf life. Store away from vegetables. Store in a portable bin, baskets, boxes, or perforated plastic bags. To help maintain moisture, you may want to consider lining with plastic or foil. It's recommended to wrap individually in paper or newspaper to get the best storage life. Check routinely for any that are beginning to rot. One apple could ruin the whole bunch.

Food	Temperature	Humidity	How Long It Will Last	Tips
Asparagus	33–40°F (0–4°C)	90–95% humidity	3–5 months	Store large, mature roots of asparagus in tub of soil in the fall. Bring to room temperature during the winter to force a winter harvest.
Beets	32–40°F (0–4°C)	90–95% humidity	4–6 months	Harvest mature beets before frost. Immature beets can remain in the ground under a thick layer of mulch. Break off stems, leaving 1 inch of stem, when harvesting. Spread an inch-thick layer of damp sawdust, sand, or leaves in a carton or box. Place beets side by side on top of the bedding in a single layer. Place another layer of bedding on top of beets and repeat until carton or box is full. Store them by grouping by size. Use the smallest ones first as they deteriorate more quickly. Beets that have gone soft in storage are still good to eat after being boiled.
Brussels Sprouts	32–40°F (0–4°C)	90–95% humidity	Sprouts that have been picked off the plant: 3–5 weeks Bare-root stalk full of sprouts: 1-2 months	Best when picked after several frosts. Store picked sprouts in perforated plastic bags. You can replant the sprout stalk (if you have the space in your root cellar) in a bucket or tub. Brussels sprouts have shallow root systems, making this fairly easy. Last option is to hang the bare-root stalk and take sprouts off as you need them.

Root Cellaring

Food	Temperature	Humidity	How Long It Will Last	Tips
Cabbage	32–40°F (0–4°C)	90–95% humidity	Up to 6 months	Store firm and solid heads for longest storage. Loose heads don't keep well. Place the heads on shelves with several inches between them, or tie a string around the root and suspend from a rafter, or layer heads in hay or wrapped in newspaper. If cabbage freezes, it can be used when it thaws but will not keep well raw after it thaws.
Carrots	32–40°F (0–4°C)	90–95% humidity	4–6 months	Break off stems when harvesting. Spread an inch-thick layer of damp sawdust, sand, or leaves in a carton or box. Place carrots side by side on top of the bedding. Carrots can touch but should be in a single layer. Place another layer of bedding on top of carrots and repeat until carton or box is full. Carrots may also be left right in the garden. Spread at least one to two feet of mulch over the row before the ground freezes. You may want to put a layer of hardware cloth or screening on top of the carrots before mulching to prevent mice from eating them. Store them by grouping by size. Use the smallest ones first as they deteriorate more quickly.

Food	Temperature	Humidity	How Long It Will Last	Tips
Cauliflower	32–40°F (0–4°C)	90–95% humidity	2–4 weeks	Store only solid heads. Pull out by the roots and either replant in sand, hang by the roots, or store on shelves. Enclose the heads with plastic bags for longest storage life.
Celeriac (Celery Root)	32–40°F (0–4°C)	90–95% humidity	3–6 months	Cover roots with damp sawdust, moss, or sand.
Celery	32–40°F (0–4°C)	90–95% humidity	5–8 weeks	Dig and replant in boxes of sand or soil, putting them close together. Don't get the leaves wet when watering. Keep away from turnips and cabbage.
Crabapples	32–40°F (0–4°C)	80–90% humidity	Several months after being picked	May be hung in net bags in the root cellar.
Garlic	32–55°F (0–12°C)	60–70% humidity	2–3 months for hardneck varieties	Will keep best if harvested before cloves burst through the papery sheaths (they often do this when left in the ground until the tops die back and fall over).
			4–5 months for softneck varieties	Store in a bin, basket, or braid, and hang from the ceiling.
Ginger Root	40–50°F (4–10°C)	80–90% humidity	Up to 6 months	Store in a sand can, wooden box with lid, or baskets.

Root Cellaring

Food	Temperature	Humidity	How Long It Will Last	Tips
Grapefruit	33–40°F (0–4°C)	80–90% humidity	4–6 weeks	Store in a portable bin.
Grapes	40°F (4°C)	80% humidity	1–2 months	Should be spread in shallow layers, one bunch deep, in trays or baskets OR hang in bunches from dowel rods.
Horseradish	32–40°F (0–4°C)	90–95% humidity	4–6 months	Dig up large roots in late fall (before a freeze) and store in damp sand or sawdust.
Jerusalem Artichoke	32–40°F (0–4°C)	90–95% humidity	2–4 weeks	Best kept in the ground. Mulch with straw. If stored in root cellar, they won't last long as their thin skin makes them dry up quickly. May be able to prolong storage (by a month) by putting them in damp soil.
Kohlrabi	32–40°F (0–4°C)	90–95% humidity	3–4 months	Pack in damp sand or sawdust.
Leeks	32–40°F (0–4°C)	80–90% humidity	2–3 months	Can be kept in the garden if mulched. Dig up, root and all, and replant in a box or tub of sand or soil.
Lemons and Limes	40–50°F (4–10°C)	60–70% humidity	1–3 weeks	Store in portable bins or mesh bags to maximize air flow.

Food	Temperature	Humidity	How Long It Will Last	Tips
Melon (Honeydew or Cantaloupe)	33–40°F (0–4°C)	80–90% humidity	1–2 weeks	Handle gently when placing on shelves.
Onions	32–50°F (0–10°C)	60–70% humidity	4–6 months	Best keepers are late-maturing onions with thin necks. Store in mesh bags, slatted crates, or cartons with holes in the sides. Or braid and hang from the rafters. If braiding be sure the onions are well cured and dry at the neck, otherwise they may rot. They'll sprout above 50°F/10°C but will take off above 60°F/16°C.
Oranges	32–40°F (0–4°C)	80–90% humidity	1–2 months	The skin sometimes browns when held at 32°F/0°C. Sort fruit from time to time to remove any squishy or moldy fruits.

Food	Temperature	Humidity	How Long It Will Last	Tips
Parsnips	32–35°F (0–2°C)	90-95% humidity	4–6 months	Going through a few frosts improves the flavor.
				They can overwinter for harvest in early spring when the soil starts to thaw. You can also mulch, store them in a hole-in-the-ground cellar pit (like a garbage can), or trench them.
				For indoor storage, spread an inch-thick layer of damp sawdust, sand, or leaves in a carton or box. Place parsnips side by side on top of the bedding. Parsnips can touch but should be in a single layer. Place another layer of bedding on top of parsnips and repeat until carton or box is full.
				Store them by grouping by size. Use the smallest ones first as they deteriorate more quickly.
Pears	32–40°F (0–4°C)	80–90% humidity	2–3 months	Best when picked mature but not ripened on the tree. Wrap pears individually in paper and spread them in shallow layers in small cartons. When you want to eat some, place them in a warmer room and let them ripen at 60–65°F/16–19°C for several days.

Food	Temperature	Humidity	How Long It Will Last	Tips
Potatoes	36–40°F ideal (2–4°C)	80–90% humidity	4–6 months	Store at least 6 feet (1.8 m) away from apples to prevent premature sprouting. Store in complete darkness. They should be cured before putting in storage. The easiest way to keep them is right in the garden if you're in a location that doesn't have many hard freezes. Simply cover with a heavy layer of mulch. Indoors, store in a portable bin, sand can, wooden box with lid, or paper bag. Bins can be stacked as long as there's good airflow between them.
Pumpkin	50–55°F (10–13°C)	70–75% humidity	5-6 months	High storage temperatures make them stringy. Use pumpkins that no longer have their stem first as they will go bad the quickest. Store on shelves or hang in mesh bags.
Quince	32–40°F (0–4°C)	80–90% humidity	Usually last until spring	Let the fruit ripen on the bush until they've turned yellow.

Root Cellaring

Food	Temperature	Humidity	How Long It Will Last	Tips
Rutabagas	33–40°F (0–4°C)	80–90% humidity	2–4 months (without treatment) 5–6 months (with treatment)	Can be stored outdoors with a thick layer of mulch. Indoors, store in a sand can or wooden box with lid. Dip rutabagas in melted food-grade wax (beeswax is recommended) to reduce moisture loss. This extends their storage life.
Salsify	32–40°F (0–4°C)	90-95% humidity	4–6 months	Going through a few frosts improves the flavor. They can overwinter for harvest in early spring when the soil starts to thaw. You can also mulch, store them in a hole-in-the-ground cellar pit (like a garbage can), or trench them. For indoor storage, spread an inch-thick layer of damp sawdust, sand, or leaves in a carton or box. Place salsify side by side on top of the bedding; should be in a single layer. Place another layer of bedding on top of the salsify and repeat until carton or box is full. Store them by grouping by size. Use the smallest ones first as they deteriorate more quickly.
Squash, Acorn	40–50°F (4–10°C)	60–70% humidity	2–4 months	Pick before first frost. Do NOT cure. Acorn squash does not last as long as other squash, so use them up first. Store on shelves, not touching.

Food	Temperature	Humidity	How Long It Will Last	Tips
Squash, Winter	50–55°F (10–13°C)	60–75% humidity	4–6 months	Pick before first frost. Cure before storing. Store on shelves, not touching. You may find that the root cellar is too cold. A side room, attic, heated basement, under the bed, etc., may be a better storage place.
Sweet Potatoes	50–60°F (10–15°C)	80–90% humidity	2–3 months	Must be cured before storing. Temperatures below 50 °F (10°C) promote rot. Avoid handling too much; movement promotes rot. Use bruised and small potatoes first. Wrap individually in paper and place on shelves or shallow crates.
Tangerines	32–40°F (0–4°C)	80–90% humidity	A month or two	The skin sometimes browns when held at 32°F. Sort fruit from time to time to remove any squishy or moldy fruits.
Turnips	33–40°F (0–4°C)	90–95% humidity	4–5 months	Bring in summer-planted crop before a heavy freeze. Spread an inch-thick layer of damp sawdust, sand, or leaves in a carton or box. Place turnips side by side on top of the bedding. Turnips can touch but should be in a single layer. Place another layer of bedding on top of the turnips and repeat until the carton or box is full. Store them by grouping by size. Use the smallest ones first as they deteriorate more quickly.

Food	Temperature	Humidity	How Long It Will Last	Tips
Zucchini	40–50°F (4–10°C)	80–90% humidity	1–2 weeks for small zukes Up to 3 months for large zukes	Store in a portable bin or individually on shelves.

Sweet Potatoes

For sweet potatoes, lay out the tubers (be careful not to bruise or puncture them) and allow them to dry for up to two weeks at 80-85°F/27-30°C with 80% humidity. The higher the temperature the faster they'll cure, so if temps are lower than 80°F/27°C, go the full two weeks. The curing time and higher temperatures also help develop the starches and sugars that make sweet potatoes, well, sweet.

Store sweet potatoes between 55-60°F/13-16°C. Even if you don't have perfect temperatures for curing, don't worry about it; just do your best.

Winter Squash

To cure winter squash, pick when squash is ripe; indicators of ripeness are color change, skin toughening, and a drying stem.

When picking, leave about two inches of the stem; this helps prevent oxygen from getting into the squash and improves storage time.

Wipe off dirt and dry thoroughly (I will often use a vinegar-dampened towel) and lay in a well-ventilated area at 80°F/27°C with the humidity 80-85% for 10 to 14 days.

After curing winter squash for two weeks, store in a cool, dry area at around 55°F/12°C.

I store the majority in my back pantry with a few in the kitchen where the temps are closer to the low- to mid-sixties, and my butternut, acorn, and spaghetti squash last between four and six months.

Squash in the cooler part of the house will last six months plus, with our spaghetti and delicata squash lasting the longest.

Overall Sucess Tips

Make sure to check routinely for any soft spots or rot. During storage, ensure garlic, onions, potatoes, and sweet potatoes have adequate air flow and aren't exposed to light.

I hang up my braids of onions and garlic and store potatoes in mesh bags in our pantry closet. Any containers used to hold potatoes or onions should be breathable; cardboard boxes and paper bags also work well. If using plastic containers, make sure they're not sealed and have a way to breathe or vent.

There is much debate if onions and apples should be stored near potatoes. Many studies show the ethylene gas produced by apples helps to *prevent* sprouting of potatoes (I know, I know, I've read the opposite advice for years too).

Onions should *not* be stored near potatoes (due to moisture), *but* if your potatoes start to sprout, putting an apple in with them can prevent or stop further sprouting.[5] Make sure you check the apple and replace it if it starts to go bad.

CHAPTER 7
Freeze-Drying

Freeze-drying is a relatively new food-preservation method, developed during WWII. It's only been in the past decade that home models have been available. While not a cheap form of food preservation, it allows you to preserve many forms of foods that aren't safe to do with any other method.

I initially was quite hesitant to use one, but Harvest Right sent me a machine to try for free. After using the machine, it quickly became one of my favorite tools in my preservation tool belt—mainly because it opened up the door to preserve shelf-stable food previously not safe or possible.

The texture (both in the freeze-dried state and rehydrated) is incredible. Unlike traditionally dehydrated food, freeze-dried food rehydrates to that of fresh. No rubbery or chewy foods.

A freeze-dryer uses a technique called sublimation—the food is first frozen inside the unit to negative 40 to 50°F. The moisture is turned into a small ice crystal form and the vacuum pump sucks it out. Food is dehydrated with heat in the final step.

This results in a crunchy shelf-stable food, with very little shrinkage (unlike a regular dehydrator), which means food is crisp, not chewy, but still extremely light. Freeze-dried food retains almost 97% of its nutrients, much higher than regular dehydrated or canned food.

Freeze-dried food is shelf stable for up to 25 years.

The biggest benefit is, you can freeze-dry many items you can't safely dehydrate, like:

- Raw eggs
- Raw meat
- Dairy, including milk and cheese

- Ice cream
- Desserts (cheesecake bites)
- Candy
- Full meals/leftovers
- Broth
- Coffee (hello homemade instant coffee or lattes)
- Any food you can regularly dehydrate (vegetables, fruit, herbs, etc.)

Freeze-Drying Equipment

Must-Have Items for Freeze-Drying	Recommended Items (they make life easier)
Freeze-dryer—At the time of this writing there is only one manufacturer, Harvest Right, of home freeze-dryer units.	Mylar Bags with Impulse Sealer or Hot Iron—Best for long-term food storage of foods.
Glass Jars, Lids and Bands, OR Glass Ball Type Jars with Rubber Gaskets—Needed to store freeze-dried foods; best for foods that will be eaten within a year.	Food Processor—Helpful for large batches of shredded vegetables and powdered finished freeze-dried food (8-cup is ideal).
Knife and Cutting Board—Try to keep food as uniform as possible so it dries evenly.	Oxygen Absorbers—Can be used safely in foods with 10% moisture content or lower, especially important for long-term food-storage items.
Hot Pads—Protects hands when handling frozen trays.	Vacuum Sealer with Mason Jar Attachment—Allows you to suck oxygen out of a Mason jar and seal it to store freeze-dried food.
	Silicone Mats—Nice to line trays when dealing with sticky foods.

How to Freeze-Dry Food

You can freeze-dry raw or cooked foods. Keep food as close to the same size as possible for even drying times. Wash and dry raw fruits and vegetables; remove blemished or bruised parts. Fruits and vegetables should either be peeled or halved (or sliced/diced depending on fruit/vegetable) to allow water to be extracted. The decision for slicing or dicing is dependant on how you plan on eating it later. For snacking I prefer slices; for cooking, usually diced. The exception to this is berries like raspberries or blackberries. These freeze-dry whole for me perfectly fine. See the checking of fruit on page 68 for preparation methods. Prepare specific food types for trays.

1. Line trays with food. If freeze-drying sticky fruits, you can line the trays with silicone liners or parchment paper. For liquids, I find it easiest to put trays in the machine, pull out a few inches, and then pour liquids into trays. Don't fill trays higher than the tray lip even with non-liquid foods. Place trays into the machine and select the appropriate setting.

2. Once the cycle is finished, test to see if food needs to cycle longer. Find the largest (or thickest) area of foods and test for any cold spots. If any cold is detected, it's not finished and should go back into the machine for more drying time.

3. When food is fully dry, remove and immediately seal in moisture- and oxygen-proof packaging. If food is left out it will begin to absorb moisture. Label contents (always label if raw eggs or meat), including the date, and store in a cool, dry, dark place.

Freeze-Drying Tips

You can pre-freeze trays in your regular freezer ahead of time. This reduces the amount of freezing time in the machine. Since your deep freeze is already running all the time, it also cuts back on your energy use. Purchasing an extra set of trays is helpful so you can have the next batch of food prepared and frozen while the current batch is running in the freeze-dryer.

Storing Freeze-Dried Food

Like any preserved food, storing in a cool, dry, and out-of-direct-sunlight place is best.

Mason jars or glass jars with a rubber gasket are excellent choices. If the food will be eaten within six months, I do not add an oxygen absorber. If jars are for long-term storage, I do add an oxygen absorber.

If you use an oxygen absorber, once the jar is reopened, the oxygen absorber is no longer good (which is why I don't use it in jars we're currently eating from or will be eating within the next few months). Harvest Right says that if using an oxygen absorber in Mason jars, there is no need to vacuum seal it shut; simply put food and oxygen absorber in the jar, place the lid on, and twist the band down.

Mylar bags will provide the longest shelf life when paired with oxygen absorbers (up to a 25-year shelf life).

Vacuum-sealed plastic bags are not recommended for meats or high-protein foods and should only be used for short-term storage. They're not recommended for long-term storage with freeze-dried food (they're more porous than glass or Mylar bags).

CHAPTER 8

Infusion

Infusions are simply infusing a liquid (oil, alcohol, honey, vinegar, etc.) with a fresh or dried solid matter for flavor. After the infusion period (which varies based upon the solid matter and the liquid type), the solid matter is strained out of the liquid, leaving behind an infused finished product.

These are delightfully easy to make. If you can make tea, you've got the skill set for making infusions. There are however a few safety issues you must be aware of. Botulism (I know, that word again) isn't just a danger with canning; any low-acid oxygen-absent environment where moisture is present can be a breeding ground. However, once armed, you know how to avoid it, so let's dive in.

Must-Have Items for Infusing	Recommended Items (they make life easier)
Glass Jars and Lids — Small jars work well here; I prefer wide-mouths because they're easier to pack in and strain out the solids.	Funnels — Gets the liquid in the jars without spilling all over the counter.
Strainer — These work well for the initial straining OR when you have large solids.	Tea Balls — Helpful for small batches or small herbs.
Coffee Filter/Cheesecloth — If you're dealing with finer items (crushed herbs) or sediment, these help get every bit filtered out.	Labels/Jar Pen — Paint pens or sharpies (which will wash off of glass) or labels for date made, name, and/or ingredients.

Types of Infusions

Infused Vinegar. You can use any type of vinegar you wish (white, apple cider, rice wine, red wine, etc.). I prefer to use raw apple cider in most cases, especially if I'm infusing herbs and/or fruit into it. One of my favorites is cherry-pit infused vinegar; it makes a delightful salad dressing and gives another use for those pits!

Infused Honey. Honey ranges in acidity and pH levels (from 3.5 to 7) and is not recommended for children under one year of age due to possible botulism concerns. You've likely seen recipes for raw-garlic infused honey; however, garlic is a root crop (higher chance of botulism) and non-acidic. I can't find any tested sources to ensure this wouldn't be a potential harbor for botulism, so I only infuse honey with spices or dried solids.

Infused Oil. Oil is not acidic and infused oils have tested positive for botulism. There are safe tested ways to infuse oils. When infusing oils with raw ingredients, you must acidify them first. If you don't acidify them, the infused oil must be stored in the fridge and used within 4 days. You may freeze it for long-term storage. Acidifying instructions are for garlic, basil, oregano, or rosemary only; you can find exact instructions from University of Idaho here http://www.extension.uidaho.edu/publishing/pdf/PNW/PNW664.pdf.

Extracts. Solids are placed in alcohol (vodka, rum, brandy, or even whiskey), allowed to steep, and then strained. Extracts are used in cooking, baking, or cocktails—think vanilla, lemon, almond, etc. While tinctures are alcohol based, they're for medicinal purposes and should be done by specific weight based upon the medicinal herb and aren't used for cooking/flavoring.

How to Infuse Step-by-Step Tutorial

1. Fill a clean glass jar halfway with dried or acidified herbs/spices of choice (fresh ingredients may be used with vinegar and alcohol). Fill the jar with liquid of choice based on infusion type to the top shoulder of the jar, leaving a 1- to 2-inch headspace.

2. Ensure all contents are submerged beneath the liquid level. Place a lid on the jar and put it in a spot where you'll remember to shake the jar at least once a day. If the dried matter absorbs the liquid after a few days, add more liquid to keep solids completely covered.

3. Allow to infuse for a minimum of one week, up to three to four weeks. Begin taste-testing at one week. Once desired strength is reached, strain out the solids through a fine mesh-strainer, coffee filter, or cheesecloth.

4. Pour infused liquid into a glass container and seal. Label with contents and date, then store in a dark, cool, and dry environment (or fridge/freezer depending on infused oil recipe). Strained herbs/spices can be used in teas or the compost pile.

Troubleshooting

Mold/Scum: Usually this appears when the solids aren't kept beneath the liquid level. Use a weight if the solids are floating on the surface to keep them submerged. If scum develops on the surface, skim it off, wipe clean the inside of the jar, and double-check the solids are beneath the liquid. If mold develops (especially pink mold), dispose and don't consume. If despite using a weight you still develop mold, sterilize the jar with boiling water for five minutes before filling.

Kahm yeast. This tends to happen more with vinegar infusions in my experience, especially if they involve fruit with higher sugar contents. These are harmless (though can affect flavor); skin them off, and allow to continue infusing.

Bubbles. With canning, bubbles are a bad sign, but infusions can ferment, especially when doing fruit-type vinegars or fruit-based alcohol infusions. Don't be alarmed if you see bubbles with vinegar and alcohol infusions (but when using fruit with these two infusion types, consider placing the jar in a rimmed container or tray in case it bubbles over).

CHAPTER 9
Salting and Smoking

While most of us think of using salt or smoke to "cure" meat, you can also use salt to preserve herbs, eggs, and some citrus fruits.

Salt pulls moisture out, which decreases the ability for bacteria to proliferate. Specific cuts/types of meat will require curing salt with nitrates to avoid botulism. Some methods pull the curing salt into the meat. Along with the salt, dehydrating or smoking is used to further dry the meat.

There are full books on smoking, curing, and charcuterie alone. An excellent source is Brandon Sheard from farmsteadmeatsmith.com. This is a brief overview, and there are a few of our favorite recipes in the meat section starting on page 375.

Must-Have Items for Smoking/Salting	Recommended Items (they make life easier)
Salt—For herbs and smoking I use Redmond's Real Salt. (Can you tell it's my all-around go-to?) Specific meat recipes/processes require curing salt that contains nitrates/nitrites in order to prevent botulism.*	Curing chamber—Most cured meats will need to be stored after smoking/curing in a cool, humidity-controlled environment.
Glass jar and lid—For salted herbs.	Meat grinder—If you plan on making your own sausage, you'll need a meat grinder, unless you can get your butcher to do it for you.

Must-Have Items for Smoking/Salting	Recommended Items (they make life easier)
Food scale—Used for measuring meat and salt for curing/salting specific recipes/methods.	Packaging—Dependent on method and type of cured/salted meat.
Hardwood chips/pellets—Our favorites are alder, apple, cherry, and hickory. Each type provides a different flavor. Pellets or chips depend on the smoker type.	
Wire racks—Used to smoke meat and/or hang or drape meat over for drying.	
Deep trays or baking dishes—Large enough for slabs of meat when brining prior to smoking OR to hold meat while packed with salt that will not react with the salt.	
Smoker—Some BBQs can be used to smoke, or there are a plethora of smokers on the market, from small electrical units to larger units for hot or cold smoking.	

Curing Safety

There is much confusion on using salt for curing meat. Himalayan Pink salt and Redmond Real salt both have a pink color to them but they're pure salt with naturally occurring minerals that give them their pink hue and do not have sodium nitrate or nitrite added to them. NEVER confuse the two; whereas Himalayan Pink or Redmond Real salt are safe to consume, the same amount of curing salt could be lethal.

Pink curing salt usually has food dye added to bring about its bright pink color AND includes sodium nitrite and/or sodium nitrate and sodium chloride. The sodium nitrite is important to avoid botulism.

Prague Powder #1, Insta Cure #1, or Pink Curing Salt #1. Includes sodium nitrite and sodium chloride; generally used for recipes/methods where the meat is cured for 30 days or less (short-term curing) and the meat will be cooked before serving.

Prague Powder #2, Insta Cure #2, or Pink Curing Salt #2. Includes sodium nitrate, sodium nitrite, and sodium chloride; generally used in longer cures where the bacteria convert the nitrate to nitrite. Sodium nitrate is NOT safe to consume, which is why it's only used in recipes/methods where it will be cured long enough for the conversion to happen, and these meats shouldn't be cooked at high heat.

Always follow a tested recipe/procedure and follow the instructions that come with your curing salts. Do not attempt to make up your own recipes or conversions.

Types of Curing

Dry curing. This is something homesteaders of old used, where meat hangs from hooks. A scale must be used to ensure the correct percentage of liquid has been reduced before consuming, along with controlled humidity levels during the curing process. Dry curing is generally recommended as something you learn from someone who is experienced as there is a large margin of error possible.

Wet curing/brining. Meat is submerged in a salted brine solution, often with other spices, and stored for a day up to a week in the solution in a cold environment (usually the fridge). This is a safer method for beginners to try.

Smoking

Smoking can be used for flavor, cooking, and preservation of foods. Most often it's associated with meat but can be used for cheese and vegetables. Smoking dries out meat, much like salt, but uses the smoke to do so instead of salt (though some cuts do use a salt brine).

Hot smoking. Meat is surrounded both by smoke and hot air temperatures, generally temperatures from 212°-280°F/100°-140°C. Oftentimes meat is brined before smoking. You can use a dedicated smoker or turn your BBQ into a smoker. There are some great online tutorials showing how to do this. I found EatCuredMeat.com to have some great resources for this.

Cold smoking. Meat is generally first dry-cured or brined. It imparts the smoky flavor but slowly dries out the meat and preserves it. Temperatures are between 68-86°F/20°-30°C.

PART 3
Recipes

CHAPTER 10
How to Preserve Vegetables

You'll find vegetables in alphabetical order in this section. Each vegetable will have listed the safe methods to preserve it, favorite recipes, and notes. For exact step-by-step instructions on specific preservation techniques, visit that section in the earlier chapters. Example: See how to dehydrate zucchini in Vegetable Dehydrating Chart in chapter 3 starting on page 63.

Always pick firm, at peak, disease- and blemish-free produce to can. Do not use anything that's started to go bad or has disease.

Pressure Canning Processing Charts

Below are pressure canning charts with processing times for your convenience when canning the individual foods and when doing combination recipes. Always process the vegetable or food that has the longest processing time when doing combination products.

When processing vegetables and meats (with the exception of sauerkraut, which is 5 pounds of pressure), if you're at an altitude of 1,000 feet or lower, you will use 10 pounds of pressure. See the altitude chart on the next page to adjust for your specific needs.

Low-Acid Altitude Processing Pressure Adjustment Chart

Feet	Meters	Dial Gauge	Weighted Gauge
0-1,000	0-305	11	10
1,001-2,000	306–609	11	15
2,001-4,000	610–1,219	12	15
4,001-6,000	1,220–1,828	13	15
6,001-8,000	1,829–2,438	14	15
8,001-10,000	2,439–3,048	15	15

Processing Times in Alphabetical Order

Vegetables

Pressure Canning Processing Time (in minutes)			
Vegetables			
	8 oz	Pint	Quart
Asparagus	-	30	40
Beans, dry	-	75	90
Beans, green	-	20	25

Pressure Canning Processing Time (in minutes)

Vegetables

	8 oz	Pint	Quart
Beans, lima (aka butter)	-	40	50
Beets	-	30	35
Carrots	-	25	30
Corn, cream style	-	85	-
Corn, whole kernel	-	55	85
Leafy greens	-	70	90
Mushrooms, cultivated	45	45	-
Okra	-	25	40
Peas, black-eyed	-	40	50
Peas, dry	-	75	90
Peas, sweet green	-	40	40
Peppers, bell	35	35	-
Peppers, hot	35	35	-

Pressure Canning Processing Time (in minutes)

Vegetables

	8 oz	Pint	Quart
Peppers, pimiento	35	35	-
Potatoes, sweet	-	65	90
Potatoes, white	-	35	40
Pumpkin	-	55	90
Root vegetables	-	30	35
Sauerkraut	-	10	15
Squash, winter	-	55	90

Processing Times Sorted by Time Order

Pressure Canning Processing Time (in minutes)

Vegetables

	8 oz	Pint	Quart
Sauerkraut*	-	10	15
Beans, green	-	20	25

*Sauerkraut also has a raw pack method. The times are 20 minutes for pints and 25 minutes for quarts.

Pressure Canning Processing Time (in minutes)

Vegetables

	8 oz	Pint	Quart
Carrots	-	25	30
Corn, cream style	-	85	-
Okra	-	25	40
Asparagus	-	30	40
Beets	-	30	35
Root vegetables	-	30	35
Peppers, bell	35	35	-
Peppers, hot	35	35	-
Peppers, pimiento	35	35	-
Potatoes, white	-	35	40
Beans, lima (aka butter)	-	40	50
Peas, black-eyed	-	40	50

Pressure Canning Processing Time (in minutes)

Vegetables

	8 oz	Pint	Quart
Peas, sweet green	-	40	40
Mushrooms, cultivated	45	45	-
Corn, whole kernel	-	55	85
Pumpkin	-	55	90
Squash, winter	-	55	90
Potatoes, sweet	-	65	90
Leafy greens	-	70	90
Beans, dry	-	75	90
Peas, dry	-	75	90

Asparagus

	Water-bath Can	Steam Can	Pressure Can	Dehydrate	Freeze	Freeze-Dry	Ferment	Root Cellar
ASPARAGUS	✓	✓	✓	✓	✓	✓	✓	✓
Notes	Pickled only!	Pickled only!	Raw or hot-pack, combination recipes		Must be blanched	Whole or chunks	Whole spears	Roots can be stored to force winter sprouting

Vegetable	Preparation	Jar Size	Pressure Canning Processing Time at 10 lbs. of Pressure*
Asparagus 3 to 4 pounds per quart	**Raw-Pack:** Whole or cut into 1-inch pieces. Tightly pack with the tips down (if packing whole) into hot jars. Don't crush the asparagus.	Pint	30 min
	Hot-Pack: Cut into 1-inch pieces. Combine asparagus and boiling water to cover in a stainless-steel saucepan. Bring to a boil over medium-high heat and let boil for 3 minutes. You want them to be tender-crisp. Drain, reserving liquid for packing the jars. Place the hot asparagus into hot jars.	Quart	40 min

*__Altitude adjustments__: If above 1,001 feet, increase to 10 lbs. of pressure on weighted gauge; for dial gauge, increase by 1 pound for every additional 2,000 feet in altitude.

Asparagus can be both pressure canned and water-bath canned when pickled.

Choose tender spears that are 4 to 6 inches long. Wash and drain, then remove the tough ends and peel off scales, if desired. Wash again.

Pressure Can Asparagus

Raw-Pack: Whole or cut into 1-inch pieces. Tightly pack with the tips down (if packing whole) into hot jars. Don't crush the asparagus.

Hot-Pack: Cut into 1-inch pieces. Combine asparagus and boiling water to cover in a stainless-steel saucepan. Bring to a boil over medium-high heat and let boil for 3 minutes. You want them to be tender-crisp. Drain, reserving liquid for packing the jars. Place the hot asparagus into hot jars.

1. Cover with just-off-the-boil water. Must have 1-inch headspace. Add salt if desired, ½ teaspoon per pint or 1 teaspoon per quart. Be sure to remove air bubbles and check headspace. Adjust as needed. Wipe rim; place lid and band on.
2. Place in a prepared pressure canner. When all the jars are filled and in the canner, place the lid on your pressure canner. Turn heat to medium-high and allow steam to vent through the vent pipe for 10 minutes. After 10 minutes, place the weighted pressure gauge on at 10 pounds pressure (or close vent depending on model); dial-gauge-only pressure canner, use 11 pounds PSI.*
3. Process pints for 30 minutes and quarts for 40 minutes.
4. Turn off heat and allow pressure to reduce to zero naturally. When pressure is completely reduced, remove the lid and wait an additional 10 minutes. Remove jars, place on towels in a draft-free area, cool for 24 hours, check seals, and store.

***Altitude adjustments** *see chart on page 50*

Pickled Asparagus

Yield: 6 quarts

INGREDIENTS

180 spears of asparagus (depending on size, about 30 per quart)

6½ cups water

8½ cups vinegar (always use 5% acidity when canning/pickling. White or ACV. White helps keep the green color of the asparagus)

6 tablespoons pickling salt (regular salt makes the brine cloudy)

1 to 2 cups sugar

1½ teaspoons celery seed

12 teaspoons mustard seed

12 teaspoons dill weed (or 2 heads fresh dill tucked in with the asparagus)

18 cloves garlic

1. Wash jars in hot soapy water. Wide-mouth jars work best.
2. Prepare a water-bath or steam canner, jars, lids, and bands.
3. Put 3 cloves garlic, 2 teaspoons mustard seed, and 2 teaspoons dill in the bottom of each jar.
4. Rinse asparagus in cold water. Measure and chop end off so that heads fill jars with ½-inch headspace. Pack tightly.
5. Put water, vinegar, sugar, salt, and celery seed in a large pot and bring to a boil, stirring occasionally. Once liquid has boiled, fill each jar to the top of the spears, leaving ½-inch headspace.
6. Wipe rims, put on lids, and screw on bands. Place jars in canning rack/basket in water-bath canner. Process for 10 minutes.
7. Let sit on a towel on a counter in a draft-free area for 24 hours. Check for seal, remove rings, and store in a dark, cool place.

Altitude adjustments: *If you're 1,001 to 3,000 feet increase processing time by 5 minutes, 3,001 to 6,000 feet increase processing time by 10 minutes, if above 6,001 feet increase 15 minutes processing time.*

Beans, Dry (Shelled)

	Water-bath Can	Steam Can	Pressure Can	Dehydrate	Freeze	Freeze-Dry	Ferment	Root Cellar
BEANS, DRY (SHELLED)			✓	✓		✓		
Notes			MUST be soaked before canning	Shelled and air-dried		Cooked		

Vegetable	Preparation	Jar Size	Pressure Canning Processing Time at 10 lbs. of Pressure*
Bean, dried 1½ cups per quart	Pretreat beans with a long or quick soak method.	Pint	75 min
		Quart	90 min

*__Altitude adjustments__: If above 1,001 feet increase to 10 lbs. of pressure on weighted gauge; for dial gauge increase by 1 pound for every additional 2,000 feet in altitude.

How to Pressure Can Dried Beans

Canning dried beans is very frugal and saves a lot of time when you need a quick supper. Canning dried beans plain allows you to quickly make refried beans, and add them to soups, salads, chili, and stews.

Having home-canned beans on hand means not having to plan ahead by soaking or cooking for long periods of time. In an emergency or power outage, you don't have to worry about finding extra water to soak or cook your beans with; you just pop off the lid, heat, and eat!

You can also can homemade beans with a molasses sauce for your own pork and beans at home.

On average ¾ cup dried beans equals one pint canned (and 1½ cups dried for a quart jar).

Soaking Methods to Prepare Dried Beans for Canning

If canning plain dried beans, you can soak beans for 12 to 18 hours, especially if you're planning ahead.

If not, you'll need to use the quick soak method. To quick soak, cover beans with water about 2 to 3 inches over the top, and bring to a boil. Boil for 2 minutes, remove from heat, and allow to soak for 1 hour.

Pressure Can Dried Beans

1. Using either method of soaking (but you must have soaked and rehydrated them via one of the two methods), drain and cover beans with fresh water. Bring to a boil and boil for 30 minutes.

2. While beans are cooking, prepare pressure canner (for more information see pages 48-49).

3. Remove beans from heat. Have hot clean jars ready with ½ teaspoon salt in pint jars and 1 teaspoon salt in quart jars. Fill jars with beans and cooking water to a 1-inch headspace.

4. Remove air bubbles; double-check headspace (add more of the cooking water to reach 1-inch headspace if necessary). Wipe rims clean and place on lids and bands and put jars in a pressure canner.

5. When all the jars are filled and in the canner, place the lid on your pressure canner. Turn heat to medium-high and allow steam to vent through the vent pipe for 10 minutes. After 10 minutes, place the weighted pressure gauge on at 10 pounds pressure (or close vent depending on model); dial-gauge-only pressure canner, use 11 pounds PSI.* Process pint jars for 75 minutes and quart jars for 90 minutes.

6. Turn off heat and allow pressure to reduce to zero naturally. When pressure is completely reduced, remove the lid and wait an additional 10 minutes. Remove jars, place on towels in a draft-free area, cool for 24 hours, check seals, and store.

***Altitude adjustments** *see chart on page 50*

Home-Canned Pork and Beans Molasses Style

One thing to remember is that home-canned foods will develop more flavor as they sit on the shelf. Second, if you want more flavor, at the time of cooking (not canning) you can add a few cloves, minced garlic, or minced onion and let it simmer for 10 minutes with the jar of beans before serving. However, we usually just eat these as is.

Yield: Approximately 9 pints

INGREDIENTS

5 cups dried beans

¾-inch cube of bacon, pork, or ham to each jar

Molasses Sauce (the original recipe called for half of this amount, but it wasn't enough to fill all of my jars when doing pints)

8 cups cooking liquid from beans or water

6 tablespoons dark molasses

2 tablespoons vinegar

4 teaspoons salt and dash of pepper to taste

1½ teaspoons dry mustard powder

1 tablespoon Worcestershire sauce

Altitude adjustments see chart on page 50

1. Rinse and sort dried beans. Put in a large pot and cover with water to about 3 inches over the top of the beans. Bring to a boil and boil for 2 minutes. Remove from heat and let soak for 1 hour and drain.

2. While beans are soaking, prepare pressure canner (for more information see pages 48-49).

3. Measure out ingredients for sauce and put in a saucepan on the stove.

4. Using either method of soaking (but you must have soaked and rehydrated them via one of the two methods), drain and cover beans with fresh water. Bring to a boil.

5. While the beans are coming to a boil with the fresh water for the second time, bring molasses sauce to a boil, stirring frequently.

6. When both the beans and sauce have reached a boil, carefully use your slotted spoon to fill your jar with hot beans ¾ of the way full. Add in the cube of pork, ham, or bacon to the jar. Cover with the molasses sauce to a 1-inch headspace. Remove air bubbles and recheck your headspace. Add more molasses sauce if needed.

7. Wipe clean the rim of the jar and place the lid and band on. Screw to fingertip tight and place the jar on the rack in pressure canner.

8. Fill the rest of your jars following the above procedure.

9. When all the jars are filled and in the canner, place the lid on your pressure canner. Turn heat to high and allow steam to vent through the vent pipe for 10 minutes. After 10 minutes, place the weighted pressure gauge on at 10 pounds pressure* and process pint jars for 65 minutes and quart jars for 75 minutes. If using a dial-gauge-only pressure canner, use 11 pounds PSI.* Follow pressure level according to your altitude and type of gauge (see chart at beginning of the chapter).

10. Turn off heat and allow pressure to reduce to zero naturally. When pressure is completely reduced, remove the lid and wait an additional 10 minutes. Remove jars, place on towels in a draft-free area, cool for 24 hours, check seals, and store.

Beans, Snap (Green Bush or Pole)

	Water-bath Can	Steam Can	Pressure Can	Dehydrate	Freeze	Freeze-Dry	Ferment	Root Cellar
BEANS, SNAP (GREEN BUSH OR POLE)	✓	✓	✓	✓	✓	✓	✓	
Notes	Pickled only!	Pickled only!	Raw or hot-pack or part of a combination recipe	Must be blanched OR leather britches (no blanching)	Must be blanched	Whole, pieces	Whole, pieces	

Vegetable	Preparation	Jar Size	Pressure Canning Processing Time at 10 lbs. of Pressure*
Beans, Snap 1½ to 2 pounds per quart	Rinse, drain (string per variety), trim ends, and snap into 1-inch pieces (or leave whole).	Pint	20 min
		Quart	25 min

***Altitude adjustments**: If above 1,001 feet increase to 10 pounds of pressure on weighted gauge; for dial gauge increase by 1 pound for every additional 2,000 feet in altitude.

How to Preserve Vegetables | 177

Pressure Can Green Beans (Raw-Pack Method)

INGREDIENTS

14 pounds for 7 quarts

9 pounds for 9 pints

salt

1. Wash beans and trim ends (remove strings on string varieties). Leave whole or snap into 1-inch pieces.

2. Prepare pressure canner (for more information see pages 48-49), jars, lids, and bands.

3. Fill jars with snapped beans, leaving a 1-inch headspace.

4. Add salt (1 teaspoon for quarts and ½ teaspoon for pints).

5. Add boiling water, leaving 1-inch headspace. Remove air bubbles and add more water if needed to maintain 1-inch headspace.

6. Wipe rims; put lids and bands on to fingertip tight.

7. When all the jars are filled and in the canner, place the lid on your pressure canner. Turn heat to high and allow steam to vent through the vent pipe for 10 minutes. After 10 minutes, place the weighted pressure gauge on at 10 pounds pressure* and process pint jars for 20 minutes and quart jars for 25 minutes. If using a dial-gauge-only pressure canner, use 11 pounds PSI. Follow pressure level according to your altitude and type of gauge (see chart at beginning of the chapter).

8. Turn off heat and allow pressure to reduce to zero naturally. When pressure is completely reduced, remove the lid and wait an additional 10 minutes. Remove jars, place on towels in a draft-free area, cool for 24 hours, check seals, and store.

***Altitude adjustments** see chart on page 50*

Dilly Beans

Yield: Approximately six pints

INGREDIENTS

4 to 5 pounds green beans, trimmed to fit inside jar

6 cloves peeled garlic

6 to 12 heads of fresh dill (may sub ½ teaspoon dill seed or dill weed)

3 cups water

3 cups vinegar

3 tablespoons pickling/canning salt

1. Prepare a water-bath or steam canner, jars, lids, and bands.

2. Place 1 clove of garlic and 1 to 2 heads of dill in each jar. Trim beans to fit inside jars with a generous ½-inch headspace remaining. Pack beans fairly tight.

3. Put vinegar, water, and salt in a large stainless-steel pot and bring to a full boil. Pour over beans to a ½-inch headspace. Remove air bubbles and add more brine if needed for ½-inch headspace.

4. Wipe the rim of the jars clean; place the lid and band on. Screw down to fingertip tight and place jars in a water-bath or steam canner. Process pints for 10 minutes.*

5. Follow instructions for a water-bath or steam canner at the end of processing time. Place on the counter on a folded kitchen towel. Cool for 24 hours, check the seals, and then store.

Altitude adjustments: *If you're 1,001 to 3,000 feet increase processing time by 5 minutes, 3,001 to 6,000 feet increase processing time by 10 minutes, if above 6,001 feet increase 15 minutes processing time.*

Fermented Garlic Green Beans

Yield: 1 quart

INGREDIENTS

4 cups washed, strung, and snapped fresh green beans

3 cloves garlic, peeled

2 tablespoons sea salt

3 cups water (distilled or unchlorinated)

1 teaspoon dried or 1 tablespoon fresh herb of choice

1. Place garlic and herbs in the bottom of a clean quart-sized Mason jar.
2. Dissolve salt in warm water and allow it to cool to room temperature.
3. Tightly pack jar with green beans to the shoulder to a scant 1-inch headspace. Pour salt water over top to 1-inch headspace. Place fermenting weight and ensure all contents are beneath the liquid level.
4. Place either a fermenting airlock lid on jar or a two-piece metal canning lid and band. If using a metal lid and band, tighten fully and then back it off a half turn, and make sure to burp the jar.
5. Set at room temperature for one to two weeks. Check for desired flavor at one week; move to cold storage once desired flavor is reached.

Leather Britches

Leather britches are green beans that have been preserved by stringing and drying, rather than canning or other forms of preservation.

The great thing about this method of preservation is that you don't have to heat up your house with a pressure canner or even a dehydrator to preserve them safely.

During the great depression, my grandmother did can some food, but they had a limited number of jars, so she really had to choose what food went into jars versus other forms of food preservation that were available to her.

Traditionally, leather britches were done with a greasy bean, an heirloom bean that is slick, without fuzz on the pod. Any hardy, non-fuzzy green bean will dry well and make great leather britches. It's best to choose a variety that has thicker skin and larger beans.

Use beans that aren't overripe. They should be in the perfect eating stage, tender and crisp when snapped. Some green beans are referred to as string beans because they have a long, fibrous "string" that grows on one side of the bean. Green beans are also referred to as snap beans because of the noise they make when you're snapping the ends off the beans. If the variety of bean that you have has the string, it needs to be removed. No one likes a piece of floss-like material in their mouth while enjoying dinner!

How to Make Leather Britches

1. Give the beans a quick rinse, then string them by snapping off one end and pulling the string-like membrane off the bean. Then snap the other end of the bean off.
2. Grab an older sewing needle and a long piece of thread and double thread your needle. The beans can get heavy if doing a long strand, so doubling the thread is highly recommended. Tie off a large knot at the end of the string. If the knot is too small, the beans will just slip right over it.
3. Take the bean and poke the needle through the middle of the bean. I like to poke through one of the actual beans rather than just through the green fleshy part; this will help the beans stay in place.
4. Continue stringing your beans until you have a nice long line of beans. I like to do mine in about one- to two-foot sections, but ultimately it depends on how many beans you're harvesting at a time for how long your strand will get OR how much your family will eat at one sitting.
5. Make a big loop at the top of the string and hang it from a hook where it's out of the way, preferably in a warm, dry area with good airflow.

As the beans dry, they will start to look leathery, hence the name "leather britches."

Store them in a cool, dark, dry area of your home.

Leather britches need to be rehydrated before cooking. Cover 4 cups of leather britches with 6 cups hot water (make sure they're covered by a couple of inches) and let soak for 2 hours, or until the beans are soft and pliable.

Rinse them and place in the insert pot of a pressure cooker. Add water, enough to cover by a couple of inches, 1 slice of bacon that has been chopped, 1 teaspoon of salt, and 1 clove of minced garlic. Cook on high for 20 minutes. Let the pressure release naturally for 15 minutes, then manually release any remaining pressure.

Beets

	Water-bath Can	Steam Can	Pressure Can	Dehydrate	Freeze	Freeze-Dry	Ferment	Root Cellar
Beets	✓	✓	✓	✓	✓	✓	✓	✓
Notes	Pickled only!	Pickled only!	Hot-pack	Must be cooked	Must be cooked	Sliced	Sliced, chunks, shredded, and Kvass	Leave an inch of stem, store by size, using the smallest ones first

Vegetable	Preparation	Jar Size	Pressure Canning Processing Time at 10 lbs. of Pressure*
Beets 3 pounds per quart	Blanch and peel. Beets 1- to 2-inch diameter may be canned whole. Quarter larger beets.	Pint	30 min
		Quart	35 min

__Altitude adjustments__: If above 1,001 feet increase to 10 lbs. of pressure on weighted gauge; for dial gauge increase by 1 pound for every additional 2,000 feet in altitude.

Pressure Can Beets

INGREDIENTS

21 pounds beets for 7 quarts

or

13½ pounds beets for 9 pints

1. Prepare a pressure canner (see pages 48-49 for more information), jars, lids, and bands.
2. Beets should be 1- to 2-inch diameter for whole packing. Beets larger than 3 inches in diameter are usually fibrous and not ideal.
3. Trim off beet tops, leaving an inch of stem and roots to reduce bleeding. Scrub well.
4. Cover beets with boiling water and boil until the skins come off easily. This will take approximately 15 to 25 minutes, depending on the size. Rinse immediately under cool water and allow to cool until you can handle the beets without burning your fingers. The skins will just slip off.
5. You can leave baby beets whole. Cut larger beets into ½-inch cubes or slices. Halve or quarter large slices.
6. Add 1 teaspoon of salt per quart or ½ teaspoon salt per pint. Salt isn't required, so this is your preference.
7. Fill jars with hot beets and fresh hot water that has been boiled. Leave 1-inch headspace. Remove air bubbles and add more water if needed to maintain 1-inch headspace.
8. Wipe rims; put lids and bands on to fingertip tight.
9. When all the jars are filled and in the canner, place the lid on your pressure canner. Turn heat to high and allow steam to vent through the vent pipe for 10 minutes. After 10 minutes, place the weighted pressure gauge on at 10 pounds pressure* and process pint-sized jars for 30 minutes and quart-sized jars for 35 minutes. If using a dial-gauge-only pressure canner, use 11 pounds PSI. Follow pressure level according to your altitude and type of gauge (see chart at beginning of chapter).
10. Turn off heat and allow pressure to reduce to zero naturally. When pressure is completely reduced, remove the lid and wait an additional 10 minutes. Remove jars, place on towels in a draft-free area, cool for 24 hours, check seals, and store.

***Altitude adjustments** see chart on page 50*

How to Preserve Vegetables | 185

Pickled Beets

You must peel your beets to lower the bacteria load, and pickled beets are done using a hot-pack method. You can lower the sugar but never alter the water-to-vinegar ratio. You'll likely want a small amount of sugar to help counter the pucker punch of the vinegar because we're using quite a bit more vinegar than we do with cucumbers.

How to Peel Beets for Canning

To peel beets, cut tops to 2 inches (this helps reduce bleeding and gives you something to hold on to when peeling and chopping later). Cover in a large pot with water and boil until beets are just fork tender (you don't want them overcooked), usually around 20 minutes or so depending on the size of the beets.

Rinse immediately under cool water and allow to cool until you can handle the beets without burning your fingers. The skins will just slip off. Allow them to cool enough to chop (they'll be hot on the inside still).

Make sure you dump out the water you used to boil the beets for peeling.

Sweet Cinnamon Pickled Beets

This recipe is based on the Ball Complete Book of Home Canning *and I've altered the sugar and spices only.*

Yield: Approximately 6 pints

INGREDIENTS

7 pounds of beets, peeled and chopped/diced (it's about 8 cups of prepared beets)*

5 cups vinegar (apple cider or white but must be 5% acidity)

2 cups water

1½ cups sugar (original recipe called for 2 cups sugar)

1 four-inch cinnamon stick broken up

*Baby beets may be canned whole; slice or quarter larger beets.

1. Prepare your water-bath or steam canner, jars, lids, and bands.
2. Prepare your brine recipe and place spices in a tea ball or tea bag and boil for 15 minutes. Remove spices.
3. Add peeled and chopped/diced beets to brine and bring back to a boil.
4. Use a slotted spoon to spoon beets into prepared canning jars (I prefer wide-mouth) to a generous ½-inch headspace. Use the hot pickling brine to top off to ½-inch headspace; remove air bubbles, recheck headspace, and add more brine if needed to stay at ½-inch headspace.
5. Wipe rim, place on lid, and screw band down to fingertip tight. Place in a water-bath or steam canner.
6. Repeat with each jar. Process pint jars for 30 minutes. Follow instructions for a water-bath or steam canner at the end of processing time. Place on the counter on a folded kitchen towel. Cool for 24 hours, check the seals, and then store.

Altitude adjustments: *If you're 1,001 to 3,000 feet increase processing time by 5 minutes, 3,001 to 6,000 feet increase processing time by 10 minutes, if above 6,001 feet increase 15 minutes processing time.*

FLAVOR VARIATIONS:

- Ball specifies you can cut back the beets by 2 cups and sub in an equal amount of sliced onions to make pickled beets and onions. Add the onions to the brine with the spices and cook the whole time the spices are infusing.
- Use regular pickling spices in place of the cinnamon sticks.
- Use 10 whole cloves of garlic with the cinnamon sticks.

Broccoli

	Water-bath Can	Steam Can	Pressure Can	Dehydrate	Freeze	Freeze-Dry	Ferment	Root Cellar
BROCCOLI				✓	✓	✓	✓	
Notes				Must be blanched	Must be blanched	Florets or diced	Stems, spears (not florets)	

Brussels Sprouts

	Water-bath Can	Steam Can	Pressure Can	Dehydrate	Freeze	Freeze-Dry	Ferment	Root Cellar
BRUSSELS SPROUTS				✓	✓	✓		✓
Notes				Must be blanched	Must be blanched			

Cabbage

	Water-bath Can	Steam Can	Pressure Can	Dehydrate	Freeze	Freeze-Dry	Ferment	Root Cellar
CABBAGE	✓	✓		✓	✓		✓	✓
Notes 25 pounds to 9 quarts	Pickled, relish, or sauerkraut only!	Pickled, relish, or sauerkraut only!		Must be blanched	Must be blanched		Chopped, shredded	Use firm heads for longest storage

How to Preserve Vegetables

Traditional Sauerkraut

INGREDIENTS

1 head cabbage (purple or green)

1 tablespoon sea salt

FLAVORING OPTIONS HERBS AND SPICES:

- caraway seeds
- chili flakes
- cumin
- dill
- fennel seeds
- ginger
- juniper berries
- whole black peppercorn

FLAVORING OPTIONS FRUITS AND VEGETABLES:

- sliced apples
- shredded carrots
- garlic
- lemon peel, zested
- sliced pears
- peppers
- diced pineapple

1. Sliced cabbage using either a knife or a food processor.
2. Place in a large bowl, sprinkle salt over, and mix. Let sit for at least 30 minutes.
3. Stir and let sit for another 20 to 30 minutes, until you have enough juices to cover the cabbage when packed into your jar or fermenting vessel.
4. Transfer to your container. A wide-mouth Mason jar, either a quart or ½-gallon, works great.
5. Press down hard on the cabbage so the liquid rises to the top and covers the cabbage.
6. Place your fermenting weight on top to hold the cabbage down beneath the brine level.
7. Put your lid or airlock on top. If using band, tighten fully and then back it off a half turn; make sure to burp jar.
8. Allow to ferment for 7 days and then check for flavor. Depending on the temperature of your home and your preference, it may take anywhere from 1 to 4 weeks.
9. After it's reached its desired flavor, remove the weight or airlock, and transfer to cold storage (usually your fridge).

Curtido

There are many ways you can flavor your sauerkraut, and one of our favorites is this Spanish-flavored version. It's delicious on sandwiches, on top of eggs, hamburgers, hotdogs, salads, and on top of tacos.

My version doesn't use jalapeños as I don't like much heat, but I included it as an option for you in the recipe below.

INGREDIENTS

1 head small/medium cabbage

1½ tablespoons sea salt

2 carrots

1 small/medium onion

4 to 5 cloves garlic

(optional) 1 to 2 jalapeños, deseeded

1 tablespoon dried oregano OR 2 to 3 tablespoons fresh oregano, chopped

1. Rinse and shred cabbage, carrots, onion, and garlic, either with a knife or in a food processor.
2. Place shredded cabbage, carrots, onion, and garlic in a large bowl and sprinkle with sea salt. Mix the salt and vegetables.
3. Allow to sit for 30 to 60 minutes, until juices are present in the bowl. Stir in oregano.
4. Pack into a clean quart-sized Mason jar (or ½-gallon depending on the size of your cabbage).
5. Push firmly until the juices rise above the level of the vegetables. Place fermenting weight inside, making sure the vegetables are below the level of the brine.
6. Put the lid and/or air lock device on top. If using band, tighten fully and then back it off a half turn, making sure to burp jar.
7. Allow to sit and ferment for 5 days. Taste-test to see if it's where you like it. May ferment longer, depending on taste. The warmer your home the faster it will ferment.
8. Once it reaches the desired flavor, remove the airlock lid, cover the container, and place in the fridge.

Carrots

	Water bath Can	Steam Can	Pressure Can	Dehydrate	Freeze	Freeze-Dry	Ferment	Root Cellar
CARROTS	✓	✓	✓	✓	✓	✓	✓	✓
Notes	Only in a tested recipe that has the safe ratio of acid to vegetable, such as a relish, salsa, jam, or pickle	Only in a tested recipe that has the safe ratio of acid to vegetable, such as a relish, salsa, jam, or pickle	Raw or hot-pack or part of a combination recipe	Must be blanched	Must be blanched	Sliced, diced, or shredded	Sliced, diced, shredded	Store them by size and use the smallest ones first

Vegetable	Preparation	Jar Size	Pressure Canning Processing Time at 10 lbs. of Pressure*
Carrots 2 to 3 pounds per quart	Wash and peel. Rinse again and slice or dice.	Pint	25 min
		Quart	30 min

*__Altitude adjustments__: *If above 1,001 feet increase to 10 pounds of pressure on weighted gauge; for dial gauge increase by 1 pound for every additional 2,000 feet in altitude.*

How to Preserve Vegetables | 193

Pressure Can Carrots

INGREDIENTS

17½ pounds (tops removed) for 7 quarts

11 pounds (tops removed) for 9 pints

1. Prepare a pressure canner (see pages 48-49 for more information), jars, lids, and bands.
2. Select non-fibrous, smaller carrots.
3. Wash, peel, and rinse again. Slice or dice (I prefer sliced rounds).
4. Add 1 teaspoon of salt per quart or ½ teaspoon salt per pint. Salt isn't required, so this is your preference.
5. **Hot-pack**—Cover prepared carrots with water and bring to a boil; cook for 5 minutes. Pack into prepared jars to a 1-inch headspace.
6. **Raw-pack**—Pack carrots tightly to a 1-inch headspace. Pour just-off-the-boil water over them to a 1-inch headspace.
7. Remove air bubbles and add more water if needed to maintain 1-inch headspace.
8. Wipe rims; put lids and band on to fingertip tight.
9. When all the jars are filled and in the canner, place the lid on your pressure canner. Turn heat to high and allow steam to vent through the vent pipe for 10 minutes. After 10 minutes, place the weighted pressure gauge on at 10 pounds pressure* and process pint jars for 25 minutes and quart jars for 30 minutes. If using a dial-gauge-only pressure canner, use 11 pounds PSI. Follow pressure level according to your altitude and type of gauge (see chart at beginning of chapter).
10. Turn off heat and allow pressure to reduce to zero naturally. When pressure is completely reduced, remove the lid and wait an additional 10 minutes. Remove jars, place on towels in a draft-free area, cool for 24 hours, check seals, and store.

***Altitude adjustments** see chart on page 50*

Fermented Carrots

This can be made into carrot sticks or shred it for more of a salad or side condiment.

Yield: 1 quart

INGREDIENTS

2 pounds carrots, washed and peeled

2 tablespoons sea salt

4 cups water (distilled or unchlorinated)

1 tablespoon grated fresh ginger (optional)

FLAVOR VARIATIONS

- 2 heads of fresh dill
- 2 to 3 cloves of peeled garlic
- ¼ teaspoon whole black peppercorn
- ¼ teaspoon whole allspice

1. To shred, place carrots in a food processor or grater and then place the shredded carrots in a large bowl with ginger. Sprinkle salt over top and massage in with your hands for 10 to 15 minutes until you've drawn out moisture. Tightly pack carrots and ginger into the jar, pressing down firmly often. Pour remaining liquid from the bowl over the top.

2. For sticks, slice carrots into desirable sizes. Mix salt in water until fully dissolved (I find heating the water helps dissolve the salt; then cool to room temperature). Place carrots and spices, if using, in a clean quart Mason jar. Pour brine over top to a 1-inch headspace.

3. Place your weight on top to ensure all the solids are beneath the liquid level. Put the air-lock lid on or a two-piece metal lid and band (if using a band, tighten fully and then back it off a half turn, making sure to burp the jar).

4. Place filled jars on counter and allow to ferment for three to seven days. Begin checking flavor profile at three days, and then put in cold storage when desired flavor is reached. Warmer room temperatures will cause faster fermentation.

Cauliflower

	Water-bath Can	Steam Can	Pressure Can	Dehydrate	Freeze	Freeze-Dry	Ferment	Root Cellar
CAULIFLOWER	✓	✓		✓	✓	✓	✓	✓
Notes	Pickled only!	Pickled only!		Must be blanched	Must be blanched	Floret	Floret	Store only tight, solid heads

How to Preserve Vegetables | 197

Jardiniere Recipe

Adapted from Mixed Vegetable Pickles in Ball Complete Book of Home Preserving

Yield: 6 pints

INGREDIENTS

1¼ pounds pickling cucumbers, ends removed, sliced into 1-inch pieces

2 cups carrots peeled, sliced into 1½-inch pieces

2 cups celery, sliced into 1½-inch pieces

2 large red bell peppers, seeded and sliced into ½-inch strips

3 cups cauliflower florets

2 hot red peppers, seeded and cut into ½-inch thick rings (optional)

1 cup salt

Water

6½ cups vinegar (5% acidity)

2 cups sugar

¼ cup mustard seeds

2 tablespoons celery seeds

¼ teaspoon whole cloves (optional)

1. Combine prepared vegetables in a large glass or stainless-steel bowl. Mix salt with 1 gallon of water; stir until salt is dissolved. Pour over vegetables, cover, and place in the fridge for 12 to 18 hours.
2. Pour vegetables into a colander, drain, rinse thoroughly with cold water, and allow to drain.
3. Prepare a water-bath or steam canner for a hot-pack, jars, lids, and bands.
4. In a large non-reactive pot, mix vinegar, sugar, seeds, and spices. Over medium-high heat, bring to a boil and boil for 3 minutes. Add drained vegetables and simmer for 5 minutes.
5. Pack hot vegetables into prepared jars, leaving ½-inch headspace.
6. Remove air bubbles and add more brine if needed for ½-inch headspace.
7. Wipe the rims of the jars clean; place the lid and band on. Screw down to fingertip tight and place jars in a water-bath or steam canner. Process pints for 15 minutes.*
8. Follow instructions for a water-bath or steam canner at the end of processing time. Place on the counter on a folded kitchen towel. Cool for 24 hours, check the seals, and then store.

***Altitude adjustments**: If you're 1,001 to 3,000 feet increase processing time by 5 minutes, 3,001 to 6,000 feet increase processing time by 10 minutes, if above 6,001 feet increase 15 minutes processing time.*

Celery

	Waterbath Can	Steam Can	Pressure Can	Dehydrate	Freeze	Freeze-Dry	Ferment	Root Cellar
CELERY	✓	✓	✓	✓	✓	✓	✓	✓
Notes	Only as part of a tested relish or pickle recipe	Only as part of a tested relish or pickle recipe	Only as an ingredient in a combination recipe	Must be blanched	Must be blanched	Stalks, diced, leaves	Stalks, leaves	Only if plant is transferred to boxes of sand or soil

This preservation method can be used with any leafy herb such as:

- Basil
- Celery leaf
- Cilantro
- Chives
- Dill leaf
- Lemon balm
- Parsley
- Rosemary

Celery Salt

Use in place of salt in any cooking recipe. This is ideal because it keeps the bright fresh flavor of herbs (especially wonderful with basil, which typically loses its flavor with plain dehydrating). If you'd like to do different or larger amounts, just keep the ratio 4 parts fresh herb to 1 part salt.

INGREDIENTS

½ cup celery leaves (leaves and stems, fresh, finely chopped)

2 tablespoons mineral salt

1. Rinse leaves and allow to air-dry on an absorbent towel.
2. Finely chop the herbs.
3. Place herbs and salt into a food processor and pulse until thoroughly combined.
4. Put in a glass jar with a lid and store in the fridge for up to a year.

Corn, Sweet

	Water-bath Can	Steam Can	Pressure Can	Dehydrate	Freeze	Freeze-Dry	Ferment	Root Cellar
CORN, SWEET	✓	✓	✓	✓	✓	✓	✓	
Notes	Only as part of a tested relish recipe	Only as part of a tested relish recipe	Raw or hot-pack	Must be blanched	Must be blanched	Kernel	Kernel, salsa	

Vegetable	Preparation	Jar Size	Pressure Canning Processing Time at 10 lbs. of Pressure*
Corn, sweet 6 to 16 ears (4½ pounds) per quart	Husk, remove silk, and rinse. Blanch for 3 minutes. Cut off kernels.	Pint	55 min
		Quart	85 min

__Altitude adjustments__: If above 1,001 feet increase to 10 pounds of pressure on weighted gauge; for dial gauge increase by 1 pound for every additional 2,000 feet in altitude.

Corn – How to Freeze

INGREDIENTS

Corn on the cob

1. The natural sugars in corn turn to starch quickly after ripening, so pick ears as soon as they ripen. Husk and remove the silks. Wash the ears.
2. **Whole cobs:** If you are freezing whole cobs, choose small ears. Blanch three ears at a time in steam or boiling water for 3 to 6 minutes. Cool and pack, grouping enough for one meal. Wrap ears in freezer paper or a plastic freezer bag.
3. **Cut corn:** Blanch corn while still on the cob for 3 to 6 minutes. Cool and then remove the kernels with a sharp knife or corn cutter. Cut the kernels off by placing the cob on a nail embedded in a block of wood or by pushing it into the hole of a tube pan. Pack enough for one meal into freezer bags.

Pressure Can Corn

The natural sugars in corn turn to starch quickly after ripening, so pick ears as soon as they ripen. Husk and remove the silks. Wash the ears. The sugar content of young ears and sweet varieties may cause browning. This doesn't affect the quality of the corn.

INGREDIENTS

31½ pounds (in husk) sweet corn for 7 quarts

20 pounds (in husk) sweet corn for 9 pints

1. Prepare a pressure canner (see pages 48-49 for more information), jars, lids, and bands.
2. Husk, remove silk, and rinse. Blanch for 3 minutes in boiling water.
3. Remove the kernels with a sharp knife or corn cutter (not scraping; you want a clean cut of ¾ of the kernel).
4. **Raw-pack**—Pack kernels into hot jars with a generous 1-inch headspace. You can add ½ teaspoon of salt per pint jar or 1 teaspoon per quart jar if you'd like, but it's not necessary.
5. Ladle boiling water into jars to cover vegetables, leaving a 1-inch headspace.
6. **Hot-pack**—For every 4 cups (1 quart) of kernels, place into 1 cup hot water. Bring to a boil and simmer for 5 minutes. Pack into jars with both the kernels and cooking liquid to a 1-inch headspace.
7. Remove air bubbles and add more water if needed. Wipe rims and place lids and bands on to fingertip tight.
8. Place jars into the prepared pressure canner. When all the jars are filled and in the canner, place the lid on your pressure canner. Turn heat to high and allow steam to vent through the vent pipe for 10 minutes. After 10 minutes, place the weighted pressure gauge on at 10 pounds pressure* and process pint jars for 55 minutes and quart jars for 85 minutes. If using a dial-gauge-only pressure canner, use 11 pounds PSI. Follow pressure level according to your altitude and type of gauge (see chart at beginning of chapter).
9. Turn off heat and allow pressure to reduce to zero naturally. When pressure is completely reduced, remove the lid and wait an additional 10 minutes. Remove jars, place on towels in a draft-free area, cool for 24 hours, check seals, and store.

__Altitude adjustments__ see chart on page 50

Cucumber

	Water-bath Can	Steam Can	Pressure Can	Dehydrate	Freeze	Freeze-Dry	Ferment	Root Cellar
CUCUMBER	✓	✓		✓		✓	✓	
Notes 8 pounds pickling cucumber to 3 to 4 quarts	Only as a tested pickle, relish, or salsa!	Only as a tested pickle, relish, or salsa!		Slices		Slices	Whole, spears, slices	

Fermented Pickles

Yield: 1 half-gallon or 2 quarts

INGREDIENTS

2 tablespoons sea salt

4 cups water

cucumbers to fill wide-mouth ½-gallon jar

2 heads dill

4 to 5 cloves garlic

1. Make your brine, using 2 tablespoons of salt to 1 quart of water (4 cups). Stir salt into water until it's dissolved.
2. Pack your vegetables into the clean container, leaving a 2-inch headspace (space between top of jar and the top of the food). Just like any pickle making, the freshness and quality of ingredients going in determines the end product. As fresh as possible is best.
3. Fill the jar with the brine to a 1-inch headspace. Place a weight into the jar to keep the food beneath the brine surface to ensure solids stay beneath the liquid.
4. Put the air-lock lid on or a two-piece metal lid and band (if using the band, tighten fully and then back it off a half turn, making sure to burp the jar).
5. Place on the counter and allow to ferment for four days. Taste the pickles; if they're not "tangy" enough, let them continue to ferment. It sometimes takes up to 10 days if the room is cold.
6. Take off the fermenting lid and replace with a two-piece metal canning lid and band. They will keep for months in the fridge, but they're not shelf stable for the pantry.
7. When they're done fermenting, they must be moved to the fridge or a similar cold area.

Notes

- You can add 1 fresh grape leaf to the bottom of the jar for a crispier pickle.
- Make sure you remove both ends of the pickles.

How to Make Pickles

You'll want to use canning or pickling salt to avoid a cloudy, discolored brine. The fresher the cucumber, the crisper the pickle, so if you can start the process right at picking time, you'll have the absolute best product, but otherwise, try to get them as fresh and as soon as possible after picking. Make sure you use pickling cucumbers if you're purchasing them and not regular cucumbers (many English cucumbers are covered in wax at the store and not a candidate for pickling). Check the ends of the pickle when purchasing; if they're already soft, they won't crisp back up and will make a mushy pickle.

Try to purchase cucumbers no bigger than 5 inches; larger cucumbers make softer pickles. You can use the larger ones for relishes or chopped pickle recipes, but they won't create that crisp whole or spear pickle.

Brine safety: Always make sure you're using vinegar that is 5% acidity—homemade apple cider vinegar is not a candidate to use when canning. I make my own but it's for cooking and baking, not our canning. You may use either white vinegar or apple cider (note: apple cider vinegar will produce a darker brine) but it must be 5% acidity.

When using older pickling recipes or ones passed down, never dilute your vinegar more than equal parts with water. Example, 1 cup vinegar to 1 cup water. Vinegar used to be made at 7%, so older recipes were measured with a higher acidic vinegar. If you're following an updated pickling recipe from the USDA sites or the newer *Ball Book of Canning* and their brine ratio is more water than vinegar, that is a tested recipe and safe to use, but if it's from a blog or an older book, I never drop below the equal ratio on the brine.

Garlic Dill Pickles

Yield: Approximately 4 quarts

INGREDIENTS

7 to 8 pounds of pickling cucumbers (rinsed and blossom ends removed; you may also cut into spears)

½ cup pickling salt

4 cups cold water

BRINE

5 cups water

5 cups vinegar

¼ cup sugar (more to taste if you prefer sweeter)

5 tablespoons pickling salt

2 tablespoons of your preferred pickling spices

PLACE IN EACH QUART (HALF THIS FOR PINTS)

2 cloves peeled garlic

2 teaspoons whole mustard seed

2 to 3 heads fresh dill heads (or 2 tablespoons dill seed or chopped dill weed)

1. Wash cucumbers well in cold water; gently scrub off any dirt. Remove $1/16$ to ¼ inch from the blossom end of the cucumber (enzymes around the blossom end will produce a softer pickle). Place all of your cucumbers in a large glass or stainless-steel bowl. If more than a few layers deep of cucumbers, layer ice between the layers of cucumbers; if it's a smaller amount, place ice on top of cucumbers.

2. Mix ½ cup of pickling/canning salt with 4 cups of cold water (double this as needed if doing a larger batch of pickles). Pour over top of cucumbers, adding more cold water if necessary to cover the tops of the cucumbers. Use a clean plate and place on top of the cucumbers to keep them under the surface of the ice salt water. Fill a pint-sized Mason jar with water (use a lid) and set it on top of the plate to act as a weight. Put the bowl in the fridge overnight or for 12 hours.

3. After soaking cucumbers, pour out salt water and rinse thoroughly with cold water and allow cucumbers to drain.

4. While cucumbers are draining, begin heating up the water in your water-bath canner. Place brine ingredients in a large stainless-steel pot and bring to a low boil; stir to dissolve the sugar and salt. Allow to simmer for about 10 to 15 minutes or until the spices have seeped into and flavored the brine.

5. Wash and rinse jars in hot soapy water. Place garlic and mustard seed in each jar. I prefer to use a wide-mouth when making pickles. Using the larger cucumbers first, pack your jars, tucking the smaller cucumbers up around the top to a generous 1-inch headspace. Add your dill heads, slipping them down around the cucumbers.

6. Remove your spices from the brine and pour the hot brine over the cucumbers to a ½-inch headspace. Remove air bubbles and recheck your headspace. Add more brine if needed. Wipe the rims clean and put the lids and bands on, then screw down to fingertip tight.

7. Place prepared jars into a water-bath or steam canner. Process quart jars for 15 minutes and pints for 10 minutes. Follow instructions for a water-bath or steam canner at the end of processing time. Place on the counter on a folded kitchen towel. Cool for 24 hours, check the seals, and then store.

Altitude adjustments: If you're 1,001 to 3,000 feet increase processing time by 5 minutes, 3,001 to 6,000 feet increase processing time by 10 minutes, if above 6,001 feet increase 15 minutes processing time.

Pickles develop their flavor profile over a few months, so try to let them sit and deepen in flavor for at least a few weeks before eating (if you can; they're so tempting).

Melissa's Pickling Spice

Makes 2 tablespoons

1 tablespoon celery seed

½ tablespoon whole black peppercorns

½ tablespoon allspice

Ball Homemade Pickling Spice

Yield: ½ cup

INGREDIENTS

1 cinnamon stick, broken into pieces

5 bay leaves, crushed

2 tablespoons mustard seeds

1 tablespoon whole allspice

1 tablespoon coriander seeds

1 tablespoon whole black peppercorns

1 tablespoon ground ginger

1 tablespoon dill seeds

2 teaspoons cardamom seeds

1 to 2 teaspoons hot pepper flakes

2 teaspoons whole cloves

1. Combine all ingredients together in a small bowl. Omit any ingredient you don't care for or don't have on hand. This is for flavoring the brine, so you can't go wrong.

Mustard Pickle Relish
(my husband's grandmother's recipe)

Yield: Approximately 4 pints

INGREDIENTS

6 cups washed and diced pickling cucumbers

2 cups diced onion

1 cup canning/pickling salt

8 cups water

4 cups vinegar (5% acidity)

4 tablespoons sugar

2 tablespoons Clear Jel® (optional, but produces a thicker relish)

6 tablespoons dry mustard

2 tablespoons dry turmeric

2 teaspoons celery salt (you can use regular salt, but the celery salt adds to the flavor)

½ cup water

1. Place cucumbers and onions in a large stainless steel or glass bowl.
2. Mix 1 cup of pickling/canning salt with 8 cups of cold water (double this as needed if doing a larger batch of pickles). Pour over top of cucumbers and onions, adding more cold water if necessary to cover the tops of the cucumbers. Use a clean plate and place on top of the cucumbers to keep them under the surface of the ice salt water. Fill a pint-sized Mason jar with water (use a lid) and set it on top of the plate to act as a weight. Put the bowl in the fridge overnight or for 12 hours.
3. After soaking cucumbers and onions, pour out salt water and rinse thoroughly with cold water and allow cucumbers to drain.
4. Prepare a water-bath or steam canner, jars, lids, and bands.
5. In a large stainless-steel pot, combine sugar, dry mustard, turmeric, celery salt, and Clear Jel, then pour in ½ cup of water, whisking until combined and smooth. Pour in vinegar and bring to a full boil while stirring. Once it's reached a full boil, lower heat to a simmer and stir until it thickens up, then add the cucumbers and the onions and bring to a boil. When it reaches a boil with the vegetables added, keep at a low boil and cook for 15 minutes, stirring as needed.
6. In jars that have been washed in hot soapy water and rinsed, pack the relish/pickle mixture to ½-inch headspace. Remove air bubbles and add more product if needed to keep the ½-inch headspace. Clean the rims, put on lids and bands, and screw down to fingertip tight.
7. Place filled jars into your water-bath or steam canner. Process pints for 10 minutes.* Follow instructions for a water-bath or steam canner at the end of processing time. Place on the counter on a folded kitchen towel. Cool for 24 hours, check the seals, and then store.

****Altitude adjustments**: If you're 1,001 to 3,000 feet increase processing time by 5 minutes, 3,001 to 6,000 feet increase processing time by 10 minutes, if above 6,001 feet increase 15 minutes processing time.*

How to Preserve Vegetables

Bread and Butter Refrigerator Pickle

INGREDIENTS

2 cups sliced and trimmed pickling cucumbers

½ cup sliced onion

½ cup each sliced red and yellow bell pepper (or any color combination you have on hand)

2 cups white vinegar

⅔ cup sugar

1 tablespoon mustard seed

1½ teaspoons celery seed

¾ teaspoon turmeric

2 whole cloves

2 teaspoons salt

1. Wash one quart-sized Mason jar and lid. Wide-mouth works best when stuffing them for pickles, but regular-mouth will work as well.

2. Rinse and scrub cucumbers. Cut off the blossom end of the cucumber (it contains enzymes that can soften pickles). Slice evenly; a mandoline works well for uniform slices when pickling. Cut up all the rest of your vegetables.

3. Layer vegetables in the clean Mason jar. Push down lightly to pack vegetables down and get a few more in. Pack vegetables into the jar within ½-inch headspace. Place the jar on a towel folded into thirds.

4. In a stainless-steel saucepan, combine vinegar, sugar, salt, and spices. Bring to a boil on medium-high heat and boil for 3 minutes.

5. Using a canning funnel and ladle, pour pickling liquid over the vegetables. You may have a slight amount left over depending on how tightly you packed your jar. Apply a lid. Allow to cool for 30 minutes and then place in the refrigerator. Pickles should marinate for 2 weeks and be used within 3 months. Confession: I taste-tested mine after 2 days and have been munching away. The flavor will intensify over time.

Eggplant

	Water-bath Can	Steam Can	Pressure Can	Dehydrate	Freeze	Freeze-Dry	Ferment	Root Cellar
EGGPLANT	✓	✓		✓	✓	✓	✓	
Notes 1 pound for 2 pints	Tested combination pickle recipe only, very limited	Tested combination pickle recipe only, very limited		Must be blanched	Must be blanched	Sliced, diced		

Garlic

	Water-bath Can	Steam Can	Pressure Can	Dehydrate	Freeze	Freeze-Dry	Ferment	Root Cellar
GARLIC	✓	✓		✓		✓	✓	✓
Notes 12 pounds for 5 quarts	Pickled or as an ingredient in a tested jelly or salsa recipe	Pickled or as an ingredient in a tested jelly or salsa recipe		Does NOT require blanching		Cloves, minced	Cloves	Soft-neck varieties store the longest

How to Preserve Vegetables

Fermented Garlic

INGREDIENTS

Garlic

Water

Salt

1. Decide the size of jar to use. Truly, you don't want to try to fill a quart jar. It'll take *forever*! I used a pint jar and even that took way longer than I wanted.
2. Peel enough cloves to fill your jar, leaving room for the glass weight.
3. Fill the jar to within an inch of the top with a salt-water brine. Proportions for the brine are ½ tablespoon sea salt to one cup water.
4. Place weight on top of the garlic to keep it submerged.
5. Place pickle pipe and ring on the jar. (You can also use an airlock or a canning lid but if you use the lid be sure to burp it every other day or so to release the built-up gas.)
6. Cover the jar with a cloth to keep out of light and leave on your countertop for about a week. Then move to your refrigerator.
7. Fermentation will continue in the refrigerator but at a slower rate. A few weeks in the fridge will give it a nice mellow flavor.

When you leave it on your counter, your home will smell like garlic!

The fermented garlic can be used just like regular garlic in recipes that don't require cooking (the cooking will kill the benefits of the fermentation!), such as salad dressings and pesto.

Use it to make garlic butter and slather on warm fresh homemade bread. YUM!

Pickled Garlic

Shared from my book, The Made-from-Scratch Life.

Yield: Approximately nine 6-ounce jars

INGREDIENTS

135 cloves peeled garlic (depending upon the size of the garlic, about 15 per jar)

3 cups vinegar

1½ cups water

2 tablespoons canning salt

9 teaspoons mustard seed

9 teaspoons black peppercorn

Red chili flakes (optional)

1. Peel the garlic.
2. Prepare a water-bath or steam canner, jars, lids, and bands.
3. Pour vinegar, water, and canning salt into a saucepan and bring to a boil. Stir until salt is completely dissolved.
4. Set jars on a folded towel on the counter. Place 1 teaspoon of mustard seeds and black peppercorns in each jar. Add a pinch of hot pepper flakes if you like a little heat in your food. (Whenever making pickles, we do two batches—one with added hot pepper for my husband and one without for me.)
5. Pack jars with the peeled garlic to a generous ½-inch headspace. Don't pack tightly.
6. Pour hot brine over the garlic to a ½-inch headspace. Remove air bubbles and add more brine if needed to maintain headspace.
7. Wipe rim of jar with a clean towel. Place canning lids on the center of the jar and screw bands down until fingertip tight.
8. Place filled jars into your water-bath or steam canner. Process pints for 10 minutes.* Follow instructions for a water-bath or steam canner at the end of processing time. Place on the counter on a folded kitchen towel. Cool for 24 hours, check the seals, and then store.

***Altitude adjustments**: If you're 1,001 to 3,000 feet increase processing time by 5 minutes, 3,001 to 6,000 feet increase processing time by 10 minutes, if above 6,001 feet increase 15 minutes processing time.*

Red Pepper Garlic Jelly

See Peppers, Sweet on page 230

Kale

	Water-bath Can	Steam Can	Pressure Can	Dehydrate	Freeze	Freeze-Dry	Ferment	Root Cellar
KALE			✓	✓	✓	✓		
Notes			Considered a leafy green for pressure canning	Must be blanched	Must be blanched			

Vegetable	Preparation	Jar Size	Pressure Canning Processing Time at 10 lbs. of Pressure*
Kale, leafy greens 4 per quart	Wash small amounts of greens thoroughly, changing water frequently. Continue rinsing until water runs clear. Remove tough stems or ribs. In a large stainless-steel pot, blanch 1 pound/500 grams of greens (use a steamer basket or cheesecloth) for 3 to 5 minutes until wilted. Drain, and dispose of blanching water.	Pint	70 min
		Quart	90 min

*Altitude adjustments: If above 1,001 feet increase to 10 lbs. of pressure on weighted gauge; for dial gauge increase by 1 pound for every additional 2,000 feet in altitude.

Leeks

	Water-bath Can	Steam Can	Pressure Can	Dehydrate	Freeze	Freeze-Dry	Ferment	Root Cellar
LEEKS				✓	✓	✓	✓	✓
Notes				Sliced		Sliced		Only if dug up and replanted in a container of sand or soil

Leekchi

INGREDIENTS

6 cups thinly sliced leeks (about 1½ pounds or 3 large leeks)

2 teaspoons sea salt

2 large cloves garlic

1 tablespoon finely grated ginger

2 teaspoons hot red pepper powder

1. Rinse leeks well because soil likes to stick in between the layers where the dark part begins to branch out.
2. Place the thinly sliced leeks in a large bowl. Sprinkle the salt on top. Using your hands, massage the leeks and salt together until the juices release (about 5 minutes). Cover and allow to rest for about 45 minutes.
3. Add the garlic, ginger, and hot pepper powder. Mix well until fully incorporated.
4. Press into a clean 2-quart Mason jar or crock, or 1-quart jars. Compress well to remove all air pockets and to allow the juices to rise to the top. The vegetables must be fully submerged to ferment properly. If you don't have enough juice, use some homemade brine (see recipe below).
5. Use a weight to keep the vegetables submerged. Place the fermenting lid on the jar.
6. Leave your leekchi at room temperature, away from direct sun, for about 1 week. The contents may bubble and seep out. Check daily to ensure the vegetables remain submerged.
7. It's ready when it has turned a yellowish color and the leeks have softened and have a sour aroma.

Adapted from
http://www.pbs.org/food/kitchen-vignettes/leekchi/

Homemade Brine (if needed)

INGREDIENTS

1 cup water

1 teaspoon salt

1. Stir salt into water until the salt has dissolved. Pour just enough of this to cover your vegetable mixture.

Lettuce

	Water-bath Can	Steam Can	Pressure Can	Dehydrate	Freeze	Freeze-Dry	Ferment	Root Cellar
LETTUCE								
Notes			I've not found a satisfactory way to preserve lettuce long term.					

Okra

	Water-bath Can	Steam Can	Pressure Can	Dehydrate	Freeze	Freeze-Dry	Ferment	Root Cellar
OKRA	✓	✓	✓	✓	✓	✓	✓	
Notes	Pickled only!	Pickled only!	Hot-pack	Does NOT need to be blanched	Must be blanched			

Vegetable	Preparation	Jar Size	Pressure Canning Processing Time at 10 lbs. of Pressure*
Okra 1½ pounds per quart	Wash and trim ends. Use whole or slice into 1-inch pieces.	Pint	25 min
	Place in a pot and cover with water; bring to a boil and cook for two minutes.	Quart	40 min

*__Altitude adjustments__: If above 1,001 feet increase to 10 lbs. of pressure on weighted gauge; for dial gauge increase by 1 pound for every additional 2,000 feet in altitude.

Summer Squash

See Tomato Zuchini Sauce (subsitute okra) page 245

Pressure Can Okra

INGREDIENTS

11 pounds for 7 quarts

7 pounds (tops removed) for 9 pints

1. Prepare a pressure canner (see pages 48-49 for more information), jars, lids, and bands.
2. Wash and trim ends. Use whole or slice into 1-inch pieces.
3. Place in a pot and cover with water; bring to a boil and cook for two minutes.
4. Add 1 teaspoon salt per quart or ½ teaspoon salt per pint. Salt isn't required, so this is your preference.
5. Pack hot okra into prepared jars to a 1-inch headspace.
6. Remove air bubbles and add more water if needed to maintain 1-inch headspace.
7. Wipe rims and put lids and bands on to fingertip tight.
8. When all the jars are filled and in the canner, place the lid on your pressure canner. Turn heat to high and allow steam to vent through the vent pipe for 10 minutes. After 10 minutes, place the weighted pressure gauge on at 10 pounds pressure* and process pint jars for 25 minutes and quart jars for 40 minutes. If using a dial-gauge-only pressure canner, use 11 pounds PSI. Follow pressure level according to your altitude and type of gauge (see chart at beginning of chapter).
9. Turn off heat and allow pressure to reduce to zero naturally. When pressure is completely reduced, remove the lid and wait an additional 10 minutes. Remove jars, place on towels in a draft-free area, cool for 24 hours, check seals, and store.

***Altitude adjustments** see chart on page 50*

Onions

	Water-bath Can	Steam Can	Pressure Can	Dehydrate	Freeze	Freeze-Dry	Ferment	Root Cellar
ONIONS	✓	✓	✓	✓	✓	✓	✓	✓
Notes	Only as an ingredient in a tested marmalade, jelly, pickle, relish, sauce, or salsa recipe	Only as an ingredient in a tested marmalade, jelly, pickle, relish, sauce, or salsa recipe	Only as an ingredient in a combination recipe	Does NOT need to be blanched	Must be blanched	Sliced, diced, minced	Sliced, rings	Late maturing onions last the longest

Radish

See Radish and Onion Pickles page 241

Parsnip

	Water-bath Can	Steam Can	Pressure Can	Dehydrate	Freeze	Freeze-Dry	Ferment	Root Cellar
PARSNIP			✓			✓		✓
Notes			Hot-pack					Store by size and use the smallest first

Vegetable	Preparation	Jar Size	Pressure Canning Processing Time at 10 lbs. of Pressure*
Parsnip 1 pound per pint	Wash and peel; rinse again. Cut into 1- to 2-inch pieces. Place in a pot and cover with water, bring to a boil, and cook for 3 to 5 minutes.	Pint	30 min
		Quart	35 min

*__Altitude adjustments__: If above 1,001 feet increase to 10 lbs. of pressure on weighted gauge; for dial gauge increase by 1 pound for every additional 2,000 feet in altitude.

How to Preserve Vegetables

Pressure Can Parsnip

INGREDIENTS

Parsnips

Boiling water

Salt

1. Prepare a pressure canner (see pages 48-49 for more information), jars, lids, and bands.
2. Wash and peel parsnips. Use whole or slice into 1-inch pieces.
3. Place in a pot and cover with water, bring to a boil, and cook for 3 to 5 minutes.
4. Add 1 teaspoon of salt per quart or ½ teaspoon salt per pint. Salt isn't required, so this is your preference.
5. Pack hot parsnips into prepared jars to a 1-inch headspace. Cover with fresh boiling water.
6. Remove air bubbles and add more water if needed to maintain 1-inch headspace.
7. Wipe rims; put lids and bands on to fingertip tight.
8. When all the jars are filled and in the canner, place the lid on your pressure canner. Turn heat to high and allow steam to vent through the vent pipe for 10 minutes. After 10 minutes, place the weighted pressure gauge on at 10 pounds pressure* and process pint jars for 30 minutes and quart jars for 35 minutes. If using a dial-gauge-only pressure canner, use 11 pounds PSI. Follow pressure level according to your altitude and type of gauge (see chart at beginning of chapter).
9. Turn off heat and allow pressure to reduce to zero naturally. When pressure is completely reduced, remove the lid and wait an additional 10 minutes. Remove jars, place on towels in a draft-free area, cool for 24 hours, check seals, and store.

***Altitude adjustments** see chart on page 50*

Pea, Field

	Water-bath Can	Steam Can	Pressure Can	Dehydrate	Freeze	Freeze-Dry	Ferment	Root Cellar
PEA, FIELD			✓	✓	✓	✓		
Notes			*Raw or hot-pack or as an ingredient in a combination recipe*	*Must be blanched*	*Must be blanched*			

Vegetable	Preparation	Jar Size	Pressure Canning Processing Time at 10 lbs. of Pressure*
Pea, field, shelled 4½ pounds per quart	Shell and rinse. **Hot-pack:** Place shelled peas in a large saucepan and cover with boiling water. Bring to a boil in a saucepan, and boil for 2 minutes. Add ½ teaspoon salt to pint jar or 1 teaspoon to quarts. Fill jars loosely with hot peas, and add cooking liquid, leaving 1-inch headspace. **Raw-pack:** Add ½ teaspoon salt to pint jar or 1 teaspoon to quarts. Fill jars with raw peas, add boiling water, leaving 1-inch headspace. Don't shake, press, or smoosh down peas.	Pint	40 min
		Quart	40 min

__Altitude adjustments__: If above 1,001 feet increase to 10 lbs. of pressure on weighted gauge; for dial gauge increase by 1 pound for every additional 2,000 feet in altitude.

Dried Peas

Canning dried peas is very frugal and saves a lot of time when you need a quick supper. Canning dried peas plain allows you to quickly add them to soups, salads, chili, and stews.

Having home-canned dried peas on hand means not having to plan ahead by soaking or cooking for long periods of time. In an emergency or power outage, you don't have to worry about finding extra water to soak or cook your peas with; you just pop off the lid, heat, and eat!

Per the National Center for Home Food Preservation, "An average of 5 pounds is needed per canner load of 7 quarts; an average of 3¼ pounds is needed per canner load of 9 pints; an average of ¾ pounds per quart."

Soaking Methods to Prepare Dried Peas for Canning

If canning plain dried peas, you can soak them for 12 to 18 hours, especially if you're planning ahead.

If not, you'll need to use the quick soak method. To quick soak, cover peas with water about 2 to 3 inches over the top, and bring to a boil. Boil for 2 minutes, remove from heat, and allow to soak for 1 hour.

Pressure Can Dried Peas

1. Using either method of soaking (but you must have soaked and rehydrated them via one of the two methods), drain and cover peas with fresh water. Bring to a boil and boil for 30 minutes.
2. While peas are cooking, prepare a pressure canner (for more information see pages 48-49), jars, lids, and bands.
3. Remove peas from heat. Have hot clean jars ready with ½ teaspoon salt in pint jars and 1 teaspoon salt in quart jars. Fill jars with peas and cooking water to a 1-inch headspace.
4. Remove air bubbles; double-check headspace (add more of the cooking water to reach 1-inch headspace if necessary). Wipe rims clean, place on lids and bands, and put jars in a pressure canner.
5. When all the jars are filled and in the canner, place the lid on your pressure canner. Turn heat to medium-high and allow steam to vent through the vent pipe for 10 minutes. After 10 minutes, place the weighted pressure gauge on at 10 pounds pressure (or close vent depending on model);

dial-gauge-only pressure canner, use 11 pounds PSI.* Process pint jars for 75 minutes and quart jars for 90 minutes.

6. Turn off heat and allow pressure to reduce to zero naturally. When pressure is completely reduced, remove the lid and wait an additional 10 minutes. Remove jars, place on towels in a draft-free area, cool for 24 hours, check seals, and store.

***Altitude adjustments** see chart on page 50*

Pea, Sugar Snap

	Water-bath Can	Steam Can	Pressure Can	Dehydrate	Freeze	Freeze-Dry	Ferment	Root Cellar
PEA, SUGAR SNAP				✓	✓	✓	✓	
Notes				Whole	Must be blanched	Whole	Whole	

How to Freeze Peas

INGREDIENTS

Peas

Water

Ice

1. Harvest when pea pods are filled with young, tender peas that are not starchy.
2. Wash and shell.
3. Bring water to boil for blanching. In the meantime, put ice in cold water in a large bowl.
4. Blanch peas 1½ to 2 minutes. Start timer right away.
5. Remove immediately when the time is up and put in the ice bath.
6. Drain and place on a towel to dry them. Don't squeeze the peas though!
7. Package into serving quantities, either in Ziplock bags or food-saver bags.
8. Label and freeze.

Blanching is the process of scalding vegetables in boiling water or steam for a short period of time. It stops enzyme actions that cause loss of flavor, color, texture, and nutrients.

Fermented Sugar Snap Peas

Recipe adapted from https://www.attainablesustainable.net/spicy-pickled-snap-peas/

Yield: 1 quart

INGREDIENTS

3 cups washed, strung, and stemmed sugar snap peas

3 to 5 cloves garlic, peeled

2 tablespoons sea salt

2 cups water (distilled or unchlorinated)

1 teaspoon dried or 1 tablespoon fresh herb of choice (basil, dill, and oregano to name a few)

1. Place garlic and herbs in the bottom of a clean quart-sized Mason jar.
2. Dissolve salt in warm water and allow it to cool to room temperature.
3. Tightly pack jar with peas to the shoulder to a scant 1-inch headspace. Pour salt water over top to 1-inch headspace. Place fermenting weight and ensure all contents are beneath the liquid level.
4. Place either a fermenting airlock lid on jar or a two-piece metal canning lid and band. If using a metal lid and band, tighten fully and then back it off a half turn; make sure to burp the jar.
5. Set at room temperature for five to seven days. Check for desired flavor at five days; move to cold storage once desired flavor is reached.

Peppers, Hot

	Water-bath Can	Steam Can	Pressure Can	Dehydrate	Freeze	Freeze-Dry	Ferment	Root Cellar
PEPPERS, HOT	✓	✓	✓	✓	✓	✓	✓	
Notes	Only as an ingredient in a tested pickle, jelly, chutney, sauce, relish, or salsa recipe	Only as an ingredient in a tested pickle, jelly, chutney, sauce, relish, or salsa recipe	Hot-pack or as an ingredient in a combination recipe	Must be blanched	Must be blanched	Sliced, diced		

Vegetable	Preparation	Jar Size	Pressure Canning Processing Time at 10 lbs. of Pressure*
Pepper, hot 1 pound per pint	Cut two small slits in small peppers and four in larger ones. **Oven Method:** Place peppers under broiler or in a 400°F oven for 6 to 8 minutes; they're ready when skins blister. Remove from the oven and place on a pan covered with a towel or into a paper bag (close bag) to cool for approximately 15 minutes. Remove skins, stems, and seeds. **Hot-Water Method:** In a large pot of boiling water, blanch peppers for 3 minutes. When skin wrinkles, remove. Small peppers are done whole, whereas large peppers should be quartered, cored, and seeded.	Half-Pint	35 min
		Pint	35 min

***Altitude adjustments**: If above 1,001 feet increase to 10 lbs. of pressure on weighted gauge; for dial gauge increase by 1 pound for every additional 2,000 feet in altitude. Average of 1 pound per pint*

How to Preserve Vegetables

Pressure Can Peppers

This method can be used for both hot or sweet peppers, including chiles, jalapeños, and pimientos. If processing hot peppers, wear gloves (plastic sandwich bags work in a pinch). Never touch your face, nose, or eyes after handling hot peppers. Wash hands well after touching and working with them.

INGREDIENTS

9 pounds for 9 pints

Prepare a pressure canner (see pages 48-49 for more information), jars, lids and bands

1. Rinse and dry peppers.
2. Peppers require a hot-pack, which can be achieved via two methods. Cut two small slits in small peppers and four in larger ones.
3. **Oven Method:** Place peppers under broiler or in a 400°F oven for 6 to 8 minutes; they're ready when skins blister. Remove from the oven and place on a pan covered with a towel or into a paper bag (close bag) to cool for approximately 15 minutes. Remove skins, stems, and seeds.
4. **Hot-Water Method:** In a large pot of boiling water, blanch peppers for 3 minutes. When skin wrinkles, remove.
5. Small peppers are done whole, whereas large peppers should be quartered, cored, and seeded.
6. Add ½ teaspoon salt per pint. Salt isn't required, so this is your preference.
7. Pack peppers into prepared jars to a 1-inch headspace. Fill jars with just-off-the-boil water.
8. Remove air bubbles and add more water if needed to maintain 1-inch headspace.
9. Wipe rims, and then put lids and bands on to fingertip tight.
10. When all the jars are filled and in the canner, place the lid on your pressure canner. Turn heat to high and allow steam to vent through the vent pipe for 10 minutes. After 10 minutes, place the weighted pressure gauge on at 10 pounds pressure* and process half-pint and pint jars for 35 minutes. If using a dial-gauge-only pressure canner, use 11 pounds PSI. Follow pressure level according to your altitude and type of gauge (see chart at beginning of chapter).
11. Turn off heat and allow pressure to reduce to zero naturally. When pressure is completely reduced, remove the lid and wait an additional 10 minutes. Remove jars, place on towels in a draft-free area, cool for 24 hours, check seals, and store.

*Altitude Adjustments *see chart on page 50*

Peppers, Sweet

	Water-bath Can	Steam Can	Pressure Can	Dehydrate	Freeze	Freeze-Dry	Ferment	Root Cellar
PEPPERS, SWEET	✓	✓	✓	✓	✓	✓	✓	
Notes	Only as an ingredient in a tested pickle, jelly, chutney, sauce, relish, or salsa recipe	Only as an ingredient in a tested pickle, jelly, chutney, sauce, relish, or salsa recipe	Hot-pack or as an ingredient in a combination recipe	Must be blanched	Must be blanched			

How to Pressure Can Peppers, Hot

See page 227

How to Preserve Vegetables | 229

Red Pepper Garlic Jelly

This is so tasty and festive when poured over a brick of cream cheese and served with crackers (I've been known to eat a few bites with a spoon too!).

Yield: 3 6-ounce jars

INGREDIENTS

1 cup minced red bell pepper

¼ cup deveined and minced jalapeños (or pepper of your choice)

5 cloves finely chopped garlic

1⅓ cups vinegar

2⅓ cups sugar (or 1½ cups honey)

1½ teaspoons pectin powder (I only use Pomona's Pectin)

2 teaspoons calcium water (comes with Pomona's Universal Pectin)

1. Prepare water-bath canner or steam canner, jars, lids, and bands.
2. Place peppers, garlic, and vinegar in a saucepan. Add calcium water and stir well. Measure ½ cup sugar into a bowl with pectin and combine.
3. Bring saucepan contents to a boil. Add pectin-sugar and stir vigorously for 2 minutes. Add remaining sugar and stir until dissolved. Return to a boil and remove from heat.
4. Fill warm jars with red pepper garlic jelly within ¼ inch from the top. Wipe the rim of the jars clean; place the lids and bands on. Screw down to fingertip tight and place jars in a water-bath or steam canner. Process pints for 10 minutes.*
5. Follow instructions for a water-bath or steam canner at the end of processing time. Place on the counter on a folded kitchen towel. Cool for 24 hours, check the seals, and then store.

***Altitude adjustments**: If you're 1,001 to 3,000 feet increase processing time by 5 minutes, 3,001 to 6,000 feet increase processing time by 10 minutes, if above 6,001 feet increase 15 minutes processing time.*

Potatoes

	Water-bath Can	Steam Can	Pressure Can	Dehydrate	Freeze	Freeze-Dry	Ferment	Root Cellar
POTATOES			✓	✓	✓	✓	✓	✓
Notes			Hot-pack	Must be blanched	Must be blanched or cooked	Hash browns, mashed, boiled, roasted		Store in complete darkness

Vegetable	Preparation	Jar Size	Pressure Canning Processing Time at 10 lbs. of Pressure*
Potatoes, white 2½ - 3 pounds per quart	Wash and peel potatoes (you MUST peel potatoes when canning due to higher botulism loads in the soil, and it's a root crop). Cut into ½-inch cubes. Place in water to prevent darkening. You may see it recommended to use an ascorbic acid solution, which you can, but my team member never has. Blanch potatoes by cooking in boiling water for 2 minutes. Drain. If using small whole potatoes, boil for 10 minutes and then drain. Optional: Add 1 teaspoon salt per quart jar (½ teaspoon if using pints).	Pint	35 min
		Quart	40 min

*__Altitude adjustments__: If above 1,001 feet increase to 10 lbs. of pressure on weighted gauge; for dial gauge increase by 1 pound for every additional 2,000 feet in altitude. Average of 1 pound per pint.

Pressure Can Potatoes

Potatoes that are 1 to 2 inches in diameter may be packed whole (must be peeled).

I like to use canned potatoes in recipes that call for leftover mashed potatoes, such as potato bread or rolls or shepherd's pie. Just heat and mash.

INGREDIENTS

20 pounds for 7 quarts

13 pounds is needed for 9 pints

Salt (optional)

1. Prepare a pressure canner (see pages 48–49 for more information), jars, lids, and bands.

2. Wash and peel potatoes (you MUST peel potatoes when canning due to higher botulism loads in the soil, and it's a root crop). Cut into ½-inch cubes. Place in water to prevent darkening. You may see it recommended to use an ascorbic acid solution, which you can, but my team member never has.

3. Blanch potatoes by cooking in boiling water for 2 minutes. Drain. If using small whole potatoes, boil for 10 minutes and then drain.

4. Optional: Add 1 teaspoon salt per quart jar (½ teaspoon if using pints). Fill jars with hot potatoes, leaving no more than 1-inch headspace.

5. Cover potatoes with fresh hot water, leaving 1-inch headspace. Be sure to use fresh hot water and not the water the potatoes were boiled in; it contains too much starch.

6. Wipe the rim of the jars clean; place the lid and band on. Screw down to fingertip tight and place jars in canner. When all the jars are filled and in the canner, place the lid on your pressure canner. Turn heat to high and allow steam to vent through the vent pipe for 10 minutes. After 10 minutes, place the weighted pressure gauge on at 10 pounds pressure* and process pint jars for 35 minutes and quart jars for 40 minutes. If using a dial-gauge-only pressure canner, use 11 pounds PSI. Follow pressure level according to your altitude and type of gauge (see chart at beginning of chapter).

7. Turn off heat and allow pressure to reduce to zero naturally. When pressure is completely reduced, remove the lid and wait an additional 10 minutes. Remove jars, place on towels in a draft-free area, cool for 24 hours, check seals, and store.

*Altitude adjustments see chart on page 50

Freezer Hash Browns

INGREDIENTS

21-24 russet or gold potatoes

1. Preheat the oven to 350°F (177°C).
2. Scrub the potatoes and then poke them a few times with a fork. Place on a baking sheet and bake for 1 hour or until fork tender.
3. Allow potatoes to cool completely and refrigerate for a few hours or overnight. This makes the grating easier.
4. Shred the cold potatoes, discarding the peel, which should slip off easily as you grate.
5. Spread the shredded potatoes on baking sheets to about a ¾-inch thickness. Cover with a piece of parchment paper and spread another layer of shredded potatoes.
6. Continue with remaining potatoes. Make sure to keep the layers at ¾-inch thickness.
7. Place in the freezer until completely frozen. Overnight is a safe bet. Once fully frozen, break apart and store in a large Ziplock bag or freezer-safe container.

To use: If in a casserole, thaw first and drain excess liquid. If cooking them on a skillet, frozen works fine.

Adapted from https://prepareandnourish.com/making-and-freezing-hash-browns/

Pumpkin

	Water-bath Can	Steam Can	Pressure Can	Dehydrate	Freeze	Freeze-Dry	Ferment	Root Cellar
PUMPKIN	✓	✓	✓	✓	✓	✓		✓
Notes	Only in a tested compote or pickle recipe	Only in a tested compote or pickle recipe	Hot-pack, chunks only!	Must be cooked. Freezing is only safe method for storing puree	Must be cooked	Cubed, puree		Stores best when the stem is left intact. Use ones that don't have a stem first

Vegetable	Preparation	Jar Size	Pressure Canning Processing Time at 10 lbs. of Pressure*
Pumpkin 2¼ pounds per quart	Wash your squash off and remove the stems. Cut in half and remove the seeds and pulps. Cut your pumpkin into quarts and then into 1-inch-long strips. Peel the rind. Cut into 1-inch cubes. Prepare a large pot with water and bring to a boil. Blanch prepared squash cubes in boiling water for 2 minutes (pumpkin may only be canned via hot-pack; do not skip this step).	Pint Quart	55 min 90 min

***Altitude adjustments**: *If above 1,001 feet increase to 10 lbs. of pressure on weighted gauge; for dial gauge increase by 1 pound for every additional 2,000 feet in altitude. Average of 1 pound per pint.*

Pressure Can Pumpkin

The pumpkin soup in the photo on the opposite page is made from canned pumpkin. To make the soup, drain (reserve some of the liquid), puree with just enough of the reserved liquid to liquify, heat, and season to taste.

INGREDIENTS

16 pounds for 7 quarts (that equaled three sugar pumpkins for me)

10 pounds per 9 pints

1. Prepare a pressure canner (see pages 48-49 for more information), jars, lids, and bands.

2. Wash your squash and remove the stems. Cut in half and remove the seeds and pulp.

3. Cut your pumpkin into quarters and then into 1-inch-long strips.

4. Peel the rind. Cut into 1-inch cubes.**

5. Prepare a large pot with water and bring to a boil. Blanch prepared squash cubes in boiling water for 2 minutes (pumpkin may only be canned via hot-pack; do not skip this step).

6. Remove from heat and with a slotted spoon, fill jars with cubes to generous 1-inch headspace (do not mash or puree while packing). Take the liquid from the pot and fill to 1-inch headspace; remove air bubbles, check headspace again, and add more water if necessary.

7. Wipe the rim of the jars clean; place the lid and band on. Screw down to fingertip tight and place jars in canner. When all the jars are filled and in the canner, place the lid on your pressure canner. Turn heat to high and allow steam to vent through the vent pipe for 10 minutes. After 10 minutes, place the weighted pressure gauge on at 10 pounds pressure* and process pint jars for 55 minutes and quart jars for 90 minutes. If using a dial-gauge-only pressure canner, use 11 pounds PSI. Follow pressure level according to your altitude and type of gauge (see chart at beginning of chapter).

8. Turn off heat and allow pressure to reduce to zero naturally. When pressure is completely reduced, remove the lid and wait an additional 10 minutes. Remove jars, place on towels in a draft-free area, cool for 24 hours, check seals, and store.

*****Altitude adjustments** *see chart on page 50*

****The Ball Book of Complete Canning* says you can peel pumpkin and place it sealed in the fridge for a day before canning. They recommend letting it come to room temp for an hour before blanching and following hot-pack canning procedures.*

Pumpkin Puree

INGREDIENTS

Sugar or pie pumpkin

Sharp knife

9x13 baking dish

Water

1. Preheat oven to 375°F (190°C).
2. Take your pumpkin and pop off the stem (or cut it if it's still a bit green). Chop the pumpkin in half.
3. Scoop out the seeds and the stringy flesh parts clinging to the seeds. Save the seeds to roast and snack on later.
4. Place each half of the pumpkin cut-side down in a 9x13 baking dish with an inch of water.
5. Bake for 30 to 40 minutes (depending on the size of your pumpkin), or until pumpkin is soft and fully cooked.
6. Remove pan from oven and allow to cool. Scoop out the soft pumpkin flesh. I use the edge of a large spoon and scrape it off the skin.
7. Place cooked pumpkin into a blender or food processor and puree. Or go old-school and use a potato masher. Sugar and pie pumpkins have drier flesh, so you might need to add a tiny bit of water.

You can use your puree right away to bake with or store in the fridge for up to 5 to 7 days. Or freeze it for later use. When freezing I like to freeze in 1- or 2-cup portions.

Having home-canned pumpkin on the shelf is a welcome treat and can be safely canned at home, provided you're using a pressure canner and doing it in cubed format.

Any smooth (not stringy) pumpkins may be canned at home in cubed format only (no pureed or mashed format). Recommended are sugar or pie pumpkins.

Radish

	Water-bath Can	Steam Can	Pressure Can	Dehydrate	Freeze	Freeze-Dry	Ferment	Root Cellar
RADISH				✓	✓	✓	✓	✓
Notes				Sliced	Must be blanched	Sliced or cubed	Pickled	Store same as carrots; will store approximately 3 months

Fermented Radish and Onion Pickles

Not only are these fermented radishes and onions delicious on a sandwich or hamburger, but they turn a beautiful bright pink color after a few days, making them one of the prettiest jars in our fridge!

Yield: 1 pint

INGREDIENTS

½ pound radishes

½ small onion

2 teaspoons sea or mineral salt

1 cup water (distilled or unchlorinated)

½ teaspoon whole black peppercorns, caraway, or herbs of choice (optional)

1. Rinse radishes well, cut off tip and tail, and slice into rounds.
2. Peel onion and slice into thin rings.
3. Dissolve salt in warm water and allow it to cool to room temperature.
4. Layer radishes and onions in a wide-mouth pint jar to a scant 1-inch headspace. Pour salt water over top to 1-inch headspace. Place fermenting weight and ensure all contents are beneath the liquid level.
5. Place either a fermenting airlock lid on the jar or a two-piece metal canning lid and band. If using a metal lid and band, tighten fully and then back it off a half turn; make sure to burp the jar.
6. Set at room temperature for five to seven days. Check for desired flavor at five days; move to cold storage once desired flavor is reached.

How to Preserve Vegetables

Rutabaga

	Water-bath Can	Steam Can	Pressure Can	Dehydrate	Freeze	Freeze-Dry	Ferment	Root Cellar
RUTABAGA					✓	✓		✓
Notes					Must be blanched			Stores best when dipped in food-grade wax

Spinach and Other Leafy Greens (beet greens, mustard greens, Swiss chard, collard greens)

	Water-bath Can	Steam Can	Pressure Can	Dehydrate	Freeze	Freeze-Dry	Ferment	Root Cellar
SPINACH & OTHER LEAFY GREENS			✓	✓	✓	✓		
Notes			Hot-pack	Must be blanched	Must be blanched			

Vegetable	Preparation	Jar Size	Pressure Canning Processing Time at 10 lbs. of Pressure*
Spinach, leafy greens 4 pounds per quart	Wash small amounts of greens thoroughly, changing water frequently. Continue rinsing until water runs clear.	Pint	70 min
	Remove tough stems or ribs. In a large stainless-steel pot, blanch 1 pound/500 grams of greens (use a steamer basket or cheesecloth) for 3 to 5 minutes until wilted. Drain and dispose of blanching water.	Quart	90 min

***Altitude adjustments**: *If above 1,001 feet increase to 10 lbs. of pressure on weighted gauge; for dial gauge increase by 1 pound for every additional 2,000 feet in altitude.*

Pressure Can Spinach and Leafy Greens

INGREDIENTS

28 pounds for 7 quarts

18 pounds for 9 pints

1. Prepare a pressure canner (see pages 48-49 for more information), jars, lids, and bands.

2. Wash small amounts of greens thoroughly, changing water frequently. Continue rinsing until water runs clear.

3. Remove tough stems or ribs.

4. In a large stainless-steel pot, blanch 1 pound/500 grams of greens (use a steamer basket or cheesecloth) for 3 to 5 minutes until wilted.

5. Drain and dispose of blanching water.

6. Add ¼ teaspoon salt to pint jar or ½ teaspoon salt to quart jar, if desired.

7. Fill jars loosely with greens to a 1-inch headspace and pour fresh boiling water over top; remove air bubbles and check headspace again, adding more water if necessary to maintain 1-inch headspace.

8. Wipe the rim of the jars clean; place the lid and band on. Screw down to fingertip tight and place jars in canner. When all the jars are filled and in the canner, place the lid on your pressure canner. Turn heat to high and allow steam to vent through the vent pipe for 10 minutes. After 10 minutes, place the weighted pressure gauge on at 10 pounds pressure* and process pint-sized jars for 70 minutes and quart-sized jars for 90 minutes. If using a dial-gauge-only pressure canner, use 11 pounds PSI. Follow pressure level according to your altitude and type of gauge (see chart at beginning of chapter).

9. Turn off heat and allow pressure to reduce to zero naturally. When pressure is completely reduced, remove the lid and wait an additional 10 minutes. Remove jars, place on towels in a draft-free area, cool for 24 hours, check seals, and store.

***Altitude adjustments** see chart on page 50*

Squash, Summer (pattypan, yellow, zucchini)

	Water Bath Can	Steam Can	Pressure Can	Dehydrate	Freeze	Freeze-Dry	Ferment	Root Cellar
SQUASH, SUMMER	✓	✓		✓	✓	✓		
Notes	Only in a tested pickle recipe	Only in a tested pickle recipe		Must be blanched; shredded does well without blanching	Must be blanched; shredded does well without blanching			

Mustard pickles
See page 208

Tomatoes and Zucchini *From the National Center of Home Food Preservation*

INGREDIENTS

12 pounds of tomatoes and 4 pounds of zucchini per 7 quarts

7 pounds of tomatoes and 2½ pounds of zucchini per 9 pints

4 to 5 pearl onions or 2 onion slices per quart jar; half this amount for pint jars (optional)

Salt - 1 teaspoon per quart or ½ teaspoon per pint

Altitude adjustments see chart on page 50

May substitute okra for the zucchini

1. Wash and rinse tomatoes and zucchini. Slice or cube zucchini.
2. Blanch tomatoes in boiling water for 30 to 60 seconds, until skins split. Dip in cold water; remove skins, core, and seeds, and quarter.
3. Prepare a pressure canner (see pages 48-49 for more information), jars, lids, and bands.
4. In a large pot, bring prepared quartered tomatoes to a boil and simmer for 10 minutes.
5. Add zucchini and gently boil for an additional 5 minutes.
6. Add salt to each jar and onion slices if using. Ladle hot mixture into each jar to a 1-inch headspace. Remove air bubbles and recheck headspace; ladle in more contents if necessary to maintain 1-inch headspace.
7. Wipe the rim of the jars clean; place the lid and band on. Screw down to fingertip tight and place jars in canner. When all the jars are filled and in the canner, place the lid on your pressure canner. Turn heat to high and allow steam to vent through the vent pipe for 10 minutes. After 10 minutes, place the weighted pressure gauge on at 10 pounds pressure* and process pint-sized jars for 30 minutes and quart-sized jars for 35 minutes. If using a dial-gauge-only pressure canner, use 11 pounds PSI. Follow pressure level according to your altitude and type of gauge (see chart at beginning of chapter).
8. Turn off heat and allow pressure to reduce to zero naturally. When pressure is completely reduced, remove the lid and wait an additional 10 minutes. Remove jars, place on towels in a draft-free area, cool for 24 hours, check seals, and store.

Squash, Winter (hubbard, banana, acorn, butternut, buttercup)

	Water-bath Can	Steam Can	Pressure Can	Dehydrate	Freeze	Freeze-Dry	Ferment	Root Cellar
SQUASH, WINTER			✓	✓	✓	✓		✓
Notes			Hot-pack, chunks only!	Must be blanched or cooked	Must be cooked			Acorn squash doesn't last as long as other winter squash. Use them first. Stems should be left intact.

Vegetable	Preparation	Jar Size	Pressure Canning Processing Time at 10 lbs. of Pressure*
Winter squash (smooth flesh) 2¼ pounds per quart	Wash your squash off and remove the stems. Cut in half and remove the seeds and pulp. Cut your pumpkin into quarters and then into 1-inch-long strips. Peel the rind. Cut into 1-inch cubes. Prepare a large pot with water and bring to a boil. Blanch prepared squash cubes in boiling water for 2 minutes (pumpkin may only be canned via hot-pack; do not skip this step).	Pint Quart	55 min 90 min

__Altitude adjustments__: If above 1,001 feet increase to 10 lbs. of pressure on weighted gauge; for dial gauge increase by 1 pound for every additional 2,000 feet in altitude. Average of 1 pound per pint.

Pressure Can Winter Squash

Having home-canned winter squash on the shelf is a welcome treat and can be safely canned at home, provided you're using a pressure canner and doing it in cubed format.

Any smooth (not stringy) winter squash may be canned at home in cubed format only (no pureed or mashed format).

Most common are butternut. It's NOT safe to can spaghetti squash due to its stringiness.

How to Can Winter Squash

Average is 16 pounds for 7 quarts

10 pounds for 9 pints

1. Prepare a pressure canner (see pages 48-49 for more information), jars, lids, and bands.
2. Wash your squash and remove the stems. Cut in half and remove the seeds and pulp.
3. Cut your winter squash into quarters and then into 1-inch-long strips.
4. Peel the rind. Cut into 1-inch cubes.**
5. Prepare a large pot with water and bring to a boil. Blanch prepared squash cubes in boiling water for 2 minutes.
6. Remove from heat and with a slotted spoon, fill jars with cubes to generous 1-inch headspace (do not mash or puree while packing). Take the liquid from the pot and fill to a 1-inch headspace. Remove air bubbles and check headspace again; add more water if necessary.
7. Wipe the rim of the jars clean; place the lid and band on. Screw down to fingertip tight and place jars in canner. When all the jars are filled and in the canner, place the lid on your pressure canner. Turn heat to high and allow steam to vent through the vent pipe for 10 minutes. After 10 minutes, place the weighted pressure gauge on at 10 pounds pressure* and process pint jars for 55 minutes and quart jars for 90 minutes. If using a dial-gauge-only pressure canner, use 11 pounds PSI. Follow pressure level according to your altitude and type of gauge (see chart at beginning of chapter).
8. Turn off heat and allow pressure to reduce to zero naturally. When pressure is completely reduced, remove the lid and wait an additional 10 minutes. Remove jars, place on towels in a draft-free area, cool for 24 hours, check seals, and store.

*****Altitude adjustments** *see chart on page 50*

**"*The* Ball Book of Complete Canning *says you can peel squash and place it sealed in the fridge for a day before canning. They recommend letting it come to room temp for an hour before blanching and following hot-pack canning procedures.*

Sweet Potatoes

	Water-bath Can	Steam Can	Pressure Can	Dehydrate	Freeze	Freeze-Dry	Ferment	Root Cellar
SWEET POTATOES			✓	✓	✓	✓	✓	✓
Notes			Hot-pack	Blanch or roast, cubed, shredded, pureed	Must be cooked	Cubed or mashed	Sliced, diced, or shredded (similar to carrots in ferments)	Must be cured before storing

Vegetable	Preparation	Jar Size	Pressure Canning Processing Time at 10 lbs. of Pressure*
Potatoes, sweet 2½ - 3 pounds per quart	Pick small to medium-sized potatoes that are firm. Don't use soft potatoes. Wash and drain sweet potatoes while you bring a large stainless-steel pot of water to a boil. Boil or steam potatoes for 15 minutes for small and 20 minutes for medium potatoes, just until the skins can easily be removed (do not fully cook). Bring a kettle of water to a boil while potatoes are cooling enough to peel (alternatively you can use syrup; see syrup chart on page 270). Let sweet potatoes cool slightly before peeling and cutting into cubes or quarters. Do NOT mash or puree.	Pint	65 min
		Quart	90 min

***Altitude adjustments**: If above 1,001 feet increase to 10 lbs. of pressure on weighted gauge; for dial gauge increase by 1 pound for every additional 2,000 feet in altitude. Average of 1 pound per pint.

Pressure Can Sweet Potatoes

INGREDIENTS

Average 16 pounds for 7 quarts

10 pounds for 9 pints

1. Prepare a pressure canner (see pages 18-19 for more information), jars, lids, and bands.
2. Wash and drain sweet potatoes while you bring a large stainless-steel pot of water to a boil. Boil or steam potatoes for 15 minutes for small and 20 minutes for medium potatoes, just until the skins can easily be removed (do not fully cook).
3. Bring a kettle of water to a boil while potatoes are cooling enough to peel (alternatively you can use syrup; see syrup chart on page 270).
4. Let sweet potatoes cool slightly before peeling and cutting into cubes or quarters. Do NOT mash or puree.
5. Pack hot potatoes into prepared jars to a 1-inch headspace and pour just-off-the-boil water or syrup over top. Remove air bubbles and add more liquid if needed to maintain the 1-inch headspace.
6. Add ½ teaspoon salt to pint jars or 1 teaspoon salt to quart jars if desired.
7. Wipe the rim of the jars clean; place the lid and band on. Screw down to fingertip tight and place jars in canner. When all the jars are filled and in the canner, place the lid on your pressure canner. Turn heat to high and allow steam to vent through the vent pipe for 10 minutes. After 10 minutes, place the weighted pressure gauge on at 10 pounds pressure* and process pint-sized jars for 65 minutes and quart-sized jars for 90 minutes. If using a dial-gauge-only pressure canner, use 11 pounds PSI. Follow pressure level according to your altitude and type of gauge (see chart at beginning of chapter).
8. Turn off heat and allow pressure to reduce to zero naturally. When pressure is completely reduced, remove the lid and wait an additional 10 minutes. Remove jars, place on towels in a draft-free area, cool for 24 hours, check seals, and store.

***Altitude adjustments** see chart on page 50*

Tomatoes

	Water-bath Can	Steam Can	Pressure Can	Dehydrate	Freeze	Freeze-Dry	Ferment	Root Cellar
TOMATOES	✓	✓	✓	✓	✓	✓	✓	✓
Notes	An acid must be added with tomatoes! Follow a tested recipe.	An acid must be added with tomatoes! Follow a tested recipe. Processing time CANNOT exceed 45 minutes.	Raw or hot-packed, or as an ingredient in a combination recipe. An acid must be added with tomatoes except when canning meats or soups!	Do NOT need to be blanched	Do NOT need to be blanched	Sliced, cubed, salsa	Whole, crushed, salsa, ketchup	Green tomatoes will store as they ripen

Summer Squash

See Tomato Zuchini Sauce page 245

Never use diseased or blemished tomatoes. Never can tomatoes that have been left on the vine and gone through a frost. When tomatoes are on the vine and go through a frost, it alters their acidity level and lowers it too much for canning. This is only for tomatoes on the vine that have been through a frost, not for tomatoes you've picked and then frozen.

Home-Canning Tomatoes

When canning tomatoes at home, it's important that you add sufficient amounts of acid to your home-canned tomato products. Tomatoes fall borderline in the pH level; they need 4.6 or lower to be safely canned via the water-bath method and tomatoes are often higher than that.

Since 1994 the safe guidelines for canning tomatoes are to add acid to the jar (to ensure each jar has enough acid) or that your salsa recipes have a sufficient amount of acid in the recipe to make it safe with the combination of vegetables.

How to Preserve Vegetables

Acid and Salt Amounts Per Jar for Tomatoes

Ingredient	Pint	Quart
Citric acid	¼ teaspoon	½ teaspoon
Bottled lemon juice	1 tablespoon	2 tablespoons
Vinegar 5% acidity	2 tablespoons	4 tablespoons
Salt (optional but better overall flavor)	½ teaspoon	1 teaspoon

Paste tomatoes have less water and are my preferred tomatoes to use for canning or salsas.

Raw-Packed Tomatoes Without Liquid (my preferred method)

INGREDIENTS

Average of 3 pounds per quart or 1½ pounds per pint

Bottled lemon juice or citric acid

1. Prepare a water-bath or pressure canner (see pages 48-49 for more information), jars, lids, and bands.

2. Peel tomatoes by blanching in boiling water for 30 to 60 seconds or until the skin starts to crack. Immerse tomatoes in cold water and slip off the skins. Remove cores and any bruised or blemished spots (sometimes they show up more after blanching). You can leave them whole, in halves, or quartered.

3. Add the acid amount from the chart on facing page to each jar.

4. Pack raw tomatoes into prepared jars with a ½-inch headspace. Press tomatoes down tight until the juice in the tomatoes fills up the spaces between tomatoes and the jar with juice. Add ½ teaspoon salt to pints or 1 teaspoon to quart, if desired.

5. Remove air bubbles, recheck headspace, and add more tomatoes if needed. Wipe down the rim of the jar. Place lid and band on and screw down to fingertip tight.

6. Place into the prepared canner on the rack.

7. **To process in a water-bath**, make sure jars are completely submerged beneath the water. Bring to a boil and process both pints and quarts for 85 minutes.* Remove canner lid and wait 5 minutes; remove jars, allow to cool, and seal for 24 hours.

8. **To process a pressure canner** (my favorite), place jars inside pressure canner. Check the vent pipe is clear and lock the lid into place and bring to a boil. Allow steam to vent for 10 minutes and then close the vent. Process pint and quart jars at 10 pounds of pressure for 25 minutes. If using a dial-gauge-only pressure canner, use 11 pounds PSI. Follow pressure level according to your altitude and type of gauge (see chart at beginning of chapter).*

9. Turn off heat and allow pressure to reduce to zero naturally. When pressure is completely reduced, remove the lid and wait an additional 10 minutes. Remove jars, place on towels in a draft-free area, cool for 24 hours, check seals, and store.

Altitude adjustments see chart on page 50

Tomatoes Packed in Water

INGREDIENTS

Average of 3 pounds per quart or 1½ lbs per pint

Bottled lemon juice or citric acid

2 teaspoons of dried herbs or spices per pint jar (optional)*

**Altitude adjustments:

Water-bath: *If above 1,000 feet above sea level increase processing time by 5 minutes; for every 3,000 feet increment, increase another 5 minutes processing time.*

Pressure canner: *If above 1,000 feet above sea level, increase pounds of pressure to 15 pounds.*

Dried spices and herbs are optional but some favorites are basil, thyme, oregano, rosemary, garlic powder, chili powder, ground cumin, and cayenne pepper.

OPTIONS

Tomatoes Packed in Tomato Juice: Provides increased flavor but increased processing time. Increase processing time for pressure canner to 25 minutes for both pint and quart jars. Water-bath time remains the same.

1. Prepare a water-bath or pressure canner (see pages 48-49 for more information), jars, lids, and bands.

2. Peel tomatoes by blanching in boiling water for 30 to 60 seconds or until skin starts to crack. Immerse tomatoes in cold water and slip off the skins. Remove cores and any bruised or blemished spots (sometimes they show up more after blanching). You can leave them whole, in halves, or quartered.

3. Add acid amount from the chart on page 252 to each jar and chosen spices if using.

4. **Raw-pack:** Boil 4 cups or so of water. Pack tomatoes to a generous ½-inch headspace. Ladle hot water into jar to cover tomatoes. Remove air bubbles, recheck headspace, and add more tomatoes if needed. Wipe down rim of jar. Place lid and band on and screw down to fingertip tight.

5. **Hot-pack:** Put peeled tomatoes into a saucepan and just cover with water. Bring to a boil and gently boil for 5 minutes, stirring often to prevent any scorching. Ladle hot tomatoes into prepared jars to a generous ½-inch headspace; add cooking liquid to the jars to a ½-inch headspace. Remove air bubbles, recheck headspace, and add more liquid if needed. Wipe down the rim of the jar. Place lid and band on and screw down to fingertip tight.

6. Place into the prepared canner on the rack.

7. **To process in a water-bath**, make sure jars are completely submerged beneath the water. Bring to a boil and process pints for 40 minutes and quarts for 45 minutes.** Remove canner lid and wait 5 minutes; remove jars, allow to cool, and seal for 24 hours.

8. **To process in pressure canner** (my favorite), place jars on canner rack inside pressure canner prepared with 2 to 3 inches of water. Check vent pipe is clear and lock lid into place and bring to a boil. Allow steam to vent for 10 minutes and then close vent and allow to build to 10 pounds of pressure.

9. Process both pint and quart jars at 10 pounds of pressure (dial-gauge-only canner use 11 pounds PSI) for 10 minutes. Turn off heat and allow pressure to cool and return to zero naturally. Remove the canner lid once pressure is completely reduced. Leave jars in the canner with the lid removed for *10 minutes,* then transfer to a folded towel and allow to cool and seal for 24 hours.

How to Make Tomato Sauce

Tomato sauce is one of the most versatile items you'll have in your pantry and food storage. It's probably my favorite tomato product, and if I only had to pick a top few (I don't think I could pick just one), then it would be on my top favorite list of home-canned items.

Tomato sauce can be turned into pasta sauce, pizza sauce, ketchup, added to soups, stews, chili, and casseroles, and of course used as tomato sauce in recipes.

Traditionally, tomato sauce took much longer to make than canning regular tomatoes, but with the help of modern appliances such as a blender, you can have homemade tomato sauce ready to can much faster than ever before.

While you can use any type of tomato, a paste tomato will reduce the boiling time and produce a thicker sauce much faster. My preference is San Marzano Lungo or Amish Paste tomatoes.

There are a few options when it comes to removing the skins on your tomatoes and making sauce.

1. **First is the traditional water blanching.** Immerse your tomatoes into boiling water for a minute or so, plunge into cold water, and remove the skins. Chop tomatoes; remove stems, cores, and any blemished areas and simmer in a large pot.
2. **Food mill or sieve.** Chop tomatoes into quarters and place into a large pot. Crush tomatoes as they're reaching a boil and continue adding new layers of tomatoes. Once they're all in the pot, let boil for 5 minutes. Then process mixture through your food mill or sieve to remove skins and seeds. Then place remaining sauce back into the pot on the stove and heat to a boil.
3. **Freeze your tomatoes whole.** Pop your ripe tomatoes into the freezer, then thaw, and rinse under warm water. The skins fall off. Scoop out seeds. Place in a blender and puree; or if you don't have a blender, chop, put in a large pot, mash with a potato masher, and bring to a boil.
4. **Roast your tomatoes.** Roast tomatoes on low broil for 30 to 45 minutes, until skins are beginning to blacken and shrivel. Allow to cool for 15 minutes (cool enough to handle), then remove the skins, puree the skinless tomato, put straight in a pot, and cook down to sauce, or run through a sieve/food mill to remove the seeds.

To prevent the tomatoes from separating, as soon as you've cut them, they need to be heated. Tomatoes contain an enzyme that when exposed to air begins to break down the pectin (which results in separation, where you see a layer of liquid and then the tomato flesh/sauce) and heat inactivates this enzyme. This is why many instructions only have you cut a few tomatoes at a time before adding them to the pot. If they do separate, it's not a safety issue; just mix back together before heating and serving or cooking.

Always use stainless-steel or a nonreactive pot when cooking tomato products.

No matter which of the above methods you used, bring sauce to a boil over medium heat, and let it simmer until some of the water has evaporated and sauce has reached its desired thickness. Using a paste tomato will result in a thicker sauce faster. Stir often so it doesn't burn or scorch. You can let the sauce reduce by half if you wish for thickness or only reduce by a third, up to you!

Once sauce is ready, prepare clean jars and add acid and salt following the chart on page 252.

> **Note:** *Headspace is different for water-bath and pressure canning. While the National Center of Home Food Preservation uses the same headspace, Ball does not. Both are tested sources (which means they're both safe) but I've found when pressure canning I have less siphoning using the headspace recommendations from Ball.*

How to Can Tomato Sauce

INGREDIENTS

Thin Sauce: Average of 5 pounds per quart or 2½ pounds per pint

Thicker Sauce: 6½ pounds per quart or 3¼ pounds per pint

Bottled lemon juice or citric acid

Salt (optional)

Herbs/spices (optional)

1. Rinse tomatoes, choose the peeling method from the previous page, and prepare sauce. Once sauce has reached desired thickness, prepare a water-bath or pressure canner (see pages 48-49 for more information), jars, lids, and bands.

2. Add lemon juice or citric acid, salt, and herbs to each jar, then fill with hot tomato sauce according to the canning method.

3. **Water-bath or steam canner instructions:** Fill jars to a ½-inch headspace. Run a spatula around the jar circumference to remove air bubbles. Add more tomato sauce if needed to keep ½-inch headspace. Wipe the rim of the jars clean; place the lid and band on. Screw down to fingertip tight and place jars in a water-bath or steam canner. Process pints for 35 minutes and quarts for 40 minutes* (if you're 1,000 feet or higher above sea level, you will need to use a water-bath and not the steam canner).

4. Follow instructions for a water-bath or steam canner at the end of processing time. Place on the counter on a folded kitchen towel. Cool for 24 hours, check the seals, and then store.

5. **Pressure-canner instructions:** Fill jars to a 1-inch headspace. Run a spatula around the jar circumference to remove air bubbles. Add more tomato sauce if needed to keep 1-inch headspace.

6. Wipe the rim of the jars clean; place the lid and band on. Screw down to fingertip tight and place jars in canner. When all the jars are filled and in the canner, place the lid on your pressure canner. Turn heat to high and allow steam to vent through the vent pipe for 10 minutes; close the vent. After 10 minutes, place the weighted pressure gauge on at 10 pounds pressure* and process pint and quart jars for 15 minutes. If using a dial-gauge-only pressure canner, use 11 pounds PSI. Follow pressure level according to your altitude and type of gauge (see chart at beginning of chapter).

7. Turn off heat and allow pressure to reduce to zero naturally. When pressure is completely reduced, remove the lid, and wait an additional 10 minutes. Remove jars, place on towels in a draft-free area, cool for 24 hours, check seals, and store.

***Altitude adjustments** see chart on page 50*

Altitude adjustments for water-bath or steam canner: *If you're 1,001 to 3,000 feet increase processing time by 5 minutes, 3,001 to 6,000 feet increase processing time by 10 minutes, if above 6,001 feet increase processing time by 15 minutes.*

FLAVOR OPTIONS:

- Add to the jar 1 fresh basil leaf, free of blemishes.

- Add to the jar 2 teaspoons of dried herbs. Examples: ½ teaspoon dried basil, ½ teaspoon dried rosemary, ½ teaspoon dried oregano, ½ teaspoon dried thyme, or any combination of dried herbs you prefer.

- You can sub out one of the ½ teaspoons of dried herbs for hot red pepper flakes if you like a little heat; however, I would try it with ¼ teaspoon first to make sure it's not too hot.

Fresh Summer Salsa Recipe

Home-canned salsa recipes are a delicious way to add flavor to dishes, with your favorite chips, or atop meats. They can be a variety of heat or sweet with fruit salsas as well.

The most important thing to remember with home-canning salsa is to always follow a canning salsa recipe. It must have a tested ratio of acid to non-acid and you can never alter that ratio. For example, you can't increase the amount of pepper, but you could use a mild pepper in place of a hot pepper, such as a New Mexico pepper instead of a jalapeño or vice versa.

To make quick work while chopping up all those veggies, use a food processor. Use care when handling or chopping hot peppers; wear gloves when handling them to avoid accidentally getting pepper juice where you don't want it. A plastic baggy works great as a makeshift glove.

Yield: Approximately 6 pints

INGREDIENTS

- 12 cups peeled, cored, and diced tomatoes
- 2 cups chopped onion
- 1 cup chopped green bell pepper
- 1½ cups fresh finely chopped cilantro
- 6 jalapeño peppers, seeded and chopped (if you want more heat, leave the seeds in)
- 15 cloves garlic, chopped finely
- 1 tablespoon salt
- ¼ cup lime juice
- ¾ cup vinegar
- ¾ teaspoon hot pepper flakes (optional)

1. Prepare a water-bath or steam canner (see pages 48-49 for more information), jars, lids, and bands.
2. In a large pot combine all ingredients and bring to a boil over medium-high heat. Stir often and gently boil for 10 minutes, until slightly thickened.
3. Ladle hot salsa into jars to a ½-inch headspace. Remove air bubbles and adjust headspace if needed by adding more salsa.
4. Wipe the rim of the jars clean; place the lid and band on. Screw down to fingertip tight and place jars in a water-bath or steam canner. Process pints for 15 minutes.*
5. Follow instructions for a water-bath or steam canner at the end of processing time. Place on the counter on a folded kitchen towel. Cool for 24 hours, check the seals, and then store.

***Altitude adjustments**: If you're 1,001 to 3,000 feet increase processing time by 5 minutes, 3,001 to 6,000 feet increase processing time by 10 minutes, if above 6,001 feet increase 15 minutes processing time.*

Bruschetta in a Jar

This recipe is adapted from Ball's Book of Complete Home Canning. *I was on the hunt for some way to can the cherry tomatoes I had, and this is one of the few recipes that doesn't require you to peel the tomatoes, because both the acid level and processing times were tested with the peels on (never leave the peels on if the recipe says peeled).*

Yield: Approximately 6 to 7 half-pint jars (250ml)

INGREDIENTS

9 cups chopped, cored plum tomatoes or cherry tomatoes (about 4 lbs.)

5 cloves garlic, minced

1 cup dry white wine

1 cup white wine vinegar**

½ cup water

2 tablespoons sugar

2 tablespoons dried basil

2 tablespoons dried oregano

2 tablespoons balsamic vinegar

1½ teaspoons salt

1. Prepare a water-bath or steam canner (see pages 48-49 for more information), jars, lids, and bands.

2. Combine garlic, wine, wine vinegar, water, sugar, basil, oregano, balsamic vinegar, and salt. Bring to a rolling boil over high heat. Reduce the heat and let it simmer for 5 minutes to let the garlic heat through. Remove from heat.

3. Put the tomatoes in the hot jars, leaving a generous ½-inch headspace. Fill the jars with the hot brine over the tomatoes to a ½-inch headspace.

4. Remove air bubbles, and add more hot brine if needed to maintain headspace. Wipe the rim of the jars clean; place the lid and band on. Screw down to fingertip tight and place jars in a water-bath or steam canner.

5. Process half-pints for 20 minutes.*

6. Follow instructions for a water-bath or steam canner at the end of processing time. Place on the counter on a folded kitchen towel. Cool for 24 hours, check the seals, and then store.

*****Altitude adjustments**: *If you're 1,001 to 3,000 feet increase processing time by 5 minutes, 3,001 to 6,000 feet increase processing time by 10 minutes, if above 6,001 feet increase processing time by 15 minutes.*

****You can use any vinegar as long as it's 5% acidity. It's okay if you need to make additional brine if needed as long as you use the same ratios as listed in the recipe.*

Fermented Salsa

Yield: Approximately ½ gallon

INGREDIENTS

3 pounds of tomatoes, diced (paste varieties keep it nice and thick)

2 bell peppers, deseeded and diced

2 onions, diced

8 to 12 cloves of garlic, minced

1 jalapeño, seeded and diced (or hot pepper of choice)

1 cup cilantro or parsley (for those cilantro haters), finely chopped

2 tablespoons mineral or sea salt

1½ teaspoons ground cumin

1 tablespoon fresh lime juice (optional)

1. Combine all ingredients in a large bowl and mix well. Alternatively, you could pulse everything together in a food processor, but I like a little chunk in my salsa.

2. Pack into one clean half-gallon or two quart Mason jars, leaving a generous 1- to 1½-inch headspace. Push down to remove any air pockets and bring the liquid level up over the solids.

3. Place a weight inside to keep solids submerged. Put on an airlock lid or two-part metal lid and band. If using a band, tighten down until you feel resistance and then back it off approximately a half turn (still check and burp daily if pressure builds).

4. Set on the counter, out of direct sunlight, and ferment for 2 to 3 days. Taste-test on day 2; if it's to your liking, place a metal lid and band on and move to the fridge or cold storage.

Turnips

	Water-bath Can	Steam Can	Pressure Can	Dehydrate	Freeze	Freeze-Dry	Ferment	Root Cellar
TURNIPS				✓	✓	✓	✓	✓
Notes				Blanch, sliced or mashed	Must be blanched	Sliced or shredded	Group them by size and use smallest ones first	

How to Preserve Vegetables

CHAPTER 11
How to Preserve Fruits

This chapter shares general guidelines on how to can fruit by itself, old-fashioned jams and jellies, fruit butters, fruit juice, and pie fillings. Following these, you'll find fruit in alphabetical order in this section. Each fruit will have listed the safe methods to preserve it, favorite recipes, and notes.

For exact step-by-step instructions on specific preservation techniques, visit that section in the earlier chapters. As an example, how to can apples is under the canning fruit section, whereas freezing apple instructions are in the freezing chapter. All water-bath recipes may be used with a steam canner (follow steam canner instructions for time adjustments at the end of processing).

If purchasing fruit, it's helpful to know how many pounds are needed for the number of jars you wish to put up when canning. This varies by recipe type, but I have included amounts where applicable.

While bushels and pecks aren't used as much when buying at grocery stores, they are still helpful units of measure to know in the following chart.

Bulk Conversion Chart

Bushel	Peck	Quart	Pint
4 pecks	8 quarts	2 pints	2 cups
8 gallons	16 pints	4 cups	
32 quarts	32 cups		
64 pints			
128 cups			

Canning Fruit Product Guidelines

For specific fruit recipes, go to that fruit. Below are the guidelines for canning different fruit products.

How to Can Fruit

To can fruit you can use both the water-bath or pressure canner at lower pounds of pressure than non-acidic foods; just note that if you use the pressure canner, follow the processing time carefully (don't cut it short) and be aware that overcooking the fruit will make it mushy and is easier to do with the pressure canner.

To can fruit you'll add liquid to the jar, usually in the form of syrup. You may make a syrup with sugar or honey, and some people also can with fruit juice or water. If you choose fruit juice or water, you must hot-pack your fruit.

I prefer a raw-pack and a light sugar syrup. You can make your syrup with varying amounts of sugar; I usually prefer the super-light or pretty-light syrup unless the fruit is quite tart to begin with.

To keep fruit from browning you can put peeled fruit into a water mixture of citric acid or ascorbic acid until it goes in the jar or syrup.

If I want to keep fruit from browning (I don't bother doing this with peaches, but I do with apples), the simplest way is to put prepared fruit in a bowl of cold water and lemon juice or another browning preventative.

Browning Preventative	How Much	Water
Lemon juice	½ cup	½ gallon (8 cups)
Citric acid	1 teaspoon	1 quart (4 cups)
Ascorbic acid (Vitamin C)	1 teaspoon	1 gallon (16 cups)

Note: Citric acid and lemon juice are not as effective in preventing browning as ascorbic acid solutions.

How to Preserve Fruits | 269

To Make Syrups

For syrup, measure water into a heavy-bottomed saucepan and pour in sugar (or honey). Heat over medium-low until it reaches a boil, stirring frequently to prevent scorching. Turn heat to low, but keep syrup hot, until ready to pour over fruit or pour fruit in, depending upon raw- or hot-pack method.

The below calculations are for approximately 8 pints or 4 quarts of fruit. You can also halve the recipe if you're getting toward the last few jars and realize you're going to need more syrup to finish it off. I usually use between 1½ to 2 cups of syrup per quart jar, especially with larger fruit like peaches.

Syrups for Canning Fruit Chart

Syrup Type	Cups of Sugar	Cups of Water	Other Sweetener
Super-light	¾ cup	6½ cups	
Pretty-light	1½ cups	5¾ cups	
Light	2¼ cups	5¼ cups	
Medium	2¼ cups	5¼ cups	
Heavy	3¼ cups	5 cups	
Honey-light		5 cups	1½ cups honey
Honey-medium		4 cups	2 cups honey

Old-Fashioned Jam and Jelly Master Recipe

Your great-grandmother likely didn't use store-bought pectin to make her jam or jelly. It wasn't until the early 1900s that store-bought pectin was invented (originally in the form of a syrup).

Prior to that, jam and jelly were made for years with fruit and sugar. Jam is a fruit spread that uses the whole pieces of fruit. Jelly uses just the juice of the fruit.

You'll find on the next page the master formula I use to make my own combinations of jams and jellies without store-bought pectin. Refer to the Canning Problems and Troubleshooting section for tips on reaching the gelling point.

Pay attention to the fruits that require added acid per cup to maintain a 4.6 pH level or lower for safety.

Jam and Jelly Master Recipe

Fruit—8 cups low or medium pectin level fruit (strawberry, blueberry, blackberry, etc.). Never use fig, melon, bananas, or elderberries (new testing shows elderberries are not acidic enough for canning unless using a specific tested recipe by weight per the University of Wisconsin-Madison Division of Extension)[6] as they're not high enough in acid to be safe.

Sugar—2½ to 4 cups sugar (dependent upon taste and if jam is setting properly. If you're struggling to get a gel, add ¼ to ½ cup more sugar.)

Acid—Fresh or bottled lemon juice depending on fruit. High-acidic fruits are fine to use fresh lemon or lime juice with, but others (see list below) require bottled. When acid is needed for safety, only bottled lemon juice is recommended. Fresh varies greatly in pH level based on type and time of harvest.

Pectin—High-level source: zest of 2 limes and ¼ cup of lime juice; zest of 2 lemons and ¼ cup of lemon juice (if you have super big lemons, one might be enough); zest of 1 orange and ¼ cup lemon juice; 1 or 2 large, grated green apples (when using apples, 1 tablespoon of bottled lemon juice per cup of grated apple is needed); 2 cups currant juice; or a combination. I've done 1 cup currant juice with the zest of 1 lemon and had great results.

The below fruits require 1 tablespoon bottled lemon juice from concentrate per cup of mashed/pureed fruit for acidity levels.[7]

- Apricot
- Apple
- Blueberry
- Sweet Blackberry
- Sweet Cherry
- Mulberry
- Ripe Quince
- Sweet Plum
- Peach (white peaches shouldn't be used as they're lower in acid in these recipes)

- Pear (do not use Asian pear; they're lower in acid in these recipes)

You may choose to use either the lime/lemon zest OR a grated, peeled, and cored apple (green/tart apples are high in pectin) in any of the below recipes, BUT you must use 1 tablespoon bottled lemon juice per cup of apple when using the apple as your pectin source.

Pro Tips

- Underripe fruit, just a bit under—not totally green—has more pectin. Select up to a quarter of slightly underripe fruit for a better gel.
- If you put a high-level pectin fruit with a lower-level pectin fruit, you can use a small amount of higher-level pectin fruit in place of store-bought pectin. One of my favorites is red raspberry and currant.

Three Ways to Test Your Jam "Set" or "Gel"

The sheet test and the one I use most often. Take a large metal spoon and put it in the fridge or freezer when you begin making your jam. Dip the spoon into the boiling jam and hold it up so that the spoon is sideways and the jam can drip off the side/edge of the spoon. If it just runs off, it's not ready. Large drops mean you're almost there; and the sheeting is when the jelly/jam drips off the spoon in one sheet instead of individual drops, hence the name "sheet test."

Cold plate test. Put a saucer or small plate in the freezer. Put a small spoonful of jam on the chilled plate and put it in the freezer for a minute. Pull it out and push against the edge of jam with the tip of your finger. If you can run your finger through it and it stays separated and/or the surface shows wrinkles where you've pushed it, then it's done.

Candy thermometer. Use a candy thermometer, making sure you don't touch the bottom of the pan (directly on the heat source) with the end of the thermometer. The goal is 220°F/104°C. It's important to note that if you're at high altitude, 1,000 feet/305 meters above sea level, then you need to subtract 2° for every 1,000 feet/305 meters above sea level.

When you're doing these tests, pull your jam onto a cool burner so you don't overcook it if it's indeed at the gel stage.

Gelling Temperatures for Altitudes Difference
(per National Center of Home Food Preservation)

Sea level - 999 ft	1,000– 1,999 ft	2,000– 2,999 ft	3,000– 3,999 ft	4,000– 4,999 ft	5,000– 5,999 ft	6,000– 6,999 ft	7,000– 7,999 ft	8,000– 8,999 ft
220°F (104°C)	218° F (103°C)	216° F (102°C)	214°F (101°C)	212° F (100°C)	211° F (99°C)	209° F (98°C)	207°F (97°C)	205°F (96°C)

Troubleshooting Tips When No-added-pectin Jam Won't Set

If you do the gel-stage tests and your jam isn't quite there, you have a few options. The first is to simply let it cook for 5 minutes and test it again. I generally have to let my no-store-bought-pectin recipes cook for 20 minutes, but I start testing at 10 minutes of simmering time to avoid going over the gel or set point.

If your jam has cooked for 20 minutes and it's not showing signs of gelling, add a ¼ cup of sugar or a tad more acid such as lemon or lime juice by way of a tablespoon or two. Cook for another 5 minutes; if it's still not gelling, add another ½ cup of sugar.

If you thought your jam/jelly had set but upon cooling realize it's not really set, you have two options. Go ahead and can it up as syrup. Or put it back in the pot, bring it to a boil, and add ½ cup more sugar or more of a natural pectin source, such as more grated citrus peel or grated green apple.

Why Jam or Jelly Didn't Set

A trinity of three factors, the amount of sugar, pectin, and acid, work together to create the gelling point.

Some fruits have enough pectin in them that we don't have to add any extra, like wild grapes and apples, but others need more, like blueberries, blackberries, raspberries, and strawberries, so we add another form of pectin, either from citrus, currant juice, or green apples to boost the pectin levels. You can also add store-bought pectin, which I do on occasion, but I prefer to use old-fashioned methods when possible.

No-Sugar Jams and Jellies

You do not have to use sugar or honey when making jams and jellies, but you will need an outside pectin source to get a set.

The only store-bought pectin I use is Pomona's Pectin as it's a natural citrus pectin and doesn't have questionable ingredients or dextrose added to it. Pomona's doesn't rely on sugar for the set but the calcium. You can use stevia, Splenda, xylitol, sucanat, agave, and maple syrup with it.

How to Make and Can Fruit Juice and Syrups

The process for making fruit juice and syrup to can is very similar. You just take the fruit syrup one step further. Having home-canned fruit juice at home is great because you can control how much sugar to add to the final product—or none at all.

To make fruit syrup, we simply take the fruit juice and add a few more ingredients to create a syrup, perfect for using on pancakes, waffles, or ice cream, or in milk shakes and smoothies, or mixed into yogurts.

Using a Juicer

If you plan on making lots of jellies and juices, then a stainless-steel juicer is a great investment because it saves tons of time and manual labor. If you have a steam juicer, simply fill the bottom pan with water, stack all the pieces into place, put your fruit in the strainer, and bring to a boil. Set the timer for the correct time depending upon your fruit and collect the juice for jelly, juice, or syrup making.

Traditional Method

For the traditional juice-making method, place your fruit in a large stainless-steel pot and add enough water so it doesn't stick. For apples, stem and chop up, then bring to a boil and simmer until the fruit is soft and releases its juices.

After it is boiled, transfer to a dampened jelly bag or strainer lined with several layers of cheesecloth and put over a bowl. Allow to drain for several hours.

No-Sugar Jams and Jellies

You do not have to use sugar or honey when making jams and jellies, but you will need an outside pectin source to get a set.

The only store-bought pectin I use is Pomona's Pectin as it's a natural citrus pectin and doesn't have questionable ingredients or dextrose added to it. Pomona's doesn't rely on sugar for the set but the calcium. You can use stevia, Splenda, xylitol, sucanat, agave, and maple syrup with it.

How to Make and Can Fruit Juice and Syrups

The process for making fruit juice and syrup to can is very similar. You just take the fruit syrup one step further. Having home-canned fruit juice at home is great because you can control how much sugar to add to the final product—or none at all.

To make fruit syrup, we simply take the fruit juice and add a few more ingredients to create a syrup, perfect for using on pancakes, waffles, or ice cream, or in milk shakes and smoothies, or mixed into yogurts.

Using a Juicer

If you plan on making lots of jellies and juices, then a stainless-steel juicer is a great investment because it saves tons of time and manual labor. If you have a steam juicer, simply fill the bottom pan with water, stack all the pieces into place, put your fruit in the strainer, and bring to a boil. Set the timer for the correct time depending upon your fruit and collect the juice for jelly, juice, or syrup making.

Traditional Method

For the traditional juice-making method, place your fruit in a large stainless-steel pot and add enough water so it doesn't stick. For apples, stem and chop up, then bring to a boil and simmer until the fruit is soft and releases its juices.

After it is boiled, transfer to a dampened jelly bag or strainer lined with several layers of cheesecloth and put over a bowl. Allow to drain for several hours.

For grape juice, after draining, cover the juice and place in the fridge for 24 to 48 hours. Don't stir it. Allow the sediment to settle, then pour off the juice from the top of the sediment.

How to Can Fruit Butters

Old-fashioned fruit butters are one of my favorite things to make because they don't require an outside pectin source. They're excellent on bread, biscuits, as topping for pancakes or waffles, and perfect for jelly rolls or cake filling.

Fruit butters can only safely be made with acidic fruits. Do NOT use Asian pears, pumpkin (not even pumpkin combinations like pumpkin apple), banana, fig, melons, mango, or white peaches.

Fruit butters are thick and silky. You don't need to remove the skins on apricots, blueberries, nectarines, or plums. Rinse fruit and remove stems. For fruits with pits in them, peel if called for, cut in half, remove the pit, and place in a large heavy-bottomed pot (avoid aluminum). A pot with a wider base, as opposed to deep, has a larger surface area for evaporation and allows jams and fruit butters to thicken faster.

Follow recipes found in the individual fruit section starting on page 284.

Pie-Filling Guide

Home-canned pie filling is one of my favorites because it makes pie baking not seasonal when fruit is on, but all-year-round fun, and keeps holiday baking costs down (when fruit prices are often much higher to purchase fresh) but also saves time when we're busy. Homemade pie or dessert by just opening up the jar, dumping it into our pie crust, and baking is quick and easy.

One of the most important things to remember with home-canned pie filling is that the only safe thickener is Clear Jel, or you may can it without the thickener and add the thickener at the time of baking or preparing your dessert.

You may use frozen and then thawed fruit; this works especially well with berries and cherries, but I don't recommend that route for the apple pie or peach pie filling.

You can use the berry or fruit juice in place of water for a "fruitier" tasting pie filling.

Follow recipes found in the individual fruit section starting on page 284.

Pectin Sources

It is the combination of pectin and sugar that helps give jam and jelly its "set" or firmness. Pectin naturally occurs in fruits. Fruits high in pectin are apples, crab apples, grapes, quince, currants, lemons, and limes.

Jams are the easiest to make with natural pectin sources because they keep the skin in the product, where a higher concentration of pectin is found. But I've successfully made jelly without store-bought pectin as well.

Fruit pH and Pectin Level Chart

Fruit	PH	Pectin Level: High/Low	Pectin Level: Percent
Apple	3.3-4	High (green)/ Medium (ripe)	.71-.84
Apricot	3.3-4.8	Low	.71-1.32
Blackberry	3.85-4.5	High	.68-1.19
Blueberry	3.12-3.33	Low	
Cherry	3.2-4.54	Medium (sour)/ Low (sweet)	.24-.54
Chokeberry, Black (aka Aronia)	3.3-3.7	Low	
Crab Apple		High	

Fruit	PH	Pectin Level: High/Low	Pectin Level: Percent
Cranberry	2.3-2.5	High	
Currant	2.9	High	
Elderberry	3.8-4.5	Medium	
Fig	5.05-5.98	Low	
Gooseberry	2.8-3.1	High	
Grape	2.8-3.82	High (wild)/Medium (Concord)/Low (others)	.09-.28
Grapefruit	3.00-3.75	High (skins)/Low (flesh)	3.3-4.5
Kiwi, Hardy	3.61-3.75	Low	
Kumquat	3.64-4.25	Medium	
Lemon	2.2-2.4	High (skins)/Low (flesh)	2.8-2.99
Lime	2-2.8	High (skins)/Low (flesh)	
Lingonberry	2.95-3.18	High	

Fruit	PH	Pectin Level: High/Low	Pectin Level: Percent
Loganberry	2.7-3.5	Medium	0.59
Lychee	4.7-5.01	Low	
Mango	3.4-4.8	Low	
Mulberry	5.6	Medium	
Nectarine	3.92-4.18	Low	
Orange	3.69-4.34	High (skins)/ Low (flesh)	2.34-2.38
Papaya	5.2-6	High	
Peach	3.3-4.05	Low	
Pear	3.5-4.6	Low	
Persimmon	4.42-4.7	High	
Pineapple	3.2-4	Low	
Plum	2.8-4.3	High (most)/ Low (Italian)	
Pomegranate	2.93-3.2	High	

Fruit	PH	Pectin Level: High/Low	Pectin Level: Percent
Quince	3.12-3.4	High	
Raspberry	3.22-3.95	Low	0.97
Rhubarb	3.1-3.4	Medium	
Strawberry	3-3.9	Low	
Tangerine	3.32-4.48	High (skins)/ Low (flesh)	

How to Can Fruit Juice

Prepare jars and water-bath canner.

Place the juice in a large pot and heat to 190°F (88°C); don't boil it. Add sugar to taste if desired (general recommendations are 1 to 2 cups of sugar to 16 cups of juice). Heat at 190°F (88°C) for 5 minutes, then place it into hot and prepared canning jars, leaving ¼-inch headspace.

Fruit Juice	Processing Times* (minutes) - Pint Jars	Processing Times* (minutes) - Quart Jars
Apple	10	10
Berry	15	15
Cranberry	15	15
Grape	10	10

***Altitude adjustments:** *if 1,000 feet or higher above sea level, increase boiling time by 5 minutes for every 3,000 feet increment.*

Apple

	Water-bath Can	Steam Can	Pressure Can	Dehydrate	Freeze	Freeze-Dry	Ferment	Root Cellar
APPLE	✓	✓	✓	✓	✓	✓	✓	✓
Notes	Pie filling, jam, jelly, butter, sauce, slices in syrup	Pie filling, jam, jelly, butter, sauce, slices in syrup	Applesauce, slices	Slices, fruit leather	Slices, chunks, wedges	Slices	Vinegar, spiced apples	Whole

Fermented Sauce

See cranberries on page 317

Variety note: You can use any apple for these recipes, but for best results on pie fillings or slices, choose firm crisp apples (such as Gravenstein, Honey Crisp, Gala, or Granny Smith). For sauces, fruit butters, jams, and jellies, use softer varieties (such as Cortland, Golden Delicious, and McIntosh).

Fruit	Preparation	Jar Size	Water-Bath/Steam Canning Processing Time*	Pressure Canning Processing Time at 5 lbs. of Pressure*
Apples 1.5 pounds of apples per pint jar; 3 medium apples = 1 pound	Wash, stem, peel, and core; may either halve or cut into ¼-inch slices.	Pint	20 min	8 min
	Hot-Pack: Precook for 5 minutes in syrup, pack in jars, and add syrup to ½-inch headspace.	Quart	20 min	

__Altitude adjustments__: if you're 1,001 to 3,000 feet increase by 5 minutes processing time, 3,001 to 6,000 feet increase processing time by 10 minutes, if above 6,001 feet increase 15 minutes processing time. __Pressure canning__: if above 1,001 feet increase to 10 pounds of pressure on weighted gauge; for dial gauge increase by 1 pound for every additional 2,000 feet in altitude.

Low-Sugar Apple Pie Jam

Yield: 3 pints

INGREDIENTS

8 cups peeled, chopped, and cored apples

¾ cup dried cranberries (optional)

8 tablespoons bottled lemon juice

1 cup water

4 teaspoons calcium water*

4 teaspoons powder pectin*

1 teaspoon cinnamon

½ teaspoon nutmeg

2 cups sugar

1. Prepare jars and water-bath canner.
2. Peel, core, and chop apples.
3. Place apples in a big stainless-steel pot and add lemon juice and water. Bring to a boil and cook for 10 minutes until the apples are soft.
4. Meanwhile, mix sugar, spices, and powdered pectin together. Set aside.
5. Add calcium water (comes in the Pomona Pectin and activates the pectin) to the apples. Boil for 1 more minute.
6. Add the sugar mixture and return to a boil, stirring constantly (you don't want burnt sugar) for 2 minutes. You'll see and feel the mixture thicken up. Remove from heat.
7. Pour into clean canning jars to a ¼-inch headspace. Remove air bubbles and add more jam if needed to meet the required headspace.
8. Place in a water-bath canner, making sure the water level is 1 inch above the surface of the jars, and process for 10 minutes. Don't start the timer until the water is at a full boil.
9. Turn off heat and remove the canner lid; wait 5 minutes, and then remove the jars to a towel-covered counter. Let cool, checking seals after 24 hours. Remove bands, wipe down the surface of the jars, and store in the pantry.

You can use ¾ cup of finely chopped dried cranberries. Add them with the calcium water and spices.

*Comes with Pomona's Pectin. For a no-sugar version, follow instructions with the pectin box.

Altitude adjustments: *if you're 1,001 to 3,000 feet increase by 5 minutes processing time, 3,001 to 6,000 feet increase processing time by 10 minutes, if above 6,001 feet increase 15 minutes processing time.*

Apple Butter

INGREDIENTS

4 pounds of apples, peeled, cored, and roughly chopped (approximately 17 medium apples)

1 cup apple cider (if you don't have apple cider, use water, but you may need to increase the sugar depending upon taste)

1 cup apple cider vinegar OR ¼ cup bottled lemon juice

2 to 3 cups of sugar

2 teaspoons of your favorite ground spices

1. In a large stainless-steel pot, combine apples, cider (or water), and vinegar and bring to a boil; simmer, stirring often until apples are cooked through and soft. Puree apples (don't liquefy) with a blender, food processor, immersion blender, potato masher, or a food mill.

2. Combine apple puree, sugar, and spices into a large pot. Stir until sugar and spices are dissolved. Bring to a boil, then reduce heat to a gentle simmer, stirring often as it can scorch. Continue to cook until it's reached desired thickness.

3. To check for doneness, take out a spoonful and hold it up. The butter should stay mounded on the spoon. Or chill a plate and put a spoonful on the chilled plate. It should hold its shape and there should not be a separation of liquid. Now you're ready to jar. If it's not ready yet, simply continue cooking until it's reached the desired thickness.

4. Prepare your water-bath canner and wash jars in hot soapy water and rinse. Pour or ladle fruit butter into prepared jars to a ¼-inch headspace; remove air bubbles, check headspace, and add more if needed to the ¼-inch headspace. Wipe rims clean, place lids and bands on, and put into a prepared water-bath canner with the rack and water heated.

5. Finish filling all your jars using the above procedure. Submerge jars into water, with at least 1 to 2 inches of water over the top of the lids. Bring water to a boil. Process 8-ounce (or smaller) jelly jars and pint-sized jars for 10 minutes.

6. After processing, remove canner from heat and take off lid. Let jars sit for 5 minutes, then remove from canner onto a towel and let jars cool and set for 24 hours.

Altitude adjustments: if you're 1,001 to 3,000 feet increase by 5 minutes processing time, 3,001 to 6,000 feet increase processing time by 10 minutes, if above 6,001 feet increase 15 minutes processing time.

Apple Pie Filling (makes about 4 quarts)

This is one of my favorite jars to keep on hand. It makes a delicious pie but can be used for crisps, cobblers (they look darling served in small Mason jars as pictured on page 287), or on top of ice cream.

If you don't have Clear Jel, you can omit it. When ready to bake, drain ¼ to ⅓ cup of the liquid from the jar and whisk in 3 tablespoons cornstarch or potato starch to make a slurry. Dump the rest of the jar in a medium saucepan and bring to a simmer. Whisk in the slurry and simmer for 1 minute, then place in the prepared pie shell or recipe.

INGREDIENTS

12 cups sliced, peeled, and cored apples

2¾ cups sugar

¾ cup Clear Jel

1 teaspoon cinnamon

½ teaspoon nutmeg

½ teaspoon ginger

3¾ cups water

½ cup lemon juice

1. Place peeled, cored, and sliced apples in boiling water for 1 minute, working 6 cups of apples at a time. Blanching keeps apples from becoming mushy when canning. With a slotted spoon, place apples in a bowl and cover.

2. In a large stainless-steel pot, combine sugar, Clear Jel, spices, and water. Bring to a boil over medium-high heat (don't use a hard boil), stirring constantly, and cook until it thickens and bubbles. Add lemon juice and boil for 1 minute, constantly stirring. Remove from heat and fold in apples.

3. Ladle apple pie filling into warm prepared jars. Wide-mouth works best for this recipe, but narrow can be used. Leave 1-inch headspace; run a spatula down the inside of the jars to remove air bubbles. Wipe the rim with a damp clean towel. Center lid and screw bands down until tight.

4. Place jars filled with apple pie filling in a water-bath for 25 minutes.

Altitude adjustments: *if you're 1,001 to 3,000 feet increase by 5 minutes processing time, 3,001 to 6,000 feet increase processing time by 10 minutes, if above 6,001 feet increase 15 minutes processing time.*

Applesauce

Applesauce is one of my favorite additions to keep on hand in our home food pantry. It provides our fruit servings during the winter months when fresh fruit is more expensive and a treat, plus it goes so well over warm biscuits or even in place of syrup over pancakes.

You can mix apple varieties for different flavors. My favorite apple is a Gravenstein, though they're harder to find in the store if you're not going to an orchard. I prefer to not use tart apples in my applesauce as I have to add more sweetener.

INGREDIENTS

Apples (this method allows you to process whatever amount you have)

Water

Sweetener (optional), recommended 2 tablespoons of sugar per quart

Ground spices (optional)

Lemon juice

Wash, core, and peel your apples. If you have a sieve or food mill, you can skip peeling and coring as they'll separate out when put through it.

1. Add about 1 inch of water to the bottom of the pan. Bring to medium-high heat and place a lid on the pot so it traps the steam. Cook for 10 minutes and check the water level and doneness of the apples. Stir the apples to prevent scorching.
2. Once soft, work them through your sieve or food mill. If not using a food mill or sieve (you peeled your apples), you can use a potato masher or leave chunky.
3. Add sweetener, ground spices to taste, and bottled lemon juice.*
4. Prepare your water-bath canner and have your jars washed in hot soapy water and rinsed.
5. Fill jars with hot applesauce to a ½-inch headspace. Remove air bubbles and recheck headspace, adjusting with more sauce as needed. Wipe the rim of the jar clean; place the lid and band on. Set the jar in the prepared water-bath canner.
6. After all your jars are prepared and in the water-bath canner, increase the heat to a boil. Once the water is at a full boil, begin processing time. Pint jars are processed for 15 minutes and quarts jars for 20 minutes.
7. When time is up, remove the lid from the canner for 5 minutes, then remove jars onto a towel, cool, and store after 24 hours and seals have been checked.

*1 tablespoon of lemon juice per 4 cups of applesauce is recommended by Ball, but the National Center of Home Food Preservation doesn't require lemon juice with applesauce; use if you wish.

Altitude adjustments: *if you're 1,001 to 3,000 feet increase by 5 minutes processing time, 3,001 to 6,000 feet increase processing time by 10 minutes, if above 6,001 feet increase 15 minutes processing time.*

Applesauce Fruit Leather

INGREDIENTS

Applesauce

1 teaspoon ground cinnamon (optional)

1 teaspoon ground nutmeg (optional)

Silicone mats or parchment paper for dehydrator

1. If you just made applesauce, allow it to cool so that you don't burn yourself. If using spices, start with 2 teaspoons of ground spices to 2 cups of applesauce and thoroughly combine. Pour the applesauce onto the trays, spreading it out to an even thickness approximately ⅛- to ¼-inch thick (the thicker will take longer to dry but gives you a thicker fruit leather).

2. Turn the dehydrator to 135°F (57°C) and dry until it resembles leather. Begin checking for doneness at 4 hours (but don't be alarmed if it takes upwards of 10 hours).

3. It's done when it's not sticky to the touch and easily pulls off the trays. You don't want it crispy brittle. Cut into strips while warm. Allow to cool for 30 minutes before storing.

4. Store in a glass jar or airtight container.

Dehydrated Cinnamon Apples

INGREDIENTS

Depending on the size of your dehydrator and apples, this is approximately for four trays

4 to 5 apples

1 to 2 tablespoons ground cinnamon (optional)

1. Peel and slice the apples. Try to cut them relatively the same size and thickness for even drying.

2. Place apple slices in a container with a lid or a plastic bag. Sprinkle 1 to 2 tablespoons of ground cinnamon on top. Close the container and shake to coat evenly.

3. Place on dehydrator trays, leaving space around each slice for air flow. Set the dehydrator to 135°F (57°C) and dehydrate until fully dry. Depending on how thick you cut the apples and the water content of them, this can take anywhere from 6 to 24 hours.

4. They should be crisp and not sticky when finished.

5. Store in a sealed container and enjoy!

Raw Apple Scrap Cider Vinegar

While this ACV can't be used in canning because the acidity levels must be exact, it is great to use in your everyday cooking.

Time: 10 minutes

INGREDIENTS

Apple peels, cores, and scrap pieces of apple to fill a half-gallon glass jar

Water

2 to 4 tablespoons sugar*

Mason jar and band

Coffee filter/cheesecloth/towel/paper towel

1. Place apple peels, cores, and scrap pieces of apples into a clean wide-mouth Mason jar until two-thirds of the way full. Mix sugar with water until dissolved and cover apples with sugar water until apples are completely submerged.

2. Place a breathable material on top of the jar and hold it in place with either a metal band or a rubber band to keep out contaminants and, most importantly, to keep out fruit flies.

3. Store on the countertop or where you'll remember to keep an eye on it for 2-3 weeks. Check that the apples have remained below the surface of the water every few days. This part of the process is the first ferment.

4. After 2-3 weeks (or more, just keep an eye on the apple scraps to ensure they stay below the liquid level), strain out the solids and put the liquid into a clean Mason jar and place a breathable lid on it. Put it in a dark area and let it continue to ferment until it becomes vinegar, usually about two to three months. Once it smells and tastes like vinegar, you can put an airtight lid on it (be sure to perform the test found on page 116).

*I have successfully made apple scrap cider vinegar for years without added sugar if using sweet apples; however, the addition of the sugar helps to kick off the fermentation process and will be consumed totally by the bacteria and can produce a stronger vinegar. I do NOT recommend honey, as it is harder for the bacteria process.

Note: If you're on city water or water that has chlorine in it, either boil the water for 20 minutes and let it cool or let it sit uncovered in the fridge for 24 hours to remove most of the chlorine if you don't have a good filter system.

Apricot

	Water-bath Can	Steam Can	Pressure Can	Dehydrate	Freeze	Freeze-Dry	Ferment	Root Cellar
APRICOT	✓	✓		✓	✓	✓	✓	
Notes	Jam, conserve, butter, halves in syrup	Jam, conserve, butter, halves in syrup		Halves, fruit leather	Halves	Sliced	Vinegar	

Fruit	Preparation	Jar Size	Water-Bath/Steam Canning Processing Time*	Pressure Canning Processing Time at 5 lbs. of Pressure*
Apricots 2¼ pounds per quart	Peeling is optional: If peeling, remove skins by blanching in hot water for 30 to 60 seconds. Place apricots in cold water and remove skins; cut in half and remove pits. Pack in a jar with the pit side down to a generous ½-inch headspace. Fill with syrup to ½-inch headspace. Hot-Pack: Place prepared fruit in boiling syrup and bring to a boil. Pack hot fruit in jars to generous ½-inch headspace and fill with hot syrup to ½-inch headspace.	Pint	Hot-Pack 20 Min Raw-Pack 25 min	10 min
		Quart	Hot-Pack 25 Raw-Pack 30 Min	10 min

*__Altitude adjustments__: *if you're 1,001 to 3,000 feet increase by 5 minutes processing time, 3,001 to 6,000 feet increase processing time by 10 minutes, if above 6,001 feet increase 15 minutes processing time.* **Pressure canning**: *if above 1,001 feet increase to 10 lbs. of pressure on weighted gauge; for dial gauge increase by 1 pound for every additional 2,000 feet in altitude.*

May substitute apricots in the Peach Jam recipe on page 348.

Aronia Berry (aka Chokeberry)

	Water-bath Can	Steam Can	Pressure Can	Dehydrate	Freeze	Freeze-Dry	Ferment	Root Cellar
ARONIA BERRY				✓	✓	✓	✓	
Notes				Whole	Whole	Whole	Vinegar	

Avocado

	Water-bath Can	Steam Can	Pressure Can	Dehydrate	Freeze	Freeze-Dry	Ferment	Root Cellar
AVOCADO					✓	✓		
Notes					Best done as a puree	Sliced		

Pick ripe fruit (yields to gentle pressure) that have blemish-free rinds. Peel and remove the pit.

For better quality, add ¼ teaspoon ascorbic acid per quart or 1 tablespoon lemon juice for 2 avocados.

Pack into your container with appropriate headspace (see the chart in the Freezing chapter) and freeze.

Banana

	Water-bath Can	Steam Can	Pressure Can	Dehydrate	Freeze	Freeze-Dry	Ferment	Root Cellar
BANANA				✓	✓	✓		
Notes	Only as an ingredient in a tested recipe			Slices	Chunks or slices, jam	Sliced		

Blackberry

	Water-bath Can	Steam Can	Pressure Can	Dehydrate	Freeze	Freeze-Dry	Ferment	Root Cellar
BLACKBERRY	✓	✓		✓	✓	✓		
Notes	Framboise, syrup, jam, vinegar, preserve, jelly, whole berries in syrup	Framboise, syrup, jam, vinegar, preserve, jelly, whole berries in syrup		Whole, fruit leather	Whole without syrup, whole with syrup, whole sugared	Whole	Vinegar	

Fruit	Preparation	Jar Size	Water-Bath/Steam Canning Processing Time*	Pressure Canning Processing Time at 5 lbs. of Pressure*
Blackberries 1¾ pounds per quart	**Raw-Pack:** Wash, cap, and stem. Put ½ cup hot syrup into a jar, then fill with berries to generous ½-inch headspace. Lightly shake the jar to settle berries and fill with syrup to ½-inch headspace.	Pint	15 min	8 min
		Quart	20 min	

*__Altitude adjustments__: if you're 1,001 to 3,000 feet increase by 5 minutes processing time, 3,001 to 6,000 feet increase processing time by 10 minutes, if above 6,001 feet increase 15 minutes processing time. **Pressure canning**: if above 1,001 feet increase to 10 lbs. of pressure on weighted gauge; for dial gauge increase by 1 pound for every additional 2,000 feet in altitude.

How to Preserve Fruits

No-Pectin Old-Fashioned Blackberry Jelly

This recipe is shared from my book, The Made-from-Scratch Life.

Yield: Approximately six half-pint jars

INGREDIENTS

1 gallon ripe blackberries (16 cups)

1 large green or slightly underripe apple

4 to 5 cups sugar

6 tablespoons bottled lemon juice

1. Remove the core and grate the apple; place it with blackberries in a large pot. With a potato masher, mash up the blackberries. Boil mixture for approximately 15 minutes. Blackberries will release their juices. Put this mixture through a sieve or food mill. You'll end up with about 6 cups of blackberry juice.

2. **Note:** If you don't have a sieve or food mill, you can use a jelly bag or cheesecloth to strain the berries. Allow boiled mixture to cool enough to handle and place into the jelly bag or a few layers of cheesecloth. Tie cheesecloth closed and hang over a bowl to collect all of the juice.

3. Put blackberry juice back into your pot. Stir in 4 to 5 cups of sugar and lemon juice, until sugar is completely dissolved. I always use less sugar to begin with and taste it before adding more. Bring to a boil and simmer for 10 minutes.

4. Fill clean jelly jars with blackberry jelly to a ¼-inch headspace. Wipe rim clean and place lids and bands on jars. Process in a water-bath for 10 minutes.

Altitude adjustments: if you're 1,001 to 3,000 feet increase by 5 minutes processing time, 3,001 to 6,000 feet increase processing time by 10 minutes, if above 6,001 feet increase 15 minutes processing time.

Blackberry Pie Filling

This recipe is shared from the PNW Publication | Fruit Pie Fillings for Home Canning and based on Oregon State University Food Scientists.

Yield: 4 quarts

INGREDIENTS

14 cups fresh blackberries

4 cups sugar

5 tablespoons Clear Jel

5⅓ cups water (may use the water that is drained from berries as part of this)

5 tablespoons + 1 teaspoon bottled lemon juice

½ teaspoon ground cinnamon

1. In a large pot, bring one gallon of water to a boil. Working in batches (5 cups of berries at a time), place berries in water, return to a boil, and boil for one minute. Strain fruit from water and allow berries to drain. Keep berries warm by placing them in a covered container. Repeat with remaining fruit until all are blanched.

2. In a clean large pot, combine sugar, Clear Jel, and cinnamon. Add water, stirring until dissolved. Continue stirring over medium-high heat until it's thick and bubbly.

3. Add bottled lemon juice; stir constantly, boiling for 1 minute.

4. Fold in blanched berries. Immediately fill prepared jars to a 1¼-inch headspace. Adjust for air bubbles and add more if needed to maintain 1¼-inch headspace.*

5. Place in the prepared canner and process pints or quarts for 30 minutes.

Altitude adjustments: *if you're 1,001 to 3,000 feet increase by 5 minutes processing time, 3,001 to 6,000 feet increase processing time by 10 minutes, if above 6,001 feet increase 15 minutes processing time.*

*You must blanch the berries to remove the air; do not raw-pack. This is a slightly larger headspace than most pie fillings due to the amount of air still in the berries for expansion reasons.

Blueberry

	Water-bath Can	Steam Can	Pressure Can	Dehydrate	Freeze	Freeze-Dry	Ferment	Root Cellar
BLUEBERRY	✓	✓		✓	✓	✓	✓	
Notes	Jam, jelly, conserve, syrup, butter, preserve, pie filling, sauce, whole berries in syrup	Jam, jelly, conserve, syrup, butter, preserve, pie filling, sauce, whole berries in syrup		Whole, fruit leather	Whole, puree	Whole (checked)	Vinegar	

Fruit	Preparation	Jar Size	Water-Bath/Steam Canning Processing Time*	Pressure Canning Processing Time at 5 lbs. of Pressure*
Blueberries 1¾ pounds per quart	**Raw-Pack:** Wash, cap, and stem. Put ½ cup hot syrup into a jar, then fill with berries to generous ½-inch headspace. Lightly shake the jar to settle berries, and fill with syrup to ½-inch headspace. **Hot-Pack:** Place washed, capped, and stemmed berries into a large pot of boiling water for 30 seconds and drain. Fill jars with hot berries and pour hot liquid on top to ½-inch headspace.	Pint Quart	Raw-pack 15 min Hot-pack 15 min Raw-pack 20 min Hot-pack 15 min	8 min

*__Altitude adjustments__: if you're 1,001 to 3,000 feet increase by 5 minutes processing time, 3,001 to 6,000 feet increase processing time by 10 minutes, if above 6,001 feet increase 15 minutes processing time. **Pressure canning**: if above 1,001 feet increase to 10 lbs. of pressure on weighted gauge; for dial gauge increase by 1 pound for every additional 2,000 feet in altitude.

Low-Sugar Blueberry Jam Without Pectin

This recipe is shared from The Made-from-Scratch Life.

Yield: 3 pints

INGREDIENTS

4 cups pureed blueberries

1¼ cups sugar

Zest of 2 limes OR 1 peeled, cored, and grated apple + 1 tablespoon bottled lime or lemon juice

¼ cup lime or lemon juice

1. Combine all ingredients in a large stockpot. Bring to a boil over medium heat, stirring frequently. Simmer for 20 to 25 minutes until the jam is set.
2. Note: It's set when it sticks to the back of a metal spoon. This is called sheeting. Look at the jam dripping off the edge of the spoon. It should look like a sheet of jam, not a bunch of individual drops.
3. Remove from heat and pour into hot jars. Wipe rims with a damp towel; put on lids and bands. Submerge in a water-bath and process for 10 minutes. Remove from heat and let sit for 5 minutes before moving to a folded towel. Let sit for 24 hours before checking seals on jars.
4. Store in a cool, dark place. If any jars didn't set, store in the fridge.

You may substitute lemons for limes. Do not alter the amount of lime juice, but you may increase sugar if desired to taste.

Altitude adjustments: *if you're 1,001 to 3,000 feet increase by 5 minutes processing time, 3,001 to 6,000 feet increase processing time by 10 minutes, if above 6,001 feet increase 15 minutes processing time.*

Blubarb Jam

Adapted from "Blubarb Jam" in Allison Carroll Duffy, Preserving with Pomona's Pectin *(Beverly, MA: Fair Winds Press, 2013), 57.*

Yield: Approximately 4 half-pint jars

INGREDIENTS

1 pound blueberries (fresh or frozen and thawed)

1 pound trimmed rhubarb stalks

½ cup water

¼ cup lemon or lime juice

2 teaspoons calcium water*

1¼ cups sugar

¼ teaspoon ground ginger (optional)

2½ teaspoons Pomona's pectin powder*

*Calcium powder comes with the Pomona's pectin to make the calcium water. If you're not using Pomona's Pectin, follow the pectin instructions from the manufacturer you're using.

Altitude adjustments: *if you're 1,001 to 3,000 feet increase by 5 minutes processing time, 3,001 to 6,000 feet increase processing time by 10 minutes, if above 6,001 feet increase 15 minutes processing time.*

1. Before you begin, prepare the calcium water. Combine ½ teaspoon calcium powder with ½ cup water in a small jar with a lid. Shake well. The extra calcium water should be stored in the refrigerator for future use.

2. Prepare a water-bath or steam canner.

3. Rinse fresh blueberries, remove stems, and mash in a large bowl. Set aside.

4. Rinse rhubarb, slice stalks lengthwise into thin strips, and dice finely. Combine the rhubarb in a saucepan with ½ cup water. Bring to a boil over high heat; reduce heat and simmer, covered, for 5 minutes, stirring often. You want the rhubarb to get soft.

5. Measure out 2 cups of the mashed blueberries and 2 cups of the mashed rhubarb and combine into a saucepan. Add lemon or lime juice and calcium water; mix well.

6. In a separate bowl, combine sugar and pectin powder. Mix thoroughly and set aside.

7. Bring fruit mixture to a full boil over high heat. Slowly add pectin-sugar mixture, stirring constantly. Continue to stir vigorously for 1 to 2 minutes to dissolve pectin while the jam comes back to a boil. Once the jam comes back to a full boil, remove from heat.

8. Remove the jars from the canner and ladle jam into hot jars, leaving ¼-inch headspace. Remove trapped air bubbles, wipe rims with a damp cloth, put on lids and bands. Place in canner.

9. Return canner to a full boil and process for 10 minutes once canner is boiling. Turn off heat and allow canner to sit untouched for 5 minutes.

10. Remove jars, place on a folded kitchen towel, and let sit for 12 to 24 hours.

Blueberry Syrup

This method is from the Ball Complete Book of Home Preserving's *fruit syrup. It uses candy-making techniques to reach a specific temperature called the Thread Stage (occurs between 223°F/106 °C and 235°F/112 °C) with the sugar water.*

INGREDIENTS

8 cups blueberries, juiced (see steps 1 and 2)

2 cups water

1 lemon, zested

4 cups water

3 cups sugar

2 tablespoons lemon juice

1. If making juice the old-fashioned way, place 2 cups of water and crushed blueberries (a potato masher works great) in a large pot and bring to a boil with the zest of one lemon. Boil for 5 minutes, then transfer to a jelly bag and drain for at least 2 hours.

2. If using the stainless-steel steam juicer, just place blueberries and zest into the juicer and omit the 2 cups of water. Steam in juicer for 45 minutes; drain out juice.

3. Prepare your water-bath or steam canner and jars.

4. In a large stainless-steel pot, place 4 cups of water with 3 cups of sugar and bring to a boil over medium-high heat. Stir frequently and cook until it reaches 230°F/110°C (if you're 1,000 feet above sea level then subtract by 2° for every 1,000 feet increase; if you're at 1,001 to 2,000 feet above sea level you'll cook until 228°F/108°C).* It takes me 20 minutes to reach the correct temperature.

5. Add blueberry juice and boil for 5 minutes; be careful not to let it scorch. Take off of the heat and add in your lemon juice. Ladle into hot jars to a ¼-inch headspace. Wipe rim, put on lid, and screw down band to fingertip tight.

6. Place jars in canner; make sure water level is 1 inch above the jars. Bring to a full boil and process for 10 minutes. When done, turn off heat, remove lid, and wait 5 minutes before placing jars on a towel and allowing to cool.

*If you don't have a candy thermometer, take a cold glass of water and drop a small amount of the hot syrup in it. It should form a thread when it hits the cold water; if it forms a ball, you've cooked it too long; so test often.

Altitude adjustments: *if you're 1,001 to 3,000 feet increase processing time by 5 minutes, 3,001 to 6,000 feet increase processing time by 10 minutes, if above 6,001 feet increase 15 minutes processing time.*

Blueberry Basil Thyme Vinegar

Adapted from the Ball Complete Book of Home Preserving

INGREDIENTS

8 cups blueberries

2 cups white wine vinegar

⅓ cup basil leaves, crushed

¼ cup thyme leaves, crushed

Grated zest of 1 lemon or lime

1. In a large bowl, mash blueberries with a potato masher into 1 cup of vinegar. Pour into a quart-sized washed Mason jar. Add remaining cup of vinegar, crushed herbs, and lemon zest. Stir to combine. Cover with a lid or plastic wrap and stand in a dark, cool place. Stir every 2 to 3 days and allow it to steep up to 4 weeks. Taste weekly until you're happy with it.

2. When you're satisfied with the taste, line a strainer with layers of cheesecloth and place over a large stainless-steel pan. Strain the vinegar. Don't squeeze. When it's all strained, put the pot on the stove at medium heat until vinegar reaches 180°F/82°C.

3. Ladle the hot vinegar into prepared jars, with a ¼-inch headspace. Process in a water-bath canner for 10 minutes. Or simply put vinegar in hot jars. Let cool to room temperature, and store in the fridge.

Altitude adjustments: *if you're 1,001 to 3,000 feet increase processing time by 5 minutes, 3,001 to 6,000 feet increase processing time by 10 minutes, if above 6,001 feet increase 15 minutes processing time.*

Cantaloupe

	Water-bath Can	Steam Can	Pressure Can	Dehydrate	Freeze	Freeze-Dry	Ferment	Root Cellar
CANTALOUPE	✓	✓		✓	✓	✓		✓
Notes	As a pickle only	As a pickle only		Slices	Slices, cubes, or balls in syrup	Slices or balls		Short-term only

Cherry, Sour

	Water-bath Can	Steam Can	Pressure Can	Dehydrate	Freeze	Freeze-Dry	Ferment	Root Cellar
CHERRY, SOUR	✓	✓	✓	✓	✓	✓		
Notes	Pie filling, in syrup, chutney, jam, jelly, sauce, conserve	Pie filling, in syrup, chutney, jam, jelly, sauce, conserve		Cut in half or leave whole (must be checked)	Whole	Halved	Vinegar	

Tart Cherry Pie Filling

See Cherry, Sweet on page 309

Cherry, Sweet

	Water-bath Can	Steam Can	Pressure Can	Dehydrate	Freeze	Freeze-Dry	Ferment	Root Cellar
CHERRY, SWEET	✓	✓		✓	✓	✓	✓	
Notes	Pie filling, in syrup, chutney, jam, jelly, sauce, preserve	Pie filling, in syrup, chutney, jam, jelly, sauce, preserve		Cut in half or leave whole (must be checked), fruit leather	Whole	Halved	Vinegar	

Fruit	Preparation	Jar Size	Water-Bath/Steam Canning Processing Time*	Pressure Canning Processing Time at 5 lbs. of Pressure*
Cherries 2½ pounds per quart	**Raw-Pack:** Put ½ cup hot syrup into a jar, then fill with cherries to generous ½-inch headspace. Lightly shake the jar to settle cherries and fill with syrup to ½-inch headspace.	Pint	Raw-Pack 25 min Hot-pack 15 min	10 min
	Hot-Pack: 8 pounds pitted cherries to 2 cups sugar. Place in a large saucepan and add enough water to prevent sticking. Cook until sugar is dissolved and cherries are heated. Ladle hot cherries and syrup into jars to ½-inch headspace.	Quart	Raw-Pack 25 min Hot-pack 20 min	

*__Altitude adjustments__: if you're 1,001 to 3,000 feet increase by 5 minutes processing time, 3,001 to 6,000 feet increase processing time by 10 minutes, if above 6,001 feet increase 15 minutes processing time. **Pressure canning**: if above 1,001 feet increase to 10 lbs. of pressure on weighted gauge; for dial gauge increase by 1 pound for every additional 2,000 feet in altitude.

Low-Sugar Cherry Jam Without Pectin

Yield: 3 pints or 6 jelly jars

INGREDIENTS

6 cups sweet cherries (any variety of sweet cherry will work; if using sour or pie cherries, increase sugar to taste)

2½ to 3 cups sugar (depending on how sweet your cherries are and your preference)

6 tablespoons bottled lemon juice

1. Prepare a water-bath or steam canner, jars, lids, and bands.
2. Wash, remove stems, and pit cherries. Roughly chop up cherries.
3. Place chopped cherries in a large stockpot. Add ½ cup water to cherries. Bring to a boil and allow to simmer for 15 minutes, stirring occasionally. You'll see the cherries begin to break down and thicken.
4. Stir in sugar and lemon juice, mixing well. Bring to a full rolling boil, stirring constantly. Sugar will scorch quickly if not kept moving. Boil, uncovered, until thick, about 10 minutes, and test for set or gel. Cherry jam is not meant to be extremely thick.
5. Remove from heat and pour into hot clean jars. Wipe rims with a damp towel; put on lids and bands. Submerge in a water-bath or steam canner and process for 15 minutes.
6. Take off heat and let sit for 5 minutes before moving to a folded towel. Let sit for 24 hours before checking seals on jars. Then store in a cool, dark place for up to a year. If any jars didn't set, store in fridge.

Altitude adjustments: *if you're 1,001 to 3,000 feet increase processing time by 5 minutes, 3,001 to 6,000 feet increase processing time by 10 minutes, if above 6,001 feet increase 15 minutes processing time.*

How to Preserve Fruits | 311

Sweet Cherry Pie Filling

The cherry pie filling recipe instructions below are for frozen and then thawed cherries; if using fresh cherries, put 6 cups at a time in 1 gallon of boiling water and boil for 1 minute. Drain and process the next batch of cherries. Keep boiled cherries in a bowl or pot with a lid to keep warm.

Follow the next two recipes except you'll use water instead of the cherry juice with fresh cherries.

Yield: 8 pints or 4 quarts

INGREDIENTS

12 to 13 cups frozen then thawed and then pitted cherries

4 cups cherry juice (drained from thawing cherries) or water

2½ cups sugar

1 cup Clear Jel

⅓ cup bottled lemon juice

½ teaspoon ground cinnamon

FOR SOUR CHERRIES

Increase sugar to 3½ cups and decrease lemon juice to ¼ cup.

1. In a colander over a large bowl, drain thawed cherries until you have 4 cups or more cherry juice (you can use the extra for whatever your heart desires).

2. Prepare a water-bath or steam canner and jars.

3. In a large stainless-steel pot, whisk together 4 cups cherry juice, sugar, cinnamon, and Clear Jel. Bring to a boil over medium-high heat, stirring almost constantly until it's thick and bubbling (about 5 minutes or less). Add lemon juice, stir, and boil for 1 minute, stirring constantly. Add the cherries and fold in gently, stirring constantly, until it reaches a boil. Remove from heat.

4. Place warm clean jars on a towel and use your canning funnel (highly recommended) to ladle hot pie filling into jars to a 1-inch headspace. Remove air bubbles and recheck headspace; add more filling if needed. Wipe the rim of the jar clean and put on the lid and band. Tighten to fingertip tight and place into the canner.

5. Make sure jars are fully covered with water and bring to a boil. Process jars (both pints and quarts) for 30 minutes.

6. After processing time, remove the canner lid and wait 5 minutes. Place jars on a towel and allow to cool for 24 hours.

Altitude adjustments: if over 1000 feet above sea level process for 35 minutes, if above 3,0001 to 6,000 feet above sea level process for 40 minutes and if above 6,001 feet process for 45 minutes.

*Recipe adapted from
National Center of Home Food Preservation*

Cherry Pit Vinegar

Move over, apple scrap vinegar; you're not the only fruit that can be used twice for delicious things. While you can use cherry juice and follow the vinegar-making instructions in the Infusion chapter, I highly recommend putting the pits to work in this easy, albeit faux, vinegar version.

Yield: 2 cups

INGREDIENTS

1 cup cherry pits*

2 cups vinegar (any vinegar of your choice)

1. Place the pits (leave all the bits of cherry fruit on them you can; this helps with the flavor) in a clean glass jar. Cover with vinegar and place out of direct sunlight. White vinegar takes on some color if using red cherries, whereas apple cider vinegar won't change as much in color; but both work equally well.

2. Allow to steep for two to three weeks. Strain, place back in a glass bottle, and enjoy your cherry-pit flavored vinegar!

*Only use uncracked pits. As long as you don't try to smash them with a hammer, they're not cracked. Cherry pits (most stone fruit pits) do contain small amounts of cyanide. This is only exposed when they're cracked, smashed, or ground up.

How to Preserve Fruits

Cranberry

	Water-bath Can	Steam Can	Pressure Can	Dehydrate	Freeze	Freeze-Dry	Ferment	Root Cellar
CRANBERRY	✓	✓		✓	✓	✓	✓	
Notes	Pie filling, in syrup, chutney, jam, jelly, sauce, preserve	Pie filling, in syrup, chutney, jam, jelly, sauce, preserve		Cut in half or leave whole (must be checked), fruit leather	Whole	Halved	Vinegar	

Cranberry Sauce

Yield: 8 half-pints (8 oz.)

INGREDIENTS

2½ to 3 cups sugar, depending on your tastes

4 cups water

8 cups fresh cranberries (about 2 lbs.)

2 cinnamon sticks (approximately 4 inches) broken in half

Grated zest of 1 large orange, optional

1. Prepare a water-bath or steam canner, jars, lids, and bands.
2. Combine sugar, cinnamon sticks, and water in a large stainless-steel saucepan. Bring to a boil over high heat, stirring to dissolve sugar. Boil hard for 5 minutes. Add cranberries and return mixture to a boil. Reduce heat and boil gently, stirring occasionally, until all berries burst and liquid begins to sheet from a metal spoon, about 15 minutes. Stir in orange zest, if using, during the last few minutes of cooking.
3. Remove cinnamon sticks.
4. Ladle hot cranberry sauce into hot jars, leaving ½-inch headspace. Remove air bubbles and adjust headspace, if necessary, by adding hot cranberry sauce. Wipe rim. Center lid on jar. Apply the band until it is fingertip tight. Place the jar in a prepared water-bath or steam canner. Repeat until jars are filled.
5. Process for 15 minutes, adjusting for altitude. Remove jars and cool. Check lids for seal after 24 hours.

Altitude adjustments: *if you're 1,001 to 3,000 feet increase processing time by 5 minutes, 3,001 to 6,000 feet increase processing time by 10 minutes, if above 6,001 feet increase 15 minutes processing time.*

Cranberry Jelly

Yield: 4 half-pints (8 oz.)

INGREDIENTS

4¼ cups cranberries

1¾ cups water

2 cups sugar

1. Prepare a water-bath or steam canner, jars, and lids.
2. In a large stainless-steel saucepan, combine the cranberries and water. Bring to a boil over medium-high heat. Reduce heat and boil gently, stirring occasionally, until skins burst. Should take about 5 minutes. Remove from heat and let cool for 5 minutes.
3. Transfer cranberry mixture to a food mill or sieve and press through.
4. Return the cranberry juice to a saucepan. Add sugar and bring to a boil over medium heat. Stir until sugar dissolves. Increase the heat to high and boil hard until it begins to sheet from a metal spoon. Remove from heat and skim off foam.
5. Ladle into hot jars, leaving ½-inch headspace. Wipe the rim, center lid on the jar, and screw band on to fingertip tight.
6. Place jars in the canner. Be sure they're covered with 1-2 inches of water. Bring to a boil, then process for 15 minutes once the boil is reached. Follow instructions for a water-bath or steam canner at the end of processing time. Place jars on the counter on a folded kitchen towel. Cool for 24 hours, check the seals, and then store.

Altitude adjustments: *If you're 1,001 to 3,000 feet increase processing time by 5 minutes, 3,001 to 6,000 feet increase processing time by 10 minutes, if above 6,001 feet increase 15 minutes processing time.*

Fermented Cranberry Sauce

This recipe by Carolyn Thomas of HomesteadingFamily.com.

INGREDIENTS

2 apples, chopped (organic)

2 cups cranberries, chopped

½ cup pecans, chopped (or walnuts or other nut)

½ cup raisins (or other dried fruit) (optional)

½ cup apple cider (or apple juice, plus more if needed)

¼ cup maple syrup (or honey, or sugar)

½ cup whey (or kombucha, kefir, sauerkraut juice, etc.)

1 teaspoon salt

1. Chop apples, cranberries. and nuts and add to a large bowl.
2. Stir in the optional dried fruit, apple cider, and maple syrup.
3. Pour the starter liquid over the chopped mixture and sprinkle with salt. Then stir to combine and ladle into a quart-sized Mason jar.
4. Pack your mixture down into the jar and top with apple cider until all food pieces are covered.
5. Cover with an airtight Mason jar lid and set at room temperature.
6. Two to 4 times a day, burp your jar and give it a turn or two.
7. After 2 days, transfer the ferment to the refrigerator.

Currant

	Water-bath Can	Steam Can	Pressure Can	Dehydrate	Freeze	Freeze-Dry	Ferment	Root Cellar
CURRANT	✓	✓		✓	✓	✓	✓	
Notes	Chutney, conserve, preserve, juice, ketchup, mustard, sauce	Chutney, conserve, preserve, juice, ketchup, mustard, sauce		Whole (must be checked)	Whole	Whole (checked)	Sauce, vinegar	

Fruit	Preparation	Jar Size	Water-Bath/Steam Canning Processing Time*	Pressure Canning Processing Time at 5 lbs. of Pressure*
Currant approximately 1 pound per pint jar	**Raw-Pack:** Wash and stem. Add ½ cup hot syrup, juice, or water to each clean jar. Fill the jar with berries to ½-inch headspace. Lightly shake the jar to settle berries and fill with hot water, juice, or syrup to ½-inch headspace. **Hot-Pack:** Place washed, capped, and stemmed berries into a large pot of boiling water for 30 seconds and drain. Fill jars with hot berries and pour hot liquid on top to ½-inch headspace.	Pint Quart	Raw-pack 15 min Hot-pack 15 min Raw-pack 20 min Hot-pack 15 min	8 min

Raspberry Red Currant Jelly

See raspberry on page 361

> ***Altitude adjustments water-bath/steam canning**: If you're 1,001 to 3,000 feet increase by 5 minutes processing time, 3,001 to 6,000 feet increase processing time by 10 minutes, if above 6,001 feet increase 15 minutes processing time. **Pressure canning**: if above 1,001 feet increase to 10 lbs. of pressure on weighted gauge; for dial gauge increase by 1 pound for every additional 2,000 feet in altitude.*

Dewberry

	Water-bath Can	Steam Can	Pressure Can	Dehydrate	Freeze	Freeze-Dry	Ferment	Root Cellar
DEWBERRY	✓	✓		✓	✓	✓	✓	
Notes	Framboise, syrup, jam, vinegar, preserve, jelly, whole berries in syrup	Framboise, syrup, jam, vinegar, preserve, jelly, whole berries in syrup		Whole, fruit leather	Whole	Whole	Vinegar	

Interchangeable with blackberries.

Fruit	Preparation	Jar Size	Water-Bath/Steam Canning Processing Time*	Pressure Canning Processing Time at 5 lbs. of Pressure*
Dewberry approximately 1 pound per pint jar	**Raw-Pack:** Wash and stem. Add ½ cup hot syrup, juice, or water to each clean jar. Fill the jar with berries to ½-inch headspace. Lightly shake the jar to settle berries and fill with hot water, juice, or syrup to ½-inch headspace.	Pint	15 min	8 min
		Quart	20 min	

*****Altitude adjustments water-bath/steam canning**: *If you're 1,001 to 3,000 feet increase by 5 minutes processing time, 3,001 to 6,000 feet increase processing time by 10 minutes, if above 6,001 feet increase 15 minutes processing time.* **Pressure canning**: *if above 1,001 feet increase to 10 lbs. of pressure on weighted gauge; for dial gauge increase by 1 pound for every additional 2,000 feet in altitude.*

Fig

	Water-bath Can	Steam Can	Pressure Can	Dehydrate	Freeze	Freeze-Dry	Ferment	Root Cellar
FIG	✓	✓		✓	✓	✓	✓	
Notes	Preserves, in syrup, jam, pickled	Preserves, in syrup, jam, pickled		Halve fully ripe fruit	Whole	Halved	Wine	

Fruit	Preparation	Jar Size	Water-Bath/Steam Canning Processing Time*	Pressure Canning Processing Time at 5 lbs. of Pressure*
Fig 2½ pounds yields 1 quart	Wash, and leave on stems and peels. Bring water to a high boil and blanch figs for 2 minutes, drain; then using light or medium syrup, heat figs thoroughly in syrup (a single layer at a time, 5 minutes each layer). Add to pint jar 1½ teaspoons bottled lemon juice and to quart jar 1 tablespoon bottled lemon juice before packing hot figs into jars to a generous ½-inch headspace and pouring hot syrup over to a ½-inch headspace.	Pint	45 min	10 min
		Quart	50 min	

***Altitude adjustments water-bath/steam canning**: *If you're 1,001 to 3,000 feet increase by 5 minutes processing time, 3,001 to 6,000 feet increase processing time by 10 minutes, if above 6,001 feet increase 15 minutes processing time.*
Pressure canning: *if above 1,001 feet increase to 10 lbs. of pressure on weighted gauge; for dial gauge increase by 1 pound for every additional 2,000 feet in altitude.*

Gooseberry

	Water-bath Can	Steam Can	Pressure Can	Dehydrate	Freeze	Freeze-Dry	Ferment	Root Cellar
GOOSEBERRY	✓	✓		✓	✓	✓	✓	
Notes	Whole berries in syrup, conserve, jam	Whole berries in syrup, conserve, jam		Check whole berries	Whole	Halved	Whole	

Fruit	Preparation	Jar Size	Water-Bath/Steam Canning Processing Time*	Pressure Canning Processing Time at 5 lbs. of Pressure*
Gooseberry approximately 1 pound per pint jar	**Raw-Pack:** Wash and cut off heads and tails. Add ½ cup hot syrup, juice, or water to each clean jar. Fill the jar with berries to ½-inch headspace. Lightly shake the jar to settle berries and fill with hot water, juice or syrup to ½-inch headspace. **Hot-Pack:** Place washed, capped, and stemmed berries into a large pot of boiling water for 30 seconds and drain. Fill jars with hot berries and pour hot liquid on top to ½-inch headspace.	Pint Quart	Raw-pack 15 min Hot-pack 15 min Raw-pack 20 min Hot-pack 15 min	8 min

*__Altitude adjustments water-bath/steam canning__: If you're 1,001 to 3,000 feet increase by 5 minutes processing time, 3,001 to 6,000 feet increase processing time by 10 minutes, if above 6,001 feet increase 15 minutes processing time.

Pressure canning: if above 1,001 feet increase to 10 lbs. of pressure on weighted gauge; for dial gauge increase by 1 pound for every additional 2,000 feet in altitude.

Grape

	Water-bath Can	Steam Can	Pressure Can	Dehydrate	Freeze	Freeze-Dry	Ferment	Root Cellar
GRAPE	✓	✓		✓	✓	✓	✓	
Notes	Jelly, jam, preserves, juice, in syrup, conserve	Jelly, jam, preserves, juice, in syrup, conserve		Seedless: leave whole and check skin With seeds: cut in half and remove seeds Fruit leather	Seedless: leave whole and check skin With seeds: cut in half and remove seeds As juice	Halved	Vinegar, wine	

Fruit	Preparation	Jar Size	Water-Bath/Steam Canning Processing Time*	Pressure Canning Processing Time at 5 lbs. of Pressure*
Grapes 2 pounds per quart	**Raw-Pack:** Wash and stem. Put ½ cup hot syrup into a jar, then fill with grapes to a generous ½-inch headspace. Lightly shake the jar to settle grapes and fill with syrup to ½-inch headspace.	Pint	15 min	8 min
		Quart	20 min	

***Altitude adjustments**: If you're 1,001 to 3,000 feet increase by 5 minutes processing time, 3,001 to 6,000 feet increase processing time by 10 minutes, if above 6,001 feet increase 15 minutes processing time. **Pressure canning**: if above 1,001 feet increase to 10 lbs. of pressure on weighted gauge; for dial gauge increase by 1 pound for every additional 2,000 feet in altitude.

How to Preserve Fruits

Dehydrated Grapes (aka Raisins)

Time: Varies on grape size but 16 to 48 hours

INGREDIENTS

Fresh grapes

1. Rinse and stem grapes.
2. Grapes need to be checked. The easiest way to do this is to pop them in the freezer for a few hours.
3. Place grapes on dehydrator trays, making sure they're not touching to allow for air flow.
4. Fruit tends to be sticky when dehydrating, so you may want to use mats or line with parchment paper for easier cleanup.
5. Dehydrate at 125° to 135°F (52° to 57°C) and begin checking on your grapes at 16 hours. They're done when they're shriveled up (not rock hard) like raisins.
6. To test for doneness, while they're still warm, place them in a sealed plastic bag or sealed Mason jar. If you see moisture bead up after a few hours, then place them back in the dehydrator and dry longer.
7. When done, store in a sealed container.

Low-Sugar Vanilla Grape Jelly

Yield: 5 pint jars or 10 jelly jars

INGREDIENTS

8 cups grape juice

3 cups sugar

2 vanilla beans

½ cup lemon or lime juice

Pomona's Universal Pectin

1. Prepare your jars: either sanitize them in a pot of boiling water for 10 minutes or wash in hot soapy water. Keep them warm. Prepare your water-bath canner, keeping water hot but not boiling.

2. Place grape juice, vanilla beans, and lemon juice in a large stockpot. Add 8 teaspoons of calcium water and stir well. (Note: stir it well—otherwise you'll wind up with cloudy gelatinous globs.)

3. In a small bowl, mix 8 teaspoons of pectin and one cup of sugar. Bring contents of stockpot to a boil. Add pectin-sugar mix and stir hard for 1 to 2 minutes. Now add in the rest of the sugar and stir until dissolved. Return to a boil and remove from the stove. Take out the two vanilla beans.*

4. Fill your jars to ¼-inch headspace. Wipe rims clean and screw on your lid and band. With the rack in place, put jars in the canner and process for 10 minutes.

5. Follow instructions for a water-bath or steam canner at the end of processing time. Place on the counter on a folded kitchen towel. Cool for 24 hours, check the seals, and then store.

Altitude adjustments: *If you're 1,001 to 3,000 feet increase processing time by 5 minutes, 3,001 to 6,000 feet increase processing time by 10 minutes, if above 6,001 feet increase 15 minutes processing time.*

*Don't toss those vanilla beans! Rinse off the jelly and let the beans air-dry. Put them in a glass jar and fill it with sugar. You'll have vanilla sugar to use in your Christmas baking!

How to Can Grape Juice

INGREDIENTS

Grapes

Water

Sugar (optional)

1. Remove the grapes from the stem and place them in a large pot. Add just enough water to cover them with water.
2. Bring to a boil and boil for 5 minutes until skins split.
3. Transfer to a sieve over a deep bowl. Press juice out.
4. Cover juice and refrigerate 24 hours to allow sediment to settle. This makes the juice clearer. You can let it sit for up to 48 hours but no longer. You don't want it to start to ferment.
5. After it has hung out in the fridge, pour the cold juice into a cheesecloth over a pot. Allow to sit until all the juice has drained out. If you want it even clearer, run it through the cheesecloth again.
6. Prepare canner, jars, and lids.
7. Bring to a simmer. Add in sugar to taste. I add about ⅛ cup sugar to 3 cups of grape juice. It's a little tart but I don't want it to be too sweet.
8. To can, bring the juice to 190°F (88°C) over medium-high heat. Don't boil. Keep the juice at this temperature for five minutes. Adjust the heat as needed.
9. Put juice into hot jars. Leave ¼-inch headspace. Wipe rim, then place the band on to fingertip tight.
10. Place in the canner and process pint, quart, or half-gallon jars for 10 minutes.
11. Follow instructions for a water-bath or steam canner at the end of processing time. Place on the counter on a folded kitchen towel. Cool for 24 hours, check the seals, and then store.

Altitude adjustments: *If you're 1,001 to 3,000 feet increase processing time by 5 minutes, 3,001 to 6,000 feet increase processing time by 10 minutes, if above 6,001 feet increase 15 minutes processing time.*

Grapefruit

	Water-bath Can	Steam Can	Pressure Can	Dehydrate	Freeze	Freeze-Dry	Ferment	Root Cellar
GRAPEFRUIT	✓	✓		✓	✓	✓		
Notes	Sections in syrup, marmalade	Sections in syrup, marmalade		Slices	Section, as juice	Slices		

Fruit	Preparation	Jar Size	Water-Bath/Steam Canning Processing Time*	Pressure Canning Processing Time at 5 lbs. of Pressure*
Grapefruit 2 pounds per quart	Raw-Pack: Wash and peel. Remove as much white tissue/pith as possible to avoid bitterness. Place sections of grapefruit in a jar, then fill with hot syrup (very light to medium) to ½-inch headspace.	Pint	10 min	8 min
		Quart	10 min	10 min

*__Altitude adjustments__: If you're 1,001 to 3,000 feet increase by 5 minutes processing time, 3,001 to 6,000 feet increase processing time by 10 minutes, if above 6,001 feet increase 15 minutes processing time. **Pressure canning**: if above 1,001 feet increase to 10 lbs. of pressure on weighted gauge; for dial gauge increase by 1 pound for every additional 2,000 feet in altitude.

See marmalade recipe on page 342

Honeyberry (aka Haskap)

	Water-bath Can	Steam Can	Pressure Can	Dehydrate	Freeze	Freeze-Dry	Ferment	Root Cellar
HONEYBERRY				✓	✓	✓	✓	
Notes				Whole, fruit leather	Whole, puree	Whole		

Huckleberry

	Water-bath Can	Steam Can	Pressure Can	Dehydrate	Freeze	Freeze-Dry	Ferment	Root Cellar
HUCKLEBERRY	✓	✓		✓	✓	✓	✓	
Notes	Jam, jelly, conserve, syrup, butter, preserve, pie filling, sauce, whole berries in syrup	Jam, jelly, conserve, syrup, butter, preserve, pie filling, sauce, whole berries in syrup		Whole, fruit leather	Whole, puree	Whole		

Interchangeable with blueberries.

Fruit	Preparation	Jar Size	Water-Bath/Steam Canning Processing Time*	Pressure Canning Processing Time at 5 lbs. of Pressure*
Huckleberry approximately 1 pound per pint jar	**Raw-Pack:** Wash and cut off heads and tails. Add ½ cup hot syrup, juice, or water to each clean jar. Fill the jar with berries to ½-inch headspace. Lightly shake the jar to settle berries and fill with hot water, juice, or syrup to ½-inch headspace. **Hot-Pack:** Place washed, capped, and stemmed berries into a large pot of boiling water for 30 seconds and drain. Fill jars with hot berries and pour hot liquid on top to ½-inch headspace.	Pint Quart	Raw-pack 15 min Hot-pack 15 min Raw-pack 20 min Hot-pack 15 min	8 min

*Altitude adjustments

Water-bath/steam canning: *If you're 1,001 to 3,000 feet increase by 5 minutes processing time, 3,001 to 6,000 feet increase processing time by 10 minutes, if above 6,001 feet increase 15 minutes processing time.*

Pressure canning: *If above 1,001 feet increase to 10 lbs. of pressure.*

Kiwi

	Water-bath Can	Steam Can	Pressure Can	Dehydrate	Freeze	Freeze-Dry	Ferment	Root Cellar
KIWI	✓	✓		✓	✓	✓		
Notes	Chutney, jam, preserves	Chutney, jam, preserves		Slices, fruit leather	Slices	Slices		

Kumquat

	Water-bath Can	Steam Can	Pressure Can	Dehydrate	Freeze	Freeze-Dry	Ferment	Root Cellar
KUMQUAT	✓	✓		✓	✓	✓		
Notes	In syrup	In syrup		Slices	Slices, as juice	Slices		

Lemon

	Water-bath Can	Steam Can	Pressure Can	Dehydrate	Freeze	Freeze-Dry	Ferment	Root Cellar
LEMON	✓	✓		✓	✓	✓	✓	✓
Notes	Marmalade	Marmalade		Slices	Sections, as juice	Slices, juice	Whole, sliced	Short-term only

How to Preserve Fruits

Dehydrated Lemon Slices

I use mine in tea, one or two slices in the bottom of a cup of hot water, or several in cold water for an iced beverage.

INGREDIENTS

Whole lemons (or oranges)

1. Rinse and dry whole lemons or oranges. Personally, I use organic when consuming the peels.
2. Slice evenly, approximately ¼-inch thick (a mandoline works great) and arrange on dehydrator trays.
3. Dehydrate at 125° to 135°F (57°C). Begin checking for doneness at 3 hours; may take up to 8 to 10 hours depending upon thickness and water content.
4. Done when they break in half and are crisp. Lemons will turn a very dark orange when dried.
5. Store in an airtight container, and vacuum seal for the longest shelf life.

Fermented Lemons

While I usually do straight lemons, you can also add spices. One or two bay leaves, whole black peppercorn, or cinnamon sticks are all popular options.

INGREDIENTS

6–8 whole lemons, organic

2 tablespoons salt

1. Rinse lemons well in hot water. Wash and rinse a wide-mouth quart jar in hot soapy water.

2. Score the lemon from the stem side (pointy part) into quarters; try to leave the bottom half-inch intact because it makes the next step easier.

3. Open the lemon up and sprinkle a scant teaspoonful of salt inside. Place the lemon, cut sides up, in the jar. Repeat, packing tightly to get all of the lemons inside the jar.

4. Once lemons have reached the top of the jar shoulder, you should have enough juice to cover them. If not, you can make a saltwater brine to top it off (or use fresh-squeezed additional lemon juice). I use a 3% brine when needed, which is 1 tablespoon of Redmond's Real Salt to 2 cups of water. If any part of the lemon pops up, use a weight to keep them fully submerged.

5. Place a lid on your vessel and allow it to ferment at room temperature for 4 to 5 days.

6. Move to the refrigerator or cold room for long-term storage. Use the fermented juice in any savory dish that calls for lemon juice (adjust the salt, as your fermented lemons have salt). The rinds will soften during fermentation, so be sure to finely chop and use them in your dishes as well; it's not just about the juice!

Lemon Marmalade

This recipe is adapted from Pomona's Pectin https://pomonapectin.com/lemon-marmalade-2/

Yield: Approximately 6 half-pint jars

INGREDIENTS

8 lemons, standard size*

3½ cups water or orange juice for citrus medley

4 teaspoons calcium water

3 cups sugar

5 teaspoons Pomona's pectin powder mixed with sweetener

1. Prepare a water-bath or steam canner, jars, lids, and bands.
2. Peel four of the lemons, scraping off the white pith to avoid bitterness. Slice peel into strips about 1 to 1½ inches long. Set aside into a medium saucepan.
3. Peel remaining lemons. From all lemons, remove seeds and pith. Finely chop the pulp, keeping as much of the juice as you can.
4. Add the pulp and juice to the pan with the sliced peel. Pour in 3 cups water/orange juice and bring to a boil. Cover with lid and simmer for 20 minutes, stirring to prevent scorching.
5. When finished, remove the pan from heat, and measure out 6 cups of the mixture. If a small amount remains, save it for something else. Return the 6 cups back to the saucepan.
6. Stir in the calcium water.
7. Mix sugar and pectin powder in a bowl until well combined.
8. Bring fruit mixture and calcium water to a full boil. Stir in pectin-sugar mixture and cook for 1 to 2 minutes to fully dissolve and bring the marmalade back to a boil.
9. Remove from heat and fill hot jars to a ¼-inch headspace. Remove air bubbles and add more if needed to maintain headspace.
10. Process jars for 10 minutes. After processing time, follow instructions specific for water-bath or steam canner.

Altitude adjustments: *If you're 1,001 to 3,000 feet increase processing time by 5 minutes, 3,001 to 6,000 feet increase processing time by 10 minutes, if above 6,001 feet increase 15 minutes processing time.*

*If using Meyer lemons, increase to ten and only use the sliced peel from two; decrease sugar and water by ½ cup.

Lime

	Water-bath Can	Steam Can	Pressure Can	Dehydrate	Freeze	Freeze-Dry	Ferment	Root Cellar
LIME	✓	✓		✓	✓	✓	✓	✓
Notes	Marmalade, as an ingredient in other fruit jams and salsa	Marmalade, as an ingredient in other fruit jams and salsa		Slices	Sections, as juice	Slices, juice	Whole, slices	Short-term only

See Fermented Lemons for recipe.

Loganberry

	Water-bath Can	Steam Can	Pressure Can	Dehydrate	Freeze	Freeze-Dry	Ferment	Root Cellar
LOGANBERRY	✓	✓		✓	✓	✓		
Notes	Syrup, jam, vinegar, preserve, jelly, whole berries in syrup	Framboise, syrup, jam, vinegar, preserve, jelly, whole berries in syrup		Whole, fruit leather	Whole	Whole		

Interchangeable with blackberries and raspberries.

Fruit	Preparation	Jar Size	Water-Bath/Steam Canning Processing Time*	Pressure Canning Processing Time at 5 lbs. of Pressure*
Loganberry 1¾ pounds per quart	**Raw-Pack:** Wash, cap, and stem. Put ½ cup hot syrup into a jar, then fill with berries to generous ½-inch headspace. Lightly shake the jar to settle berries and fill with syrup to ½-inch headspace.	Pint	15 min	8 min
		Quart	20 min	

*__Altitude adjustments__: If you're 1,001 to 3,000 feet increase by 5 minutes processing time, 3,001 to 6,000 feet increase processing time by 10 minutes, if above 6,001 feet increase 15 minutes processing time. **Pressure canning**: if above 1,001 feet increase to 10 lbs. of pressure on weighted gauge; for dial gauge increase by 1 pound for every additional 2,000 feet in altitude.*

Melon

	Water-bath Can	Steam Can	Pressure Can	Dehydrate	Freeze	Freeze-Dry	Ferment	Root Cellar
MELON	✓	✓		✓	✓	✓		✓
Notes	As a pickle only	As a pickle only		Slices	Slices, cubes, or balls	Slices, cubes, or balls		Short-term only

Mulberry

	Water-bath Can	Steam Can	Pressure Can	Dehydrate	Freeze	Freeze-Dry	Ferment	Root Cellar
MULLBERRY	✓	✓		✓	✓	✓	✓	
Notes	Jam, vinegar, preserve, jelly, whole berries in syrup	Jam, vinegar, preserve, jelly, whole berries in syrup		Whole, fruit leather	Whole	Whole	Wine, vinegar	

Fruit	Preparation	Jar Size	Water-Bath/Steam Canning Processing Time*	Pressure Canning Processing Time at 5 lbs. of Pressure*
Mulberry 1¾ pounds per quart	**Raw-Pack:** Wash, cap, and stem. Put ½ cup hot syrup into a jar, then fill with berries to generous ½-inch headspace. Lightly shake the jar to settle berries and fill with syrup to ½-inch headspace.	Pint	15 min	8 min
		Quart	20 min	

*__Altitude adjustments__: If you're 1,001 to 3,000 feet increase by 5 minutes processing time, 3,001 to 6,000 feet increase processing time by 10 minutes, if above 6,001 feet increase 15 minutes processing time. __Pressure canning__: if above 1,001 feet increase to 10 lbs. of pressure on weighted gauge; for dial gauge increase by 1 pound for every additional 2,000 feet in altitude.

Nectarine

	Water-bath Can	Steam Can	Pressure Can	Dehydrate	Freeze	Freeze-Dry	Ferment	Root Cellar
NECTARINE	✓	✓		✓	✓	✓		
Notes	Jam, jelly, in syrup, halves or slices in syrup, water, or juice	Jam, jelly, in syrup, halves or slices in syrup, water, or juice		Slices, fruit leather	Slices, puree	Slices		

Fruit	Preparation	Jar Size	Water-Bath/Steam Canning Processing Time*	Pressure Canning Processing Time at 5 lbs. of Pressure*
Nectarine 2½ pounds per quart	**Raw-Pack:** It's safe to raw-pack but not recommended as many feel it produces a poor end product. Wash, cut in half, and remove the pit. Pack in a jar with the pit side down to a generous ½-inch headspace. Fill with syrup to ½-inch headspace.	Pint	Raw-pack 25 min Hot-pack 20 min	10 min
	Hot-Pack: Wash, cut in half, remove pit. Place prepared fruit in boiling syrup and bring to a boil. Pack hot fruit in jars to generous ½-inch headspace and fill with hot syrup to ½-inch headspace.	Quart	Raw-pack 30 min Hot-pack 25 min	

*****Altitude adjustments**: *If you're 1,001 to 3,000 feet increase by 5 minutes processing time, 3,001 to 6,000 feet increase processing time by 10 minutes, if above 6,001 feet increase 15 minutes processing time.* **Pressure canning**: *if above 1,001 feet increase to 10 lbs. of pressure on weighted gauge; for dial gauge increase by 1 pound for every additional 2,000 feet in altitude.*

Orange

	Water-bath Can	Steam Can	Pressure Can	Dehydrate	Freeze	Freeze-Dry	Ferment	Root Cellar
ORANGE	✓	✓		✓	✓	✓	✓	
Notes	Sections in syrup, marmalade, conserve	Sections in syrup, marmalade, conserve		Slices	Section, as juice	Slices, juice	Slices	

See Lemons for fermenting.

Papaya

	Water-bath Can	Steam Can	Pressure Can	Dehydrate	Freeze	Freeze-Dry	Ferment	Root Cellar
PAPAYA	✓	✓		✓	✓	✓	✓	
Notes	In syrup	In syrup		Slices, fruit leather	Cubes	Slices, cubes	Slices	

Mandarin Oranges

INGREDIENTS

Mandarin oranges

Syrup, water, or citrus juice

1. Wash and peel the fruit and remove the white tissue to prevent a bitter taste.
2. If you use syrup, prepare a very light, light, or medium syrup and bring to a boil.
3. Fill jars with sections and water, juice, or hot syrup, leaving ½-inch headspace.
4. Remove air bubbles and add more liquid if needed to maintain headspace. Wipe rims; place lids and bands on.
5. Process pints or quarts in a water-bath or steam canner for 10 minutes. Follow instructions at the end of processing for a water-bath or steam canner.

Altitude adjustments: *if you're 1,001 to 3,000 feet increase processing time by 5 minutes, 3,001 to 6,000 feet increase processing time by 10 minutes, if above 6,001 feet increase 15 minutes processing time.*

See **Syrups for Canning Fruits Chart** *for syrup recipe on page 270.*

Adapted from
https://nchfp.uga.edu/how/can_02/grapefruit_orange.html

Orange Leather

INGREDIENTS

4 navel oranges, peeled and sliced

¼ cup honey

1 tablespoon cornstarch

1. Combine all the ingredients in a blender until smooth. You want an applesauce consistency.
2. Heat the puree in a small saucepan. Bring it to a boil, reduce heat to medium, and simmer for 2 minutes.
3. Let cool. Then pour 1 cup of puree onto a dehydrator sheet. Level the liquid by slapping the tray on the counter a couple of times.
4. Dehydrate at 125°F (52°C) until the leather easily peels off the sheet, about 10 to 12 hours.
5. Peel off the sheet, place on a mesh dehydrator tray, and place back into the dehydrator for 2 to 3 more hours.
6. Remove, let cool slightly, and cut into strips. Cover with plastic wrap to store.

Orange Marmalade

Yield: Approximately 6 half-pint jars

INGREDIENTS

5 oranges (medium-sized)

3 cups water or orange juice

3 teaspoons calcium water

3 tablespoons lemon or lime juice, bottled

2 cups sugar

4½ teaspoons Pomona's pectin powder mixed with sweetener

1. Prepare a water-bath or steam canner, jars, lids, and bands.
2. Peel two of the oranges, scraping off the white pith to avoid bitterness. Slice peel into strips about 1 to 1½ inches long. Set aside into a medium saucepan.
3. Peel remaining oranges. From all oranges, remove seeds and membrane (the white webby part). Finely chop the pulp, keeping as much of the juice as you can.
4. Add the pulp and juice to the pan with the sliced peel. Pour in 3 cups water/orange juice and bring to a boil. Cover with lid and simmer for 20 minutes, stirring to prevent scorching.
5. When finished, remove the pan from heat. Measure out 6 cups of the mixture. If a small amount remains, save it for something else. Return the 6 cups to the saucepan.
6. Stir in the calcium water, lemon, or lime juice.
7. Mix sugar and pectin powder in a bowl until well combined.
8. Bring fruit mixture, calcium water, and lemon/lime juice to a full boil. Stir in pectin-sugar mixture and cook for 1 to 2 minutes to fully dissolve and bring the marmalade back to a boil.
9. Remove from heat and fill hot jars to a ¼-inch headspace. Remove air bubbles and add more if needed to maintain headspace.
10. Process jars for 10 minutes. After processing time, follow instructions specific for water-bath or steam canner.

Adapted from Pomona's Pectin
https://pomonapectin.com/orange-marmalade/

Peach

	Water-bath Can	Steam Can	Pressure Can	Dehydrate	Freeze	Freeze-Dry	Ferment	Root Cellar
PEACH	✓	✓		✓	✓	✓		
Notes	Jam, jelly, dilly pickles, pie filling, sauce, salsa, halves or slices in syrup, water, or juice	Jam, jelly, dilly pickles, pie filling, sauce, salsa, halves or slices in syrup, water, or juice		Slices, fruit leather	Slices, puree	Slices	Slices	

Do not use white peaches in any of the below recipes due to lower acidity content.

When canning or cooking, always opt for freestone peach varieties; the peach will easily separate from the pit on these varieties.

Fruit	Preparation	Jar Size	Water-Bath/Steam Canning Processing Time*	Pressure Canning Processing Time at 5 lbs. of Pressure*
Peaches 2½ pounds per quart	**Peaches:** Do NOT use white peaches; they're too low in acidity. Remove skins by blanching in hot water for 30 to 60 seconds. Place peaches in cold water and remove skins; cut in half and remove pits (may quarter peaches or can in halves). Pack in a jar with the pit side down to a generous ½-inch headspace. Fill with syrup to ½-inch headspace. **Hot-Pack:** Place prepared fruit in boiling syrup and bring to a boil. Pack hot fruit in jars to generous ½-inch headspace and fill with hot syrup to ½-inch headspace.	Pint Quart	Raw-pack 25 min Hot-pack 20 min Raw-pack 30 min Hot-pack 25 min	10 min

How to Preserve Fruits | 345

FLAVOR VARIATIONS

- Cinnamon sticks: Add one 4-inch cinnamon stick to pint jars and two 4-inch cinnamon sticks to quart jars.

- Star anise: Add one small star to pint jars and one large one to quart jars.

- Fresh mint leaves: May add 1 to 2 freshly washed and unbruised mint leaves to each jar of peaches.

> **Altitude adjustments: if you're 1,001 to 3,000 feet increase by 5 minutes processing time, 3,001 to 6,000 feet increase processing time by 10 minutes, if above 6,001 feet increase 15 minutes processing time.* **Pressure canning**: *if above 1,001 feet increase to 10 lbs. of pressure on weighted gauge; for dial gauge increase by 1 pound for every additional 2,000 feet in altitude.*

Peach Salsa

Yield: 5 pint jars

INGREDIENTS

½ cup apple cider vinegar

6 cups peeled, pitted, and chopped peaches

1¼ cups chopped onion

2 jalapeño peppers, seeds removed, finely chopped

2 hot yellow wax peppers, seeds removed, finely chopped

1 red bell pepper, seeded and chopped

½ cup loosely packed finely chopped cilantro

2 tablespoons honey

1 clove garlic, minced

1½ teaspoons ground cumin

1. In a large stainless-steel pot, combine vinegar and prepared peaches. Add onion, peppers, cilantro, honey, garlic, and cumin.

2. Stirring constantly, bring to a boil over medium-high heat. Reduce heat, boiling gently and stirring often, until slightly thickened, around 4 to 5 minutes. Remove from heat.

3. Ladle hot salsa into prepared jars, leaving ½-inch headspace. Remove air bubbles and wipe the rim with a clean cloth. Center lid on jar and screw band on finger tight.

4. Place jars in a water-bath or steam canner. Process for 15 minutes. Follow instructions for a water-bath or steam canner at the end of processing time. Place on the counter on a folded kitchen towel. Cook for 24 hours, check the seals, and then store.

Altitude adjustments: *if you're 1,001 to 3,000 feet increase processing time by 5 minutes, 3,001 to 6,000 feet increase processing time by 10 minutes, if above 6,001 feet increase 15 minutes processing time.*

Recipe adapted from
Ball Complete Book of Home Food Preserving

Peach Jam No Store-Bought Pectin

Yield: Approximately 3 pints or 6 jelly jars

INGREDIENTS

2 tart or green apples, grated or chopped up (only remove the blossom ends and seeds)

½ cup bottled lemon juice

6 cups chopped, pitted, and peeled peaches (never use white peaches due to lower acidity in this recipe)

3 to 4 cups sugar

1. In a large pot, combine apples and peaches with a dash of water to keep things from sticking. Over high heat, bring to a boil; reduce heat to a simmer/gentle boil for 20 minutes.

2. Put mixture through a sieve to catch any pieces of apple skin that aren't cooked down. Minus the skins and cores, put mixture back into your large pot and add sugar and lemon juice. Bring to a boil and stir frequently. Boil gently for 10 minutes; check for set. Continue to boil for another 10 minutes if not set and add additional sugar if necessary.

3. Ladle hot jam into clean warm jars with a ¼-inch headspace. Remove air bubbles and wipe rim of jar clean. Place on lids and bands. Process in a water-bath for 10 minutes. Follow instructions for a water-bath or steam canner at the end of processing time. Place on the counter on a folded kitchen towel. Cool for 24 hours, check the seals, and then store.

Altitude adjustments: *if you're 1,001 to 3,000 feet increase processing time by 5 minutes, 3,001 to 6,000 feet increase processing time by 10 minutes, if above 6,001 feet increase 15 minutes processing time.*

To make this a spicy peach jam, add 1½ teaspoons ground chipotle with the sugar.

Pear

	Water-bath Can	Steam Can	Pressure Can	Dehydrate	Freeze	Freeze-Dry	Ferment	Root Cellar
PEAR	✓	✓		✓	✓	✓	✓	✓
Notes	Jam, marmalade, jelly, butter, pickles, in syrup, compote, salsa, conserve	Jam, marmalade, jelly, butter, pickles, in syrup, compote, salsa, conserve		Slices or quarters, fruit leather	Slices, quarters	Slices, quarters	Whole, wine, vinegar	

Fruit	Preparation	Jar Size	Water-Bath/Steam Canning Processing Time*	Pressure Canning Processing Time at 5 lbs. of Pressure*
Pears, Asian[8]	**Raw-Pack:** Pick firm but ripe pears and peel, core, and halve or slice. Add 1 tablespoon bottled lemon juice per pint jar or 2 tablespoons per quart. Fill with prepared fruit to ½-inch headspace. Cover with boiling water or syrup to ½-inch headspace.	Pint	Raw-pack 25 min Hot-pack 25 min	Not Recommended
	Hot-Pack: Pick firm but ripe pears and peel, core, and halve or slice. Precook at a boil for 5 minutes in syrup; pack in jars and to ½-inch headspace. Add 1 tablespoon bottled lemon juice per pint jar or 2 tablespoons per quart jar. Fill to ½-inch headspace with syrup.	Quart	Raw-pack 30 min Hot-pack 25 min	
Pears 2½ pounds per quart	**Hot-Pack:** Pick firm but ripe pears and peel, core, and halve. Precook at a boil for 5 minutes in syrup; pack in jars and add syrup to ½-inch headspace.	Pint	20 min	10 min
		Quart	25 min	

*__Altitude adjustments__: If you're 1,001 to 3,000 feet increase by 5 minutes processing time, 3,001 to 6,000 feet increase processing time by 10 minutes, if above 6,001 feet increase 15 minutes processing time. **Pressure canning**: if above 1,001 feet increase to 10 lbs. of pressure on weighted gauge; for dial gauge increase by 1 pound for every additional 2,000 feet in altitude.

Spiced Pear

Yield: 4 quarts

INGREDIENTS

12 pounds of peeled, halved, and cored pears (about 3 to 4 pears per quart jar)

5¾ cups water

1½ cups organic sugar

2 4-inch cinnamon sticks per quart

Powdered ginger, if desired

1. Prepare your water-bath or steam canner, jars, bands, and lids.
2. Peel pears by hand, or blanch for 15 seconds in hot water, plunge into warm water, and peel. Keep peeled pears in a solution of lemon water (about ¼ cup lemon juice to 4 cups of water) to keep them from turning brown.
3. In a large stainless-steel pot, mix water with the sugar; stir until sugar is dissolved over medium heat to almost a boil. Place pears in the hot syrup in a single layer and let heat through, about 5 minutes.
4. Fill jars with 2 cinnamon sticks each and a pinch of ginger, if desired. Add the hot pears using a slotted spoon, leaving a ½-inch headspace.
5. Using a ladle, pour the syrup over the pears to a ½-inch headspace. Remove air bubbles; double-check the headspace, adding more syrup if needed.
6. Wipe the rim of the jars clean and put on the lid and bands. Tighten fingertip tight and place in canner. Process for 20 minutes for pints and 25 minutes for quarts.
7. Follow instructions for a water-bath or steam canner at the end of processing time. Place on the counter on a folded kitchen towel. Cool for 24 hours, check the seals, and then store.

> **Altitude adjustments**: *If you're 1,001 to 3,000 feet increase processing time by 5 minutes, 3,001 to 6,000 feet increase processing time by 10 minutes, if above 6,001 feet increase 15 minutes processing time.*

Pear Butter

Yield: 4 pints

INGREDIENTS

4 pounds of pears, peeled, cored, and roughly chopped (approximately 17 medium pears)

1 cup apple cider (if you don't have apple cider, use water, but you may need to increase the sugar depending upon taste)

1 cup apple cider vinegar OR ¼ cup bottled lemon juice

2 to 3 cups of sugar

2 teaspoons of your favorite ground spices

1. In a large stainless-steel pot, combine pears, cider (or water), and vinegar and bring to a boil; simmer, stirring often, until pears are cooked through and soft. Puree pears (don't liquefy) with a blender, food processor, immersion blender, potato masher, or a food mill.

2. Combine pear puree, sugar, and spices into a large pot. Stir until sugar and spices are dissolved. Bring to a boil, then reduce heat to a gentle simmer, stirring often as it can scorch. Continue to cook until it's reached desired thickness.

3. To check for doneness, take out a spoonful and hold it up. The butter should stay mounded on the spoon. Or chill a plate and put a spoonful on the chilled plate. It should hold its shape and there should not be a separation of liquid. Now you're ready to jar. If it's not ready yet, simply continue cooking until it's reached the desired thickness.

4. Prepare your water-bath or steam canner, jars, lids, and bands.

5. Pour or ladle fruit butter into prepared jars to a ¼-inch headspace. Remove air bubbles, check headspace, and add more if needed to the ¼-inch headspace. Wipe rims clean, place lids and bands on, and put into a prepared canner.

6. Finish filling all your jars using the above procedure. Process 8-ounce (or smaller) jelly jars and pint-sized jars for 15 minutes.

7. Follow instructions for a water-bath or steam canner at the end of processing time. Place on the counter on a folded kitchen towel. Cool for 24 hours, check the seals, and then store.

Altitude adjustments: If you're 1,001 to 3,000 feet increase processing time by 5 minutes, 3,001 to 6,000 feet increase processing time by 10 minutes, if above 6,001 feet increase 15 minutes processing time.

Pineapple

	Water-bath Can	Steam Can	Pressure Can	Dehydrate	Freeze	Freeze-Dry	Ferment	Root Cellar
PINEAPPLE	✓	✓		✓	✓	✓	✓	
Notes	Conserve, jam, in syrup, salsa, topping	Conserve, jam, in syrup, salsa, topping		Slices	Slices or chunks	Slices, chunks	Wedges	

Fruit	Preparation	Jar Size	Water-Bath/Steam Canning Processing Time*	Pressure Canning Processing Time at 5 lbs. of Pressure*
Pineapple 3 pounds per quart	**Hot-Pack:** Peel, core, and cut into ½-inch slices or into 1-inch wedges. Add pineapple to syrup, bring to a boil, and simmer for 10 minutes. With a ladle, pack jars with hot pineapple to a generous ½-inch headspace; fill with hot syrup to ½-inch headspace. I prefer to use light-syrup ratio.	Pint	15 min	15 min
		Quart	20 min	

***Altitude adjustments**: If you're 1,001 to 3,000 feet increase by 5 minutes processing time, 3,001 to 6,000 feet increase processing time by 10 minutes, if above 6,001 feet increase 15 minutes processing time.

Plum

	Water-bath Can	Steam Can	Pressure Can	Dehydrate	Freeze	Freeze-Dry	Ferment	Root Cellar
PLUM	✓	✓		✓	✓	✓	✓	
Notes	Jam, butter, conserve, pickled, jelly, preserve, sauce, in syrup	Jam, butter, conserve, pickled, jelly, preserve, sauce, in syrup		Whole if small, halves or slices for larger plums, fruit leather	Slices, halves	Slices, halves	Halves	

Fruit	Preparation	Jar Size	Water-Bath/Steam Canning Processing Time*	Pressure Canning Processing Time at 5 lbs. of Pressure*
Plums 2 pounds per quart	**Raw-Pack:** Prick whole plums on both sides with a fork. Pack plums to a generous ½-inch headspace and cover with hot syrup to ½-inch headspace.	Pint	20 min	10 min
		Quart	25 min	

***Altitude adjustments**: If you're 1,001 to 3,000 feet increase by 5 minutes processing time, 3,001 to 6,000 feet increase processing time by 10 minutes, if above 6,001 feet increase 15 minutes processing time. **Pressure canning**: if above 1,001 feet increase to 10 lbs. of pressure on weighted gauge; for dial gauge increase by 1 pound for every additional 2,000 feet in altitude.

Plum Butter *Yield: 5 half-pint jars*

INGREDIENTS

5½ cups plum puree (with the skin on)

2 cups sugar

½ teaspoon vanilla extract

½ teaspoon ground cinnamon

5 tablespoons plus 1 teaspoon bottled lemon juice

Altitude adjustments: If you're 1,001 to 3,000 feet increase processing time by 5 minutes, 3,001 to 6,000 feet increase processing time by 10 minutes, if above 6,001 feet increase 15 minutes processing time.

Slow-Cooker Option: You can make your fruit butter in the slow cooker, cooking it on low for 8 to 10 hours with the lid removed to allow for evaporation. Stir often, because it can scorch in the slow cooker.

1. Add a small amount of water, about ¼ cup, to the pot to keep the fruit from scorching, and bring to a simmer. Heat, stirring often as fruit will scorch (and we don't want it to burn), for about 15 to 20 minutes, until all the fruit is heated thoroughly.

2. Take an immersion blender and carefully (the fruit is hot) puree all of the fruit to a smooth consistency. You may also use a blender if you don't have an immersion blender, but don't liquefy it. You could use a potato masher, but this takes longer and usually isn't quite as smooth a consistency.

3. Add sugar. Mix together thoroughly until sugar is dissolved. You can add more sweetener to taste, and you may use brown sugar for a slightly different flavor twist.

4. Add your flavors or spices, a bit of ground cinnamon, nutmeg, ginger, cloves, and a dash of vanilla extract. You don't have to add any spices, but it's fun to create your own flavor variation with the spices. Just start with ½-teaspoon amounts and add more to taste, as you can't take it back out once it's added in. Generally, 1 or 2 teaspoons of ground spices is enough for an entire batch.

5. Keep on a simmer, stirring often (this will scorch easily, and even a little bit of burning will flavor the whole batch), and allow the butter to thicken up. Depending upon the amount of liquid in the fruit, this usually takes anywhere from 30 to 60 minutes. (My plum butter took 72 minutes.)

6. To check for doneness, take out a spoonful and hold it up. The butter should stay mounded on the spoon. Or chill a plate and put a spoonful on the chilled plate. It should hold its shape and there should not be a separation of liquid. Now you're ready to jar. If it's not ready yet, simply continue cooking until it's reached the desired thickness.

7. Pour or ladle fruit butter into prepared jars to a ¼-inch headspace; remove air bubbles, check headspace, and add more if needed to the ¼-inch headspace. Wipe rims clean, place lids and bands on, and put into a prepared water-bath or steam canner.

8. Finish filling all your jars using the above procedure. Process 8-ounce (or smaller) jelly jars and pint-sized jars for 15 minutes. Follow instructions for a water-bath or steam canner at the end of processing time. Place on the counter on a folded kitchen towel. Cool for 24 hours, check the seals, and then store.

Plum Jam

Yield: Approximately 3 pints or 6 jelly jars

INGREDIENTS

2 tart or green apples, grated or chopped up (only remove the blossom ends and seeds)

½ cup bottled lemon juice

6 cups chopped, pitted, and peeled plums

3 to 4 cups sugar

1. Prepare water-bath or steam canner, jars, lids, and bands.
2. In a large pot, combine apples and plums with a dash of water to keep things from sticking. Over high heat, bring to a boil; reduce heat to a simmer/gentle boil for 20 minutes.
3. Put mixture through a sieve to catch any pieces of apple skin that aren't cooked down. Minus the skins and cores, put mixture back into your large pot and add sugar and lemon juice. Bring to a boil and stir frequently. Boil gently for 10 minutes; check for set. Continue to boil for another 10 minutes if not set and add additional sugar if necessary.
4. Ladle hot jam into clean warm jars with a ¼-inch headspace. Remove air bubbles and wipe the rim of the jar clean. Place on lids and bands.
5. Process jelly jars and pints for 10 minutes. Follow instructions for a water-bath or steam canner at the end of processing time. Place on the counter on a folded kitchen towel. Cool for 24 hours, check the seals, and then store.

Altitude adjustments: *If you're 1,001 to 3,000 feet increase processing time by 5 minutes, 3,001 to 6,000 feet increase processing time by 10 minutes, if above 6,001 feet increase 15 minutes processing time.*

Sweet and Spicy Plum Sauce
(recipe adapted from *Ball Complete Book of Home Preserving*)

I first tried this recipe when a neighbor brought me a box of golden plums and I had no idea what to do with them all. This recipe quickly became a favorite with chicken and meatballs.

Yield: 6 cups

INGREDIENTS

2 cups lightly packed brown sugar

1 cup sugar

1 cup apple cider vinegar

¾ cup finely chopped onion

1 tablespoon finely chopped jalapeño pepper; seeds removed

1 tablespoon finely chopped green bell pepper

2 tablespoons mustard seeds

1 tablespoon salt

2 cloves finely chopped garlic

1 tablespoon finely chopped ginger root

10 cups diced, pitted plums

1. Place the sugar, apple cider vinegar, onion, peppers, mustard seeds, canning salt, garlic, and ginger root in a heavy-bottomed stockpot. Using a thick-bottomed pot keeps your sauce from scorching. Bring to a boil, stirring often to avoid the sugar scorching.

2. Add your plums and return to a simmer. Let it simmer for approximately 1 hour and 40 minutes, stirring every now and then, until the sauce has reduced and thickened.

3. Prepare your canner, jars, and lids.

4. Ladle your sauce into hot jars (pints or smaller) with a ½-inch headspace. Process in a water-bath or steam canner for 20 minutes.

5. Follow instructions for a water-bath or steam canner at the end of processing time. Place on the counter on a folded kitchen towel. Cool for 24 hours, check the seals, and then store.

Altitude adjustments: *If you're 1,001 to 3,000 feet increase processing time by 5 minutes, 3,001 to 6,000 feet increase processing time by 10 minutes, if above 6,001 feet increase 15 minutes processing time.*

Raspberry

	Water-bath Can	Steam Can	Pressure Can	Dehydrate	Freeze	Freeze-Dry	Ferment	Root Cellar
RASPBERRY	✓	✓		✓	✓	✓	✓	
Notes	Jelly, jam, preserves, pie filling, sauce, vinegar, whole berries in syrup	Jelly, jam, preserves, pie filling, sauce, vinegar, whole berries in syrup		Whole, fruit leather	Whole	Whole	Wine, Vinegar	

Fruit	Preparation	Jar Size	Water-Bath/Steam Canning Processing Time*	Pressure Canning Processing Time at 5 lbs. of Pressure*
Raspberries 1¾ pounds per quart	**Raw-Pack:** Wash, cap, and stem. Put ½ cup hot syrup into a jar, then fill with berries to generous ½-inch headspace. Lightly shake the jar to settle berries and fill with syrup to ½-inch headspace.	Pint	15 min	8 min
		Quart	20 min	

***Altitude adjustments**: *If you're 1,001 to 3,000 feet increase by 5 minutes processing time, 3,001 to 6,000 feet increase processing time by 10 minutes, if above 6,001 feet increase 15 minutes processing time.* **Pressure canning:** *if above 1,001 feet increase to 10 lbs. of pressure on weighted gauge; for dial gauge increase by 1 pound for every additional 2,000 feet in altitude.*

Raspberry Red Currant Jelly

Yield: Approximately 4 jelly jars

INGREDIENTS

1 cup red currant juice

3 cups red raspberry juice

¼ cup lemon juice

Zest of 1 lemon

2 cups sugar

1. Prepare a water-bath or steam canner, jars, lids, and bands.

2. In a saucepan, stir together the red currant and raspberry juice, lemon juice, zest of lemon, and sugar. Bring to a hard boil and boil for 10 minutes, stirring often to keep mixture from scorching. After 10 minutes, use the drip test to check the set of the jelly.

3. Depending upon how ripe your berries are, I always recommend doing a taste test, especially with tart berries. Be careful, it's hot; don't burn your tongue. Add more sugar if desired to taste.

4. If the jelly is still too runny, allow it to continue boiling for 4 minutes and check again. The longest I've ever had to let mine boil was 25 minutes. This jelly has always set quite firmly for me.

5. Once jelly has reached its gelled point, pour into prepared jars, leaving ¼-inch headspace. Wipe rims clean and place on lids and bands. Set jars into a prepared canner. Process for 10 minutes.

6. Follow instructions for a water-bath or steam canner at the end of processing time. Place on the counter on a folded kitchen towel. Cool for 24 hours, check the seals, and then store.

Altitude adjustments: *If you're 1,001 to 3,000 feet increase processing time by 5 minutes, 3,001 to 6,000 feet increase processing time by 10 minutes, if above 6,001 feet increase 15 minutes processing time.*

Rhubarb

	Water-bath Can	Steam Can	Pressure Can	Dehydrate	Freeze	Freeze-Dry	Ferment	Root Cellar
RHUBARB	✓	✓		✓	✓	✓	✓	
Notes	Sauce, chutney, conserve, in syrup, jam, preserves, pie filling, juice concentrate	Sauce, chutney, conserve, in syrup, jam, preserves, pie filling, juice concentrate		Pieces, fruit leather	Pieces	Pieces	Diced, Vinegar	

Fruit	Preparation	Jar Size	Water-Bath/Steam Canning Processing Time*	Pressure Canning Processing Time at 5 lbs. of Pressure*
Rhubarb 1½ pounds per quart	Rinse and pat-dry rhubarb stalks. Chop into 1-inch pieces. Place into a large bowl and sprinkle 1 cup sugar for every 8 cups of rhubarb onto chopped rhubarb. Stir until well combined. Cover the bowl with a tea towel and allow it to sit for 4 hours. Dump rhubarb and syrup into a large pot. Bring to a boil and boil for 30 seconds, stirring. Take off of heat and ladle 2 cups of rhubarb into each pint jar with a generous ½-inch headspace. Pour syrup over rhubarb, dividing it evenly between the four jars to a ½-inch headspace. Remove air bubbles by running a spatula or knife around the outside of the jar and add more syrup if needed. If you run short on syrup, add boiling water.	Pint	15 min	5 min
		Quart	15 min	

***Altitude adjustments**: If you're 1,001 to 3,000 feet increase by 5 minutes processing time, 3,001 to 6,000 feet increase processing time by 10 minutes, if above 6,001 feet increase 15 minutes processing time. **Pressure canning**: if above 1,001 feet increase to 10 lbs. of pressure on weighted gauge; for dial gauge increase by 1 pound for every additional 2,000 feet in altitude.

Rhubarb BBQ Sauce

Judi Kingry and Lauren Devine, Ball / Bernardin Complete Book of Home Preserving *(Toronto: Robert Rose, 2015), 259.*

Yield: 4 pints

INGREDIENTS

8 cups chopped rhubarb

3½ cups brown sugar, loosely packed

1½ cups raisins

½ cup chopped onion

½ cup vinegar (apple cider vinegar or white)

1 teaspoon ground cinnamon

1 teaspoon ground ginger

1 teaspoon salt

1. Prepare a water-bath or steam canner, jars, lids, and bands.

2. In a large stockpot, combine all ingredients and bring to a boil over medium-high heat. Stir often and reduce heat to a low boil until sauce is thickened (a thin sauce but not syrup liquid); this takes about 30 to 40 minutes.

3. Fill warm jars with hot sauce to a ½-inch headspace. Remove air bubbles, wipe rim clean, place lid on, and screw band down to fingertip tight. Place the jar in the canner. Repeat with all jars.

4. Process for 15 minutes. Follow instructions for a water-bath or steam canner at the end of processing time. Place on the counter on a folded kitchen towel. Cool for 24 hours, check the seals, and then store.

Altitude adjustments: *If you're 1,001 to 3,000 feet increase processing time by 5 minutes, 3,001 to 6,000 feet increase processing time by 10 minutes, if above 6,001 feet increase 15 minutes processing time.*

Recipe based on
Victorian Barbecue Sauce from
Ball Complete Book of Home Preserving

Rhubarb Strawberry Pie Filling

Yield: 5 pints

INGREDIENTS

3 large apples (such as Golden Delicious, Granny Smith, Jonagold, Lady, or Rome Beauty), peeled and finely chopped

1 tablespoon grated orange zest

¼ cup freshly squeezed orange juice

7 cups sliced (1-inch thick) rhubarb

2 cups sugar

4 cups halved hulled strawberries

1. Prepare your water-bath or steam canner, jars, bands, and lids.
2. Combine the apples, orange zest, and juice in a large stainless-steel saucepan. Stir to coat the apples thoroughly. Add the rhubarb and sugar. Bring to a boil over medium-high heat. Stir constantly.
3. Reduce the heat and gently boil until rhubarb is tender. Stir frequently. It'll take about 12 minutes for the rhubarb to become tender.
4. Add the strawberries and return to a boil. Remove from heat.
5. Ladle the pie filling into hot jars. Leave 1-inch headspace. Remove any air bubbles, check headspace, and add more filling if needed to bring it up to a 1-inch headspace.
6. Wipe rim to remove any debris. Place the lid and band on the jar, and tighten to fingertip tight.
7. Put jars into the canner. Process for 15 minutes. Follow instructions for a water-bath or steam canner at the end of processing time. Place on the counter on a folded kitchen towel. Cool for 24 hours, check the seals, and then store.

Altitude adjustments: *If you're 1,001 to 3,000 feet increase processing time by 5 minutes, 3,001 to 6,000 feet increase processing time by 10 minutes, if above 6,001 feet increase 15 minutes processing time.*

Strawberry Rhubarb Jam
See recipe on pages 368-369

Blubarb Jam
See recipe on page 303

Strawberry Rhubarb Fruit Leather
See recipe on page 372

Saskatoon (aka Juneberry, Serviceberry)

	Water-bath Can	Steam Can	Pressure Can	Dehydrate	Freeze	Freeze-Dry	Ferment	Root Cellar
SASKATOON	✓	✓		✓	✓	✓		
Notes	Jam	Jam		Whole	Whole	Whole		

Strawberry

	Water-bath Can	Steam Can	Pressure Can	Dehydrate	Freeze	Freeze-Dry	Ferment	Root Cellar
STRAWBERRY	✓	✓		✓	✓	✓	✓	
Notes	Jam, jelly, sauce, pie filling, marmalade, preserves, syrup, whole berries in syrup, juice concentrate	Jam, jelly, sauce, pie filling, marmalade, preserves, syrup, whole berries in syrup, juice concentrate		Whole or sliced, fruit leather	Whole, sliced, crushed	Sliced	Wine, Vinegar	

Fruit	Preparation	Jar Size	Water-Bath/Steam Canning Processing Time*	Pressure Canning Processing Time at 5 lbs. of Pressure*
Strawberry 2 to 3 pounds per quart	For every 2 cups of rinsed and hulled strawberries, add ¼ cup sugar in a large pot. Stir to coat the berries with sugar and let sit overnight or for 6 hours. Place on medium-low heat until sugar is dissolved and strawberries are hot. Pour (or ladle) strawberries and syrup into jars with a ½-inch headspace. If you don't have enough syrup, top off with boiling water (just fill the kettle and heat in case you need it).	Pint	10 min	Not Recommended
		Quart	15 min	

*__Altitude adjustments__: If you're 1,001 to 3,000 feet increase by 5 minutes processing time, 3,001 to 6,000 feet increase processing time by 10 minutes, if above 6,001 feet increase 15 minutes processing time. **Pressure canning**: if above 1,001 feet increase to 10 lbs. of pressure on weighted gauge; for dial gauge increase by 1 pound for every additional 2,000 feet in altitude.

How to Preserve Fruits

Strawberry Rhubarb Jam Using Powdered Pectin

Yield: 4 (8 oz) jelly jars

INGREDIENTS

4½ cups diced rhubarb

4½ cups chopped strawberries

2 tablespoons lemon juice

6 tablespoons low-sugar or no-sugar powdered pectin

½ teaspoon butter (helps keep the foam down)

6½ cups sugar

1. Prepare a water-bath or steam canner, jars, lids, and bands.
2. Place fruit in a large pot over medium heat.
3. Stir in fruit mixture, lemon juice, pectin, butter. Once it begins to juice, add sugar, 1 cup at a time. Stir constantly until juice starts to simmer. Bring to a full rolling boil (means it doesn't quit boiling when you stir) and cook and stir for 1 minute.
4. Fill jars to ¼-inch headspace. Remove any air bubbles, check headspace, and add more filling if needed to bring it up to ¼-inch headspace.
5. Wipe rim to remove any debris. Place the lid and band on the jar; tighten to fingertip tight.
6. Put jars into the canner. Process for 10 minutes. Follow instructions for a water-bath or steam canner at the end of processing time. Place on the counter on a folded kitchen towel. Cool for 24 hours, check the seals, and then store.

Altitude adjustments: *If you're 1,001 to 3,000 feet increase processing time by 5 minutes, 3,001 to 6,000 feet increase processing time by 10 minutes, if above 6,001 feet increase 15 minutes processing time.*

No-Pectin Strawberry Rhubarb Jam

Yield: Approximately 4 pints or 5 (6 oz) jelly jars

INGREDIENTS

4 cups strawberries

4 cups chopped rhubarb

4 cups sugar

Zest from 2 lemons OR 1 grated, peeled, and cored apple + 1 tablespoon bottled lemon juice per cup of apple

4 tablespoons bottled lemon juice

1. Prepare a water-bath or steam canner, jars, lids, and bands.
2. Mash berries and rhubarb with a potato masher, blender, or immersion blender to desired consistency. I prefer mine chunky, but my husband likes it more pureed.
3. Place berries, rhubarb, sugar, lemon juice, and lemon zest (or grated apple) into a large pot. Stir until well combined. Bring berries to a boil.
4. If jam starts to foam, add a pat or two of butter to cut the foam.
5. Stir frequently to keep sugar from scorching. Simmer on a low boil for 10 minutes.
6. Test jam at 10 minutes for set. When jam is set or gelled, take off heat.
7. Fill jars to ¼-inch headspace. Remove any air bubbles, check headspace, and add more filling if needed to bring it up to ¼-inch headspace.
8. Wipe rim to remove any debris. Place the lid and band on the jar; tighten to fingertip tight.
9. Put jars into the canner. Process for 10 minutes. Follow instructions for a water-bath or steam canner at the end of processing time. Place on the counter on a folded kitchen towel. Cool for 24 hours, check the seals, and then store.

Altitude adjustments: *If you're 1,001 to 3,000 feet increase processing time by 5 minutes, 3,001 to 6,000 feet increase processing time by 10 minutes, if above 6,001 feet increase 15 minutes processing time.*

Low-Sugar No-Pectin Strawberry Jam

INGREDIENTS

8 cups strawberries (rinsed and hulled, before mashing)

3 cups sugar

Zest from 2 lemons

¼ cup lemon juice

1. Prepare a water-bath or steam canner, jars, lids, and bands.
2. Mash berries with a potato masher, blender, or immersion blender to desired consistency. I prefer mine chunky, but my husband likes it more pureed. Liquid or pureed berries take longer to reach the gelling point.
3. Place berries, sugar, lemon juice, and lemon zest into a large pot. Stir until well combined. Bring berries to a boil. Stir frequently to keep sugar from scorching.
4. Simmer on a low boil for 20 minutes. You can test the set of the jam by the sheeting test. Place a metal spoon in the freezer when you begin making your jam.
5. After 20 minutes of boiling, use the gelling tests on pages 273 and 274 to determine if it needs to cook longer or not.
6. Once jam has reached the gelling point, fill jars with ¼-inch headspace. Remove any air bubbles, check headspace, and add more filling if needed to bring it up to ¼-inch headspace.
7. Wipe rim to remove any debris. Place the lid and band on the jar; tighten to fingertip tight.
8. Place jars in the prepared canner. Process for 10 minutes. Follow instructions for a water-bath or steam canner at the end of processing time. Place on the counter on a folded kitchen towel. Cool for 24 hours, check the seals, and then store.

Altitude adjustments: *If you're 1,001 to 3,000 feet increase processing time by 5 minutes, 3,001 to 6,000 feet increase processing time by 10 minutes, if above 6,001 feet increase 15 minutes processing time.*

Note: Because we're not using store-bought pectin, the cook time to reach gel point can vary based on the ripeness and water content of your berries at harvest.

Strawberry Rhubarb Fruit Leather

INGREDIENTS

3 cups fresh rhubarb, washed and chopped into even chunks

2 cups strawberries

2 tablespoons honey

1. Put chopped rhubarb into a saucepan with enough water to cover it. Heat on low for about 10 minutes or until rhubarb has softened. Once softened, drain out as much water as possible from the pan. Let it cool to allow you to touch it without burning your hands. Place the rhubarb in a cheesecloth and allow the rest of the water to strain out.

2. Once the water has been strained out, put it into a large bowl and blend using an immersion blender. It should become soft and creamy. Then add the strawberries and blend until both are combined. Add the honey and blend in well.

3. Pour onto a tray with a silicone mat and spread evenly across the tray to about ¼-inch thickness. Using a silicone spatula helps to spread it. Dehydrate for about 4 hours at 130°F (54°C). It should no longer feel moist to the touch. It will feel a bit sticky and peel off the silicone mat easily.

Rhubarb Strawberry Pie Filling

See rhubarb on page 365

Watermelon

	Water-bath Can	Steam Can	Pressure Can	Dehydrate	Freeze	Freeze-Dry	Ferment	Root Cellar
WATERMELON	✓	✓		✓	✓	✓	✓	✓
Notes	As a pickle only	As a pickle only		Slices	Slices, cubes, or balls	Slices, cubes, or balls	Rind as pickles	Short-term only

CHAPTER 12
How to Preserve Meat

While there are many ways to preserve meat, most still involve some type of cold storage (with the exception of pressure canning and freeze-drying). Most of us are familiar with using the deep freezer, so I haven't devoted pages to instruction there (see the Freezing chapter on page 77 for freezer space chart).

Dehydrating meat (see salami recipe on page 389) still requires cold storage or the fridge depending on the recipe and method used, but freeze-drying allows you to preserve meat both raw and cooked.

The advantage to cooked freeze-dried meat is that you can eat it as is or simply add water and consume. Raw freeze-dried meat must be labeled as such and cooked after rehydrating. You can freeze-dry shredded, ground, or even whole cuts of meat provided they don't stick up over the edge of the trays. The manual that comes with your machine gives instructions.

The majority of this chapter we'll focus on canning meat recipes and methods.

Canning meat seems to be one of the most intimidating or last things people learn how to can, but honestly, it's one of the easiest things to can, with less hands-on time than many of the pickles or jam recipes. Having shelf-stable meat at the ready to whip up quick chicken salads, salmon patties or loaves, venison, a fast meat gravy, or adding it to casseroles—it's a busy mom's dream.

One of the differences when canning meat is that certain cuts may be canned using the raw-pack, and when using the raw-pack method with meat, you do not add liquid to the jars. This is a big difference from doing a raw-pack with fruits or vegetables.

It's important to note when canning meat that it is never fully cooked beforehand (even with a hot-pack). It is not a way to preserve your leftovers of fully cooked meats.

When using the hot-pack method, you do add liquid to the jars, in the form of boiling water, broth, or tomato juice.

When canning meat, it's advised to start with meat that has been chilled (or frozen and thawed).

You may add ½ teaspoon salt to pint jars or 1 teaspoon salt to quart jars for flavor (completely optional).

There are no safe tested times or procedures for canning cured, brined, or corned meats, with the exception of a small amount of ham or bacon in specific combination recipes.

Meat

Pressure Canning Processing Time (in minutes)				
Meats and Stock				
		8 oz	Pint	Quart
Stock, Beef		-	20	25
Stock, Chicken		-	20	25
Stock, Vegetable		-	30	35
Chicken	Bone-in	-	65	75
Duck	Bone-in	-	65	75
Game Birds	Bone-in	-	65	75
Goose	Bone-in	-	65	75

Pressure Canning Processing Time (in minutes)

Meats and Stock

Item	Type			
Turkey	Bone-in	-	65	75
Clams		60	70	-
Bear, Beef, Lamb, Pork, Sausage, Veal, Venison, Ground		-	75	90
Beef, Roast		-	75	90
Chicken	Boneless	-	75	90
Duck	Boneless	-	75	90
Game Birds	Boneless	-	75	90
Goose	Boneless	-	75	90
Lamb		-	75	90
Mutton		-	75	90
Pork		-	75	90
Turkey	Boneless	-	75	90

Pressure Canning Processing Time (in minutes)		
Meats and Stock		
Veal	-	75	90
Venison	-	75	90
Fish	100	100	-
Fish, Smoked	-	110	-

Broth

	Water-bath Can	Steam Can	Pressure Can	Dehydrate	Freeze	Freeze-Dry	Ferment	Root Cellar
BROTH			✓	✓	✓	✓		
Notes				Reduce broth	Ice cube trays or jars			

Having homemade broth sitting on the shelf is a wonderful addition to the home pantry. Not only does it make tasty meals (I like to cook rice and quinoa in broth for more nutrition and flavor), but when you're under the weather you don't have to go through the process of making broth to get a good dose in.

You can make vegetable, chicken or turkey, or beef broth. I like to have both beef and chicken broth on hand.

There are several ways to make your broth—you can do it on the stove top, in a slow cooker, or in an Instant Pot. I prefer to do the Instant Pot and slow cooker because I pour all the ingredients in, turn it on, and never touch it until it's finished. The longer the broth cooks, the richer and darker in color it will be as well.

Broth Storage Options

No matter if you're canning or not, you'll be using the fridge initially because you have to chill the broth in order to get the fat to rise to the top, because for canning, you need to remove the thick fat layer.

If you plan on leaving the **broth in the fridge**, leave that fat layer on. With poultry, I generally only get a thick fat layer on the first batch of broth when I'm initially cooking the full bird. Beef bones, however, put off a lot more fat, and I'll usually have a layer on the second batch as well.

The fat layer in the fridge acts as an oxygen barrier, which helps prolong the life in the fridge (it's why we don't want it for canning). With the fat layer on and not broken, I'll leave my broth in the fridge for up to 5 days or so. If there is no fat layer, 3 days is the rule of thumb for the fridge life.

I will often leave it in the fridge for 3 days and, if we haven't used the majority, bring it to a boil and can it. You don't have to can it the same day you make it.

The freezer is another option. You can put it in a sealed freezer container or bag. If using a bag, freeze it in a single layer lying down flat, and break off pieces as you need it. Others will freeze broth in ice cube trays for small amounts to use at a time.

You can also freeze your broth in a Mason jar. However, to avoid your jars breaking, make sure you leave at least 2 inches headspace for liquid expansion. When thawing, put the jar in the fridge to thaw to avoid extreme temperature changes. I generally don't freeze mine because my freezer is full with all of our whole meat birds and I'm not always the best at remembering to thaw it ahead of time.

Dehydrator. To dehydrate you'll want to greatly reduce the broth so it's concentrated and thick.

Freeze-Dryer. Simply pour your broth in the trays and place into the machine. When finished, powder, and store in a glass jar or Mylar bag.

Roasting Bones for Broth—To Roast or Not to Roast

Roasting the bones helps to create a deeper and stronger flavor as well as a darker color of broth. I roast my beef bones, especially the straight marrow bones (no meat on them to begin with). I don't always roast my chicken bones. It depends on how much time I have.

To roast your bones, preheat your oven to 400°F/205°C. Place the bones (I don't bother picking them clean; if there are small amounts of meat attached, it stays) in a single layer on a rimmed cookie sheet or baking pan. Roast them for 45 minutes to 1 hour.

The bones will turn a golden color and release some juices. Pop into your broth pot and go!

How Many Carcasses to Use

When it comes to chicken broth, I've noticed a vast difference in using our own organic pasture-raised birds versus store bought. If I'm using one of our own organic pasture-raised birds, I can get a gel from one carcass. If using store-bought chicken, I need two.

When I'm only using one carcass, I will use the addition of 2 or 3 chicken feet for extra gel power. If you're not getting a gel from one carcass, try adding in extra bones.

However, an Instant Pot also aids in the power of extracting the gelatin from the bones and is my favorite go-to for broth making.

How to Get More Flavor to Your Broth

If you feel like your broth doesn't have that much flavor, there are quite a few things you can do—try these tips:

1. Roast the bones.
2. If you're *not* using an Instant Pot, increase the cooking time; let it go longer.
3. If you are using an Instant Pot, make sure it's cooking at high pressure for 2 hours.
4. Add a little bit more salt. (I will drink broth like tea in the winter months. A few pints didn't have much flavor and just a sprinkle of sea salt on top made a world of difference.)
5. Add more bones (especially if you're only using one chicken carcass).
6. Add more herbs.
7. Add more onion skins (the skins create a darker color), onion, and garlic.

How to Make Your Broth

1. Place your bones (some people prefer to do just bones with bits of meat left on them; others prefer to put a whole chicken that has been cut up with the meat still on. I use soup bones with meat for my beef broth) into your pot or slow cooker. If you want to add vegetables, you may, but see our chart on processing times when using vegetables and meat together, or you may use all vegetables.
2. Add one to two tablespoons of apple cider vinegar or white vinegar. This will help break down the bones, releasing the gelatin and collagen.
3. Measure out how much water you're pouring in to cover the bones, meat, and vegetables. This will be approximately how much liquid you will get back out (minus a cup or so), so you know how many jars to prepare for canning.
4. For the **slow-cooker method**, turn it on low and let it cook for 24 hours. For the **stove-top method**, bring ingredients to a low boil and boil for 2 hours. In an **Instant Pot**, cook on high pressure for 1 hour. Some broth aficionados say broth must simmer for 72 hours. I always get a wonderful gel on mine regardless.
5. When broth is cooked, strain your broth through a fine-mesh strainer, or you can line a strainer with cheesecloth, but I just use a fine-mesh strainer and don't mind if tiny bits of meat filter through (we're talking itty bitty).
6. Place broth into the fridge until the fat layer on the top of the broth is white and turns completely solid. Skim off this fat and discard or save for another use.

I toss odds and ends pieces of vegetables into a freezer container for broth making, such as the ends of celery, onion skins, ends of carrots, or any other small amounts of vegetables I'd normally discard. We're straining the broth and not eating the vegetables, so I don't care if it's the odds and ends pieces. This is also very frugal.

Canning the Broth

1. Prepare a water-bath or pressure canner (see pages 48-49 for more information), jars, lids, and bands.

2. Place strained and skimmed broth back into a large pot and bring to a boil. Fill jars with broth to a 1-inch headspace. Wipe down the rim of the jar. Place lid and band on and screw down to fingertip tight.
3. Place into the prepared canner on the rack. Check that the vent pipe is clear and lock the lid into place and bring to a boil. Allow steam to vent for 10 minutes and then close the vent. For broth made strictly from bones, process at 10 pounds of pressure: pint jars for 20 minutes and quart jars for 25 minutes (see chart for broths made with vegetables). If using a dial-gauge-only pressure canner, use 11 pounds PSI. Follow pressure level according to your altitude and type of gauge.*
4. Turn off heat and allow pressure to reduce to zero naturally. When pressure is completely reduced, remove the lid, and wait an additional 10 minutes. Remove jars, place on towels in a draft-free area, cool for 24 hours, check seals, and store.

***Altitude adjustments** see chart on page 50*

How to Decide If You Should Reuse the Bones for a Second Batch of Broth

Using the bones for a second batch of broth is a frugal practice. In the case of beef bones, I reuse them almost every time.

For smaller bones like chicken, I do a test. I push on the bones and if they crumble (are completely soft), then I don't reuse them. They've given me all of their gelatin and collagen at this point. I find this happens when using my Instant Pot due to its effectiveness.

Always use fresh vegetables and herbs on the second batch; only the bones are reused. And if you're worried that the second batch will be weaker, consider adding extra vegetables and herbs.

Safety Notes

There is no tested time or recipe for canning **fish stock or fish broth** that I have seen.

Processing Times for Broth

Broth Type	Pounds of Pressure (see page 50 for altitude adjustments)	Processing Times: Pint Jars	Processing Times: Quart Jars
Beef Bones	10	20 min	25 min
Chicken Bones	10	20 min	25 min
Vegetable https://www.bernardin.ca/recipes/en/vegetable-stock.htm	10	30 min	35 min
Combination of beef and vegetable https://www.bernardin.ca/recipes/en/beef-stock.htm?Lang=EN-US	10	20 min	25 min
Combination of chicken and vegetable https://www.bernardin.ca/recipes/en/chicken-stock.htm	10	20 min	25 min
Vegetable broth or your own combination of chicken/beef and vegetables not from an above tested recipe	10	60 min	75 min

Note: *Vegetable broth has a longer processing time. If you're adding vegetables to your meat, then it's a combination recipe and should be canned to the longest processing ingredient. There are recipes from the Ball Complete Book of Home Preserving and Bernardin website; I've included links above that have some specified vegetable amounts with their chicken and beef stock and a shorter processing time; however, this is a tested recipe. If you're following their exact recipe, then it's fine to go with the shorter 20-minute processing time; but if you're adding in vegetables to taste (which is what I do), you must process for a longer time.*

Poultry (chicken, turkey, etc.)

	Water-bath Can	Steam Can	Pressure Can	Dehydrate	Freeze	Freeze-Dry	Ferment	Root Cellar
POULTRY			✓		✓	✓		

If using freshly processed meat, chill for 6 to 12 hours before canning.

When raw-packing meat, the jar should be room temperature and you do not preheat the water in the pressure canner.

For hot-pack, the jar should be hot, and water inside the pressure canner should be 180°F/82 °C.

1. Trim excess fat from meat. Cut meat that allows you to pack the jars—we usually do really large chunks, about 2- to 3-inch cubes when processing without the bones.
2. Prepare a pressure canner (see pages 48-49 for more information), jars, lids, and bands. Add ½ teaspoon salt to pint jars and 1 teaspoon salt to quart jars, if desired.
3. For a **hot-pack**, cook the meat to medium done or ⅔ done. Fill jars with meat to a generous 1½-inch headspace, add hot broth to 1¼-inch headspace, and remove air bubbles.
4. For a **raw-pack**, add meat to a room-temperature jar (don't pack tightly) to a 1¼-inch headspace. Do NOT add water.
5. Wipe rims clean with a towel moistened with vinegar (this helps remove any fat on the rim that can inhibit sealing). Place lid and band on and screw down to fingertip tight.
6. Place the jar into the prepared canner on the rack. Check that the vent pipe is clear and lock the lid into place and bring to a boil. Allow steam to vent for 10 minutes and then close the vent.
7. **Processing time WITHOUT bones:** Hot- and raw-pack process at 10 pounds of pressure for 75 minutes for pints and 90 minutes for quarts. If using a dial-gauge-only pressure canner, use 11 pounds PSI. Follow pressure level according to your altitude and type of gauge.*

8. **Processing time WITH bones:** Separate at joints. Hot- and raw-pack process at 10 pounds of pressure for 65 minutes for pints and 75 minutes for quarts. If using a dial-gauge-only pressure canner, use 11 pounds PSI. Follow pressure level according to your altitude and type of gauge.*
9. Turn off heat and allow pressure to reduce to zero naturally. When pressure is completely reduced, remove the lid and wait an additional 10 minutes. Remove jars, place on towels in a draft-free area, cool for 24 hours, check seals, and store.

***Altitude adjustments** see chart on page 50*

Ground or Chopped

	Water-bath Can	Steam Can	Pressure Can	Dehydrate	Freeze	Freeze-Dry	Ferment	Root Cellar
GROUND OR CHOPPED MEAT			✓	✓	✓	✓		
Notes					Dehydrated meat does not have a long shelf-life and still requires refrigeration			

Canning Ground Meat
(bear, beef, lamb, pork, sausage, veal, and venison)

There are no times that I'm aware of for ground turkey or poultry; do not substitute with those meats.

1. Prepare pressure canner (see pages 48-49 for more information), jars, lids, and bands. Add ½ teaspoon salt to pint jars and 1 teaspoon salt to quart jars, if desired.

2. Brown the meat and drain off excess fat. For meat patties or balls, form into desired shape and then brown lightly and drain off excess fat. You may also can sausage in its casing; cut it into 3- to 4-inch pieces, brown, and drain fat.

3. Pack into just-washed hot jars and add boiling meat broth, water, or tomato juice to a 1-inch headspace. Remove air bubbles and add more liquid if needed to maintain 1-inch headspace. Wipe rims clean with a towel moistened with vinegar (this helps remove any fat on the rims that can inhibit sealing). Place lid and band on and screw down to fingertip tight.

4. Place the jar into the prepared canner on the rack. Check that the vent pipe is clear and lock the lid into place and bring to a boil. Allow steam to vent for 10 minutes and then close the vent. Process at 10 pounds of pressure for 75 minutes for pints and 90 minutes for quarts. If using a dial-gauge-only pressure canner, use 11 pounds PSI. Follow pressure level according to your altitude and type of gauge.*

5. Turn off heat and allow pressure to reduce to zero naturally. When pressure is completely reduced, remove the lid and wait an additional 10 minutes. Remove jars, place on towels in a draft-free area, cool for 24 hours, check seals, and store.

*****Altitude adjustments** *see chart on page 50*

Beef Salami

This recipe is a family favorite, passed down from my father-in-law.

Yield: 5 one-pound rolls

INGREDIENTS

5 pounds hamburger

5 teaspoons (rounded) Morton's Tender Quick Salt

2 tablespoons ground black pepper (adjust to taste)

2 tablespoons brown sugar

2 tablespoons whole mustard seed

2 tablespoons ground sage

2 teaspoons smoked salt (original recipe calls for Old Hickory smoked salt)

1. Mix all ingredients together in a large bowl and cover. Put in the fridge for 3 days, mixing once per day. On day 4, shape into 5 logs and place on a broiler pan or small racks inside a larger pan. Bake for 4 hours at 140°F/60°C, then smoke for 4 hours at same temperature. If you don't have a smoker, bake for 8 hours.

2. Store in the fridge for 5 to 7 days or freeze for 6 months.

Strips, Cubes, or Chunks

	Water-bath Can	Steam Can	Pressure Can	Dehydrate	Freeze	Freeze-Dry	Ferment	Root Cellar
GROUND OR CHOPPED MEAT			✓	✓	✓	✓		
Notes			For wild game, do a water soak as explained under Rabbit.	Dehydrated meat does not have a long shelf-life and still requires refrigeration.				

For Meat Strips, Cubes, or Chunks
(bear, beef, lamb, pork, sausage, veal, and venison)

Use the same water soak as used for rabbit for any wild game that has a strong gamey taste: 1 hour in a brine of 1 tablespoon salt per 4 cups of water. Rinse then process.

If using freshly processed meat, chill for 6 to 12 hours before canning.

When raw-packing meat, the jar should be room temperature and you do not preheat the water in the pressure canner.

For hot-pack, jar should be hot, and water inside pressure canner should be 180°F/82°C.

If canning a large amount, many choose to roast a large pan of meat rather than brown in a pan. Use a preheated oven at 400°F (200°C) and sear the outside of the prepared strips. Do not fully cook the meat; this is just to brown and sear the outer edges.

If using a skillet to brown, do not use any more than 1 tablespoon of added cooking fat.

1. Trim excess fat from meat (lean cuts are recommended). Cut into ½- to 1-inch strips, cubes, or chunks.
2. Prepare a pressure canner (see pages 48-49 for more information), jars, lids, and bands. Add 1 teaspoon salt to pint jars and 2 teaspoons salt to quart jars, if desired.

3. **Hot-Pack:** Cook meat to rare by roasting, stewing, or browning, then drain off fat. Fill hot clean jars with hot meat to a generous 1-inch headspace, then add boiling broth, water, or tomato juice to a 1-inch headspace. Remove air bubbles and adjust headspace to 1 inch if needed.
   Raw-Pack: Fill clean room-temperature jars with raw meat to a 1-inch headspace. DON'T add liquid.
4. Wipe rims clean with a towel moistened with vinegar (this helps remove any fat on the rims that can inhibit sealing). Place lid and band on and screw down to fingertip tight.
5. Place the jar into the prepared canner on the rack. Check that the vent pipe is clear and lock the lid into place and bring to a boil. Allow steam to vent for 10 minutes and then close the vent.
6. For both hot- and raw-packs, process at 10 pounds of pressure for 75 minutes for pints and 90 minutes for quarts. If using a dial-gauge-only pressure canner, use 11 pounds PSI. Follow pressure level according to your altitude and type of gauge.*
7. Turn off heat and allow pressure to reduce to zero naturally. When pressure is completely reduced, remove the lid and wait an additional 10 minutes. Remove jars, place on towels in a draft-free area, cool for 24 hours, check seals, and store.

***Altitude adjustments** see chart on page 50*

Pork

	Water-bath Can	Steam Can	Pressure Can	Dehydrate	Freeze	Freeze-Dry	Ferment	Root Cellar
PORK			✓	✓	✓	✓		
Notes				Dehydrated meat does not have a long shelf-life and still requires refrigeration.				

See the sections on Ground or Chopped and Strips, Cubes, or Chunks.

Pulled Pork in a Jar

The first time I had this, a friend brought a jar over. I may have almost swooned upon the first bite. She shared her adaptations to the original recipe from The All-New Ball Book of Canning and Preserving 2016 *and it quickly became my go-to.*

Yield: Approximately 6 pint (500 ml) jars or 3 quart (1-L) jars

INGREDIENTS

4 to 5 pounds pork loin or boneless pork shoulder, cut into 1-inch chunks

1½ cups chopped onion

1½ cups ketchup

½ cup firmly packed Sucanat™**

¼ cup apple cider vinegar (5% acidity)

2 tablespoons Worcestershire sauce

2 tablespoons grainy brown mustard

2 tablespoons honey

3 cloves garlic, minced

1. Prepare a pressure canner (see pages 48-49 for more information), jars, lids, and bands for a hot-pack.

2. In a large stainless-steel pot, stir together everything BUT the pork. When blended well, fold in the pork, coating evenly. Bring contents to a boil, reduce heat, and simmer for 5 minutes.

3. Ladle mixture into prepared jars to a 1-inch headspace. Remove air bubbles and adjust headspace to 1 inch if needed.

4. Wipe rims clean with a towel moistened with vinegar (this helps remove any fat on the rims that can inhibit sealing). Place lid and band on and screw down to fingertip tight.

5. Place the jar into the prepared canner on the rack. Repeat until all the jars are filled and in the canner. Check that the vent pipe is clear and lock the lid into place and bring to a boil. Allow steam to vent for 10 minutes and then close the vent.

6. Process at 10 pounds of pressure for 75 minutes for pints and 90 minutes for quarts. If using a dial-gauge-only pressure canner, use 11 pounds PSI. Follow pressure level according to your altitude and type of gauge.*

7. Turn off heat and allow pressure to reduce to zero naturally. When pressure is completely reduced, remove the lid and wait an additional 10 minutes. Remove jars, place on towels in a draft-free area, cool for 24 hours, check seals, and store.

*****Altitude adjustments** *see chart on page 50*

**In place of Sucanat, you can substitute sugar in the raw, evaporated cane juice, coconut sugar, or light brown sugar. All will give a slightly different flavor, but the rawer versions of sugar give a deeper caramel molasses flavor.

Rabbit

	Water-bath Can	Steam Can	Pressure Can	Dehydrate	Freeze	Freeze-Dry	Ferment	Root Cellar
RABBIT			✓	✓	✓	✓		
Notes			Soak the meat for 1 hour in salt water with 1 tablespoon of salt per 4 cups of water.					

If using freshly processed meat, chill for 6 to 12 hours before canning. For rabbit it's recommended to dress and soak the meat for 1 hour (but no longer) in salt water with 1 tablespoon of salt per 4 cups of water.

When raw-packing meat, the jar should be room temperature and you do not preheat the water in the pressure canner.

For hot-pack, the jar should be hot, and water inside the pressure canner should be 180°F/82°C.

1. Trim excess fat from meat. Cut meat that allows you to pack the jars—we usually do large chunks, about 2- to 3-inch cubes when processing without the bones.
2. Prepare a pressure canner (see pages 48-49 for more information), jars, lids, and bands. Add ½ teaspoon salt to pint jars and 1 teaspoon salt to quart jars, if desired.
3. For a **hot-pack**, cook the meat to medium done or ⅔ done. Fill jars with meat to a generous 1½-inch headspace, add hot broth to 1¼-inch headspace, and remove air bubbles.
4. For a **raw-pack,** add meat to a room-temperature jar (don't pack tightly) to a 1¼-inch headspace. Do NOT add water.
5. Wipe rims clean with a towel moistened with vinegar (this helps remove any fat on the rims that can inhibit sealing). Place lid and band on and screw down to fingertip tight.
6. Place the jar into the prepared canner on the rack. Check that the vent pipe is clear, lock the lid into place, and bring to a boil. Allow steam to vent for 10 minutes and then close the vent.
7. **Processing time WITHOUT bones:** For hot- and raw-packs, process at 10 pounds of pressure for 75 minutes for pints and 90 minutes for quarts. If using a dial-gauge-only pressure canner, use 11 pounds PSI. Follow pressure level according to your altitude and type of gauge.*

8. **Processing time WITH bones:** Separate at joints. Hot and raw pack process at 10 pounds of pressure with pints for 65 minutes and quarts for 75 minutes. If using a dial-gauge-only pressure canner, use 11 pounds PSI. Follow pressure level according to your altitude and type of gauge.*

9. Turn off heat and allow pressure to reduce to zero naturally. When pressure is completely reduced, remove the lid and wait an additional 10 minutes. Remove jars, place on towels in a draft-free area, cool for 24 hours, check seals, and store.

*Altitude adjustments see chart on page 50

Fish

	Water-bath Can	Steam Can	Pressure Can	Dehydrate	Freeze	Freeze-Dry	Ferment	Root Cellar
FISH			✓	✓	✓	✓		
Notes			Not all fish are treated the same; be sure to follow the correct instructions for your particular fish.	Usually a combination of salt, smoke, heat, and air				

Fish should be cleaned within 2 hours of being caught. Do not use tins or a larger jar size than those specified.

When processing fish, you do NOT heat the water in the canner or jars. It should be room-temperature jars and water.

Due to the longer processing times, make sure you have adequate water and are using a 16- to 22-quart pressure canner for this procedure (this is the volume of water your pressure canner holds, not quart jars filled with food). Fill your pressure canner with 4 quarts (16 cups) of cool water. The liquid level will reach the bands on pint jars but shouldn't go over the tops.

Fish
(blue, mackerel, salmon, steelhead, trout, EXCEPT tuna)

INGREDIENTS

Fish

Salt (optional)

1. Prepare a pressure canner with 16 cups of cool water (see pages 48-49 for more information), jars, lids, and bands. Add ½ to 1 teaspoon salt to pint jars, if desired.

2. Wash fish well and remove blood. Cut fish in half lengthwise, then slice cleaned fish into 3½-inch-long pieces (it needs to fit in the pint-sized jar to a 1-inch headspace), removing head, tail, fins, and scales. A sharp filet knife is very handy for this part.

3. Pack the fish skin side out (skin touching the glass) into half-pint (250 ml) or pint (500 ml) room-temperature clean jars to a 1-inch headspace. Do NOT add liquid.

4. Wipe rims clean with a towel moistened with vinegar (this helps remove any fat on the rims that can inhibit sealing). Place lid and band on and screw down to fingertip tight.

5. Place the jars into the prepared canner on the rack. Check that the vent pipe is clear and lock the lid into place and bring to a boil. Allow steam to vent for 10 minutes and then close the vent.

6. Process pints at 10 pounds of pressure for 100 minutes (1 hour and 40 minutes). If using a dial-gauge-only pressure canner, use 11 pounds PSI. Follow pressure level according to your altitude and type of gauge.*

7. Turn off heat and allow pressure to reduce to zero naturally. When pressure is completely reduced, remove the lid and wait an additional 10 minutes. Remove jars, place on towels in a draft-free area, cool for 24 hours, check seals, and store.

***Altitude adjustments** see chart on page 50*

Smoked Salmon
(rockfish, sole, cod, and flounder)

We use a dry brine on our fish for canning when smoking.

We prefer a 4 to 1 ratio: 4 parts brown sugar to 1 part salt. Mix together enough to completely cover the filet. Place fish skin side down in a baking dish or food-safe tub. Liberally sprinkle the dry brine over the top of the filet. Cover with plastic wrap and place in the fridge for up to 48 hours.

Rinse fish well after brining, pat dry, and cut into slices. Lightly smoke for about 30 minutes (you don't want to smoke it like you would for regular eating; it will be too dry and too strong of a flavor). We prefer alder, apple, or cherry wood chips when smoking fish.

Do not use tins or a larger jar size than specified.

INGREDIENTS

Lightly smoked fish

16 cups cool water

1. Prepare a pressure canner with 16 cups of cool water (see pages 48-49 for more information), jars, lids, and bands.

2. Pack lightly smoked fish into clean room-temperature pint jars, skin side out to a 1-inch headspace. Do NOT add liquid. With smoked salmon it doesn't matter if it's a tight or loose pack. I try to do the larger pieces on the outside and fit a smaller piece into the center. Wide-mouth works the easiest for packing.

3. Wipe rims clean with a towel moistened with vinegar (this helps remove any fat on the rims that can inhibit sealing). Place lid and band on and screw down to fingertip tight.

4. Place the jar into the prepared canner on the rack. Check that the vent pipe is clear and lock the lid into place and bring to a boil. Allow steam to vent for 10 minutes and then close the vent.

5. Process pints at 10 pounds of pressure for 110 minutes (1 hour and 50 minutes)—yes, it is almost two hours. If using a dial-gauge-only pressure canner, use 11 pounds PSI. Follow pressure level according to your altitude and type of gauge.*

6. Turn off heat and allow pressure to reduce to zero naturally. When pressure is completely reduced, remove the lid and wait an additional 10 minutes. Remove jars, place on towels in a draft-free area, cool for 24 hours, check seals, and store.

*Altitude adjustments see chart on page 50

Tuna

Tuna should be kept on ice until ready to can. Make sure all blood has been drained and the fish is washed well.

Yield: Approximately 2 pounds to 1 pint jar

INGREDIENTS

Fish

Salt (optional)

Oil or water for hot-pack

*Altitude adjustments
see chart on page 50

1. Prepare a pressure canner with 16 cups of cool water (see pages 48-49 for more information), jars, lids, and bands.

2. **Raw-pack:** Wash fish well and remove blood. Quarter fish, peel off skin, and remove fin bases and bones. Remove the dark flesh as it's extremely strong in flavor and not recommended. Slice fish into strips (it needs to fit in the pint-sized jar to a 1-inch headspace).

3. Add 1 teaspoon salt to the jar (optional). Pack into a half-pint or pint jar to a 1-inch headspace. No added liquid is needed.

4. **Hot-pack:** Precook fish by baking at 350°F/177°C for 1 hour or steamed until the internal temperature of the fish reaches 165-175°F/74-80°C. Place cooked fish in the fridge to firm it up overnight, then remove skin, including blood vessels and any discolored areas. Fill just-washed and rinsed jars; push down gently to pack solidly. Add 1 teaspoon salt to a pint jar and water or oil to a 1-inch headspace.

5. Wipe rims clean with a towel moistened with vinegar (this helps remove any fat on the rims that can inhibit sealing). Place lid and band on and screw down to fingertip tight.

6. Place the jar into the prepared canner on the rack. Check that the vent pipe is clear and lock the lid into place and bring to a boil. Allow steam to vent for 10 minutes and then close the vent.

7. Process half-pints and pints at 10 pounds of pressure for 100 minutes (1 hour and 40 minutes). If using a dial-gauge-only pressure canner, use 11 pounds PSI. Follow pressure level according to your altitude and type of gauge.*

8. Turn off heat and allow pressure to reduce to zero naturally. When pressure is completely reduced, remove the lid and wait an additional 10 minutes. Remove jars, place on towels in a draft-free area, cool for 24 hours, check seals, and store.

Seafood

	Water-bath Can	Steam Can	Pressure Can	Dehydrate	Freeze	Freeze-Dry	Ferment	Root Cellar
SEAFOOD			✓		✓	✓		

Note: *It is only safe to can seafood in half-pints or pints!*

Pressure Can Clams

Always keep clams and crab alive and on ice until right before cooking and canning.

INGREDIENTS

Clams

Bottled lemon juice

Water

Salt

1. Prepare a pressure canner for a hot-pack (see pages 48-49 for more information), jars, lids, and bands.

2. In a double boiler or steamer, steam clams for 5 minutes and remove meat to a colander. Drain and rinse (optional: may reserve cooking liquid and strain to use as packing liquid in place of the boiling water, but make sure you bring it back to a boil).

3. Rinse in a large bowl with a mixture of 1 teaspoon salt to 4 cups water (increase as needed for volume of clams being processed). Add clam meat still in the colander, stir well, then lift up the colander and rinse and drain again.

4. Cover clam meat with boiling water that has 2 tablespoons of bottled lemon juice (or ½ teaspoon citric acid) to a gallon of water for 2 minutes; drain.

5. Pack hot and washed jars with clams and add boiling water (or boiling reserved clam juice) to a 1-inch headspace. Remove air bubbles and add more just-off-the-boil liquid if needed to maintain headspace.

6. Wipe rims clean with a moist towel. Place lid and band on and screw down to fingertip tight.

7. Place the jar into the prepared canner on the rack. Check that the vent pipe is clear and lock the lid into place and bring to a boil. Allow steam to vent for 10 minutes and then close the vent.

8. Process at 10 pounds of pressure for 60 minutes for half-pints and 70 minutes for pints. If using a dial-gauge-only pressure canner, use 11 pounds PSI. Follow pressure level according to your altitude and type of gauge.*

9. Turn off heat and allow pressure to reduce to zero naturally. When pressure is completely reduced, remove the lid and wait an additional 10 minutes. Remove jars, place on towels in a draft-free area, cool for 24 hours, check seals, and store.

***Altitude adjustments** see chart on page 50*

Pressure Can Crab
(King and Dungeness)

INGREDIENTS

Crab

Bottled lemon juice, citric acid, or vinegar

Water

Salt

1. Prepare a pressure canner for a hot-pack (see pages 48-49 for more information), jars, lids, and bands.
2. Wash and rinse crab in cold water several times. Bring water to a simmer and boil crabs for 20 minutes; add ¼ cup bottled lemon juice and 2 tablespoons of salt to each gallon of water.
3. Cool crab quickly in a cold-water bath. Drain and crack crab, removing the meat from the body and claws.
4. Soak the crab meat for 2 minutes in a salt brine of up to 1 cup of salt to a gallon of water or 2 cups lemon juice or 4 cups white vinegar. Drain and squeeze meat to expel extra water.
5. Bring a kettle of water to a boil.
6. Wash jars in hot soapy water and rinse. While jars are still hot, add 4 Tablespoons lemon juice or 1 teaspoon citric acid and crab to each pint jar to a 1-inch headspace (may use half the amount of acid for half-pint jars). Remove air bubbles and add more hot water if needed to maintain a 1-inch headspace.
7. Process jars at 10 pounds of pressure for 70 minutes for half-pints and 80 minutes for pints.
8. If using a dial-gauge-only pressure canner, use 11 pounds PSI. Follow pressure level according to your altitude and type of gauge.*
9. Turn off heat and allow pressure to reduce to zero naturally. When pressure is completely reduced, remove the lid and wait an additional 10 minutes. Remove jars, place on towels in a draft-free area, cool for 24 hours, check seals, and store.

***Altitude adjustments** see chart on page 50*

Process for crab and clams from the All-American Pressure Canner Instruction Manual

How to Freeze Crab

We've found crab meat to freeze incredibly well. Once thawed, the meat is delicious in soups, dips, or crab cakes.

1. Cook crab and shuck meat from claws and body.
2. Form and wrap meat from one crab (Dungeness) in plastic wrap into a tight log.
3. Flash freeze for approximately 10 minutes to help freeze the liquid.
4. Then vacuum freeze the wrapped log. Store in the deep freezer for up to a year.

CHAPTER 13
How to Preserve Soups and Stew

Canning combination recipes, which in usual references to canning means a combination of meat and vegetables such as a stew or soup, means ready-to-eat meals on the shelf.

When canning combination recipes, there are a few guidelines we need to follow. Remember, with soups from our Do NOT Can at Home list, no dairy, no thickeners, no pureed soups (no pureed butternut squash soup for example, but you could can it in cubes), no noodles, pasta, or rice in your soup recipes. You may can a recipe without those ingredients, such as chicken noodle soup with the chicken, broth, onions, carrots, and celery and then at the time of eating add your cooked noodles as you're heating the soup.

The rules for canning your combination recipes and soups are to follow a tested recipe from a reputable site/source such as an updated *Ball Complete Book of Home Preserving*, the USDA home food-preservation website (National Center for Home Food Preservation), or another up-to-date canning book or source. The split pea soup recipe in the *Ball Complete Book of Home Preserving* has instructions for liquefying the cooked peas in the soup and then canning, and because this is a tested recipe, we can safely follow these specific instructions. All dried beans or peas must be fully rehydrated following the instructions from our Canning Dried Beans or Peas section.

You may make up your own combination recipe by following the tested processing times and hot-pack instructions for vegetables and meats. Note: It has to be a vegetable or meat that has a tested time and process, no cabbage unless it is in an acidic sauerkraut canning recipe.

Use the vegetable processing time chart found on pages 162-166.

General guidelines are to can your soups at 10 pounds of pressure for a weighted-gauge canner and 11 pounds for dial-gauge for 60 minutes for pints and 75 minutes for quarts.

If your altitude is 1,000 feet or more above sea level, follow the altitude adjustment chart on page 50.

You must can the combination recipe to the longest processing time of your ingredients. For example, if you had leafy greens in your soup such as spinach, then you'd need to process the pints for 70 minutes and quarts for 90 minutes, not the above general guideline times.

You can use water, broth, or tomatoes for your liquid in your soups.

Prepare vegetables and meat as directed for hot-packing. Cool the meat and remove bones for anything that still has bone-in. If adding dried beans or peas, remember, for each cup of dried beans or peas, add 3 cups of water. Then boil for 2 minutes. Remove from heat and soak for 1 hour. Then heat to a boil again before draining.

When vegetables/meats are almost finished cooking for hot-pack, add your spices and seasonings/salt to taste if desired. Then, using a slotted spoon, fill your prepared clean jars with the solids of the soup ingredients to the halfway point. After all jars are filled halfway with the solid ingredients, fill to a 1-inch headspace with the liquid. Remove air bubbles and adjust if needed to a 1-inch headspace.

We fill the jars halfway with the solids to ensure each jar has the proper ratio of solids to liquid.

If you run short on liquid, have an extra kettle of hot water to top off the jar. You could also have a backup of boiling broth or tomato juice, but I find it easiest to top off with hot water. Whatever liquid you use, it must be hot at the time of adding it to the jar.

Wipe rim clean, place bands on fingertip tight, and place in prepared pressure canner. Secure lid, allow canner to vent steam for 10 minutes, then process according to time and pressure for your altitude and jars.

When done, turn off heat and allow pressure to reduce to zero naturally, then remove lid from canner. Wait 10 minutes before removing jars onto a towel and allow to cool for 24 hours. Check seals before storing.

You'll find additional tested recipes at the University of Kentucky and the Oregon State University Extension office websites.

Vegetable Soup Recipe

Adapted from Ball Complete Book of Home Preserving. *This is one of my favorite soup recipes. Not only is it a great way to preserve the summer harvest in one jar, but it has tons of flavor and is delicious for lunch, or make it for supper by dumping in a jar of canned chicken or beef.*

Yield: About 15 pints or 7 quarts

INGREDIENTS

- 10 cups of peeled and chopped tomatoes
- 5 cups peeled and chopped potatoes
- 5 cups peeled and thickly sliced carrots
- 4 cups green beans, snapped
- 4 cups fresh or frozen peas, thawed
- 2 cups sliced celery
- 2 cups chopped onions
- 8 cups water
- 4 bay leaves
- 2 tablespoons salt
- Freshly ground black pepper to taste

1. Prepare a pressure canner for a hot-pack (see pages 48-49 for more information), jars, lids, and bands.

2. In a large stainless-steel or nonreactive pot, combine all ingredients and bring to a boil. Turn down heat to a low boil and continue to cook for 15 minutes. Remove bay leaves.

3. Use a slotted spoon or ladle to fill prepared jars halfway with the solid vegetables. Pour hot liquid over solids to a 1-inch headspace, remove air bubbles, and adjust for headspace if necessary.

4. Wipe rim clean, screw bands on fingertip tight, and place in prepared pressure canner. Secure lid, allow canner to vent steam for 10 minutes, then process at 10 pounds of pressure for 60 minutes for pints and 75 minutes for quarts. If using a dial-gauge-only pressure canner, use 11 pounds PSI. Follow pressure level according to your altitude and type of gauge.*

5. Turn off heat and allow pressure to reduce to zero naturally. When pressure is completely reduced, remove the lid and wait an additional 10 minutes. Remove jars, place on towels in a draft-free area, cool for 24 hours, check seals, and store.

***Altitude adjustments** see chart on page 50

Chicken Pot Pie in a Jar

Adapted from Hearty Chicken Stew in The All-New Ball Book of Canning and Preserving

Yield: Approximately 6 pints

INGREDIENTS

3 tablespoons butter

1½ cups diced onion

1½ cups diced carrots

1 cup diced potatoes (Yukon gold or German Butterball)

½ cup diced celery

5 cups chicken broth

1 teaspoon dried oregano

1 teaspoon salt

½ teaspoon ground black pepper

3 cups 1-inch-cubed boneless, skinless, raw chicken

½ cup fresh or frozen sweet peas (thaw if using frozen)

1 tablespoon bottled lemon juice

*Altitude adjustments see chart on page 50

1. Prepare a pressure canner for a hot-pack (see pages 48-49 for more information), jars, lids, and bands.

2. In a large stainless-steel stockpot or enamel-covered Dutch oven, melt butter, and sauté onions for 3 minutes. Add carrots, potatoes, and celery and sauté another 2 minutes.

3. Stir in broth, oregano, salt, and pepper. Bring contents to a boil, reduce heat to a simmer, and cook uncovered until vegetables are soft, approximately 10 minutes. Remove from heat.

4. Stir in prepped chicken, peas, and lemon juice.

5. Ladle solids into prepared jars to half full. Ladle broth to a 1-inch headspace. Remove air bubbles and add more liquid if needed to maintain headspace.

6. Wipe rim clean, place bands on fingertip tight, and place in prepared pressure canner. Secure lid, allow canner to vent steam for 10 minutes, then process pints at 10 pounds of pressure for 1 hour and 15 minutes. If using a dial-gauge-only pressure canner, use 11 pounds PSI. Follow pressure level according to your altitude and type of gauge.*

7. Turn off heat and allow pressure to reduce to zero naturally. When pressure is completely reduced, remove the lid and wait an additional 10 minutes. Remove jars, place on towels in a draft-free area, cool for 24 hours, check seals, and store.

To make a pot pie, drain and reserve the liquid. Melt 2 tablespoons butter or lard in a 9-inch skillet over medium heat. Stir in 2 tablespoons flour and cook until it turns brown, approximately 3 to 5 minutes. Slowly whisk in broth. If you need more liquid, add in milk or additional broth. For gluten-free, reserve ½ cup of the drained broth, and pour rest in with melted fat. Whisk in 2 tablespoons cornstarch or potato starch in the ½ cup of reserved liquid. Whisk into the pan. Once it's turned bubbly and thick, fold in strained pot pie ingredients and place in the prepared 9-inch pie crust and bake.

Hearty Beef Stew

Adapted from Ball Blue Book Guide to Preserving

Yield: Approximately 14 pints or 7 quarts (recipe may be halved)

INGREDIENTS

1 tablespoon oil

12 cups peeled and cubed potatoes

8 cups peeled and thickly sliced carrots

3 cups green beans, snapped

3 cups diced celery

2 cups diced onion

4 to 5 pounds stewing beef

4½ teaspoons salt

1 teaspoon dried oregano or thyme

½ teaspoon ground black pepper

Boiling water

1. Prepare a pressure canner for a hot-pack (see pages 48-49 for more information), jars, lids, and bands.

2. In a large skillet (I prefer cast iron), heat oil over medium-high heat. Brown the beef, working in batches—do not add extra oil unless it's absolutely necessary.

3. Transfer browned beef to a large stainless-steel stockpot and add potatoes, carrots, celery, green beans, onions, and seasonings. Pour over enough boiling water to cover and bring to a boil, stirring frequently.

4. Once stew is boiling, carefully ladle into prepared hot pint or quart jars to a 1-inch headspace. Remove air bubbles; add more liquid if needed to maintain headspace. Wipe rim with a vinegar-moistened towel, place bands on fingertip tight, and place in a prepared pressure canner.

5. Secure lid, allow canner to vent steam for 10 minutes, then process at 10 pounds of pressure for 75 minutes for pints and 90 minutes for quarts. If using a dial-gauge-only pressure canner, use 11 pounds PSI. Follow pressure level according to your altitude and type of gauge.*

6. Turn off heat and allow pressure to reduce to zero naturally. When pressure is completely reduced, remove the lid and wait an additional 10 minutes. Remove jars, place on towels in a draft-free area, cool for 24 hours, check seals, and store.

*Altitude adjustments see chart on page 50

The stew you see pictured here was prepared with individual jars of canned ingredients. While it's great to have a jar of stew all in one jar for quick grab and go, you can make many a soup or stew from your individually preserved foods.

To make stew from the vegetables and meat on your shelves, follow the recipe on the next page.

Larder Stew

INGREDIENTS

1 onion, diced

1 pint canned carrots

1 pint canned green beans

1 pint canned cubed venison (or any other cubed/chunked red meat)

½ cup dehydrated* or freeze-dried red bell pepper

3 tablespoons butter, lard, or coconut oil

2 tablespoons flour (for gluten-free, see note)

1. To make stew, heat fat in a large saucepan or Dutch oven. Melt 1 tablespoon butter or lard in a 9-inch skillet over medium heat; sauté onions. When onions are translucent, melt an additional 2 tablespoons fat. Stir in 2 tablespoons flour and mix together until it forms a paste. Cook until it turns brown, approximately 3 to 5 minutes.

2. Slowly whisk in the liquid from your meat and allow to cook until it bubbles and thickens. Add in more liquid from vegetables if needed to desired consistency (I like it closer to gravy—nice and thick). When desired consistency is met, stir in the drained vegetables and freeze-dried bell pepper and allow to simmer until heated.

*30 minutes before cooking, pour 1 cup boiling water over the dehydrated bell peppers. Allow them to soak and reconstitute and then add to stew with other vegetables.

Note: Gluten-free: Reserve ½ cup of the drained broth, and pour rest in with melted fat. Whisk in 2 tablespoons cornstarch or potato starch in the ½ cup of reserved liquid. Whisk into the pan. Once it's turned bubbly and thick, stir in remaining ingredients.

Chili Con Carne

Adapted from the National Center for Home Food Preservation recipe

Yield: Approximately 9 pints

INGREDIENTS

3 cups dried pinto or red kidney beans (I like a navy or black bean)

5½ cups water

5 teaspoons salt (separated)

3 pounds ground beef or stewing meat (if using stewing meat, add 1 tablespoon oil)

1½ cups chopped onion

1 cup chopped peppers of your choice (optional)

1 teaspoon black pepper

3 to 6 tablespoons chili powder

½ teaspoon ground cinnamon (trust me, but optional)

2 quarts crushed or whole tomatoes

Boiling water

1. Prepare a pressure canner for a hot-pack (see pages 48-49 for more information), jars, lids, and bands.

2. Rinse and sort beans. Place in a large bowl and cover with 2 to 3 inches of cold water. Soak for 8 to 12 hours; drain and discard water. (To do a quick soak, see beans, dry on page 172.)

3. Combine beans in a large saucepan with 5½ cups fresh cold water and 2 teaspoons salt; bring to a boil. Reduce heat to a simmer and cook for 30 minutes. Drain and discard water.

4. In a large skillet (I prefer cast iron), heat oil over medium-high heat. Brown the beef, working in batches; do not add extra oil unless it's absolutely necessary. Sauté onions and peppers. When sautéed, drain the fat.

5. Add the remaining 3 teaspoons salt, pepper, chili powder, cinnamon, tomatoes, and drained beans. Simmer for 5 minutes only—do not keep cooking to reduce liquid or use any thickener.

6. Carefully ladle chili into prepared hot pint jars to a 1-inch headspace. Remove air bubbles; add more liquid if needed to maintain headspace (keep a kettle of just-boiled water at the ready if you don't have enough liquid). Wipe rim with a vinegar moistened towel, place bands on fingertip tight, and place in a prepared pressure canner.

7. Secure lid, allow canner to vent steam for 10 minutes, then process pints at 10 pounds of pressure for 75 minutes. If using a dial-gauge-only pressure canner, use 11 pounds PSI. Follow pressure level according to your altitude and type of gauge.*

8. Turn off heat and allow pressure to reduce to zero naturally. When pressure is completely reduced, remove the lid and wait an additional 10 minutes. Remove jars, place on towels in a draft-free area, cool for 24 hours, check seals, and store.

*****Altitude adjustments** *see chart on page 50*

Quick and Fast Larder Chili

The photo on the facing page is chili made from pantry staples, or at least my pantry staples, and now that you have this book, soon to be yours.

Yield: 4 servings

INGREDIENTS

1 pint salsa

1 pint canned shelled beans

1 pint canned ground or cubed beef or venison

1 to 2 tablespoons chili powder (or however hot you like it)

1 tablespoon ground cumin

2 teaspoons powdered garlic

2 teaspoons powdered onion

Freshly ground pepper to taste

1. Dump the contents from all three jars into a saucepan and heat to a simmer on medium heat.
2. Stir in spices and seasonings to taste.
3. Top with some sour cream (or plain yogurt), shredded cheese, and enjoy!

Freeze-Drying Soups/Stews

You can freeze-dry any soup, stew, or pot pie filling. The beauty of freeze-drying is that we don't have to be concerned with omitting ingredients for safety because freeze-dried food is well beneath the moisture percentage for botulism growth.

The below instructions are for fully cooked soups, stews, or pot pie fillings.

1. To freeze-dry, fill your trays to just below the rim (never overfill). You can pre-freeze in the deep freezer or let the machine do it.
2. Start machine.
3. When the machine is finished, check for any cold spots. I do this by taste-testing cooked foods at the thickest (or largest) piece. Alternatively, you could use an infrared thermometer to identify cold spots. If any spot is cold to the touch still, select more dry time.
4. Once food is finished, immediately crumble and place it in jars or Mylar bags and seal.
5. To serve, pour 1 part boiling water* over 2 parts freeze-dried soup/stew/pot pie filling. Add more water if needed to reach desired consistency. Allow it to absorb for a few minutes and enjoy. For pot pie filling, roll out your favorite crust, spoon the reconstituted filling inside, and bake at 400°F/204°C until crust is golden brown (approximately 30 minutes).

Start with slightly less water the first time to make sure it's the consistency you desire. You can always add more water, but you can't take it out if it's too runny.

Conclusion

While this may be the end of this book, it is just the beginning of your journey. I have been preserving food for my family for over twenty years (which seems odd to type because in my mind, I still think of myself as being in my twenties), yet two decades have passed since then, and I am still learning new recipes and methods.

Be warned, you too might be adding on a second room for a walk-in larder, and I will gladly take all the blame for it. Our food is our medicine. I know this better than most.

It should not be something we trust blindly to others and have no personal part in. If you've made it this far in the book, then you agree.

I invite you to continue your food-preserving journey with me at MelissaKNorris.com/PreservingBookResources. It is there you can join me and the thousands of others just like you who are creating art that nourishes our bodies and fills stomachs with home-preserved goodness. You'll find additional resources there. I put as much into this book as I could but, alas, there was only so much room.

Preserving food and cooking are art. And art is made to be shared, is it not?

Here's my Mason jar raised to yours as we continue on this path together.

Index

Apple
- Applesauce 289
- Apple Butter 286
- Apple Juice Canning 283
- Apple Pie Filling 288
- Apple Preserving Chart/Canning Apple Slices 284
- Blackberry Jelly 298
- Dehydrated Cinnamon Apples 292
- Dehydrating 68
- Fermented Cranberry Sauce 317
- Freezing 88
- Fruit Leather 291
- Jam/Jelly Master Recipe 272-273
- Low-Sugar Apple Pie Jam 285
- Peach Jam 348
- Pectin Source Chart 278
- Plum Jam 357
- Raw Apple Cider Vinegar 293
- Root Cellar Storage Chart 124
- Storing Apples with Potatoes 138

Apricot
- Dehydrating 68
- Freezing 88
- Jam/Jelly Master Recipe 272
- Pectin Source Chart 278
- Preserving Chart/Canning Apricots 294

Aronia berry
- Dehydrating 69
- Preserving Chart 295

Asparagus
- Asparagus Preserving Chart/Pressure Canning Asparagus 167-168
- Dehydrating 63
- Freezing/Blanching Chart 80-81
- Pickled 171
- Pressure Canning Chart 162
- Root Cellar Storage Chart 125

Avocado
- Avocado Preserving Chart 295

Banana
- Banana Preserving Chart 295
- Dehydrating 69
- Freezing 87-88
- Winter Squash Banana Preserving Chart 246

Beans
Dry
- Freezing/Blanching Chart 81
- Pork and Beans Molasses Style Recipe 176
- Pressure Canning Chart 162
- Preserving Chart, Beans, Dry, Shelled 173
- Shelled-Pressure Canning 172-174

Green
- Dehydrating 63
- Dilly Beans 179
- Freezing 81
- Fermented Garlic Green Beans 180
- Leather Britches 182-183
- Pressure Canning Chart 162
- Preserving Chart/Pressure Canning 177-178

Beef
- Beef Broth 382-384
- Beef Salami Recipe 389
- Chili Con Carne 417
- Freezer Space Chart 98
- Meat Pressure Canning Chart 376-380
- Hearty Beef Stew 413
- Larder Stew 415
- Pressure Canning Beef Strips/Cubes/Chunks 390
- Pressure Canning Ground/Chopped Beef 388
- Quick and Fast Larder Chili 419

Beets
- Dehydrating Chart 63
- Freezing/Blanching Chart 81
- Freezing Instructions 84
- Fermenting Brine Percentage Chart 106
- Root Cellar Options 119
- Root Cellar Storage Chart 125
- Pressure Canning Chart 163
- Preserving Chart/Pressure Canning 184-185
- Sweet Cinnamon Pickled Beets 187-188

Blackberry
- Blackberry Pie Filling 299
- Dehydrating 69
- Freezing 88
- Jam/Jelly Master Recipe 272
- No Pectin Old-Fashioned Blackberry Jelly 298
- Pectin Source Chart 278
- Preserving Chart/Canning Blackberries 297

Blueberry
    Blubarb Jam 303
    Blueberry Basil Thyme Vinegar 306
    Blueberry Syrup 305
    Dehydrating 69
    Freezing 88
    Jam/Jelly Master Recipe 272
    Low-Sugar Blueberry Jam Without Pectin 302
    Pectin Source Chart 278
    Preserving Chart/Canning Blueberries 301

Broccoli
    Broccoli Preserving Chart 189
    Dehydrating 63
    Freezing 81
    Fermenting Brine Percentage Chart 106

Broth
    Broth Preserving Chart 378
    Broth Processing Times Chart 384
    Broth Storage Options 379
    Chicken Pot Pie in a Jar 410
    Flavoring Broth 380
    How to Make Broth 382-383
    Larder Stew 415
    Pressure Canning tutorial 47-48
    Pressure Canning Chart 376

Brussels sprouts
    Brussels Sprouts Preserving Chart 189
    Dehydrating 64
    Freezing 81
    Root Cellar Storage Chart 125
    Seasonal Harvest Chart 24-25

Cabbage
    Cabbage Preserving Chart 189
    Curtido 192
    Dehydrating 64
    Fermenting Brine Solution Chart 106
    Freezing 81
    Root Cellar 119-120
    Root Cellar Storage Chart 126-127
    Salt Gram to Volume Fermenting Chart 110
    Sauerkraut Making Tutorial 104-105
    Seasonal Harvest Chart 24
    Traditional Sauerkraut 191

Cantaloupe
    Cantaloupe Preserving Chart 307
    Dehydrating 69
    Freezing 89
    Root Cellar Storage Chart 129

Carrots
    Broth 382
    Carrot Preserving Chart 193

Carrots (cont.)
    Chicken Pot Pie in a Jar 410
    Curtido 192
    Dehydrating 64
    Fermented Carrots 195
    Freezing 81
    Fermenting Brine Solution Chart 106
    Hearty Beef Stew 413
    Larder Stew 415
    Jardiniere Recipe 198
    Pressure Canning Chart 163 and 165
    Pressure Canning Tutorial 194
    Root Cellar Options 119
    Root Cellar Storage Chart 126
    Seasonal Harvest Chart 25
    Vegetable Soup 409

Cauliflower
    Cauliflower Preserving Chart 197
    Dehydrating 64
    Freezing 81
    Fermenting Brine Solution Chart 106
    Jardiniere Recipe 198
    Root Cellar Storage Chart 127
    Seasonal Harvest Chart 24-25

Celery
    Celery Preserving Chart and Celery Salt 199
    Chicken Pot Pie in a Jar 410
    Dehydrating 64
    Fermenting Brine Solution Chart 106
    Freezing 82
    Hearty Beef Stew 413
    Jardiniere Recipe 198
    Root Cellar Storage Chart 127
    Seasonal Harvest Chart 25
    Vegetable Soup 409

Cherry
    Cherry Pie Filling 312
    Cherry Pit Vinegar 313
    Cherry Preserving Chart - Sour 307
    Cherry Preserving Chart and Canning - Sweet 309
    Dehydrating 69
    Freezing 89
    Fruit pH and Pectin Level Chart Cherry 278
    Low-Sugar Cherry Jam Without Pectin 310
    Seasonal Harvest Chart 25

Chicken
    Broth Canning Times Chart 384
    Broth Storage Options 379
    Canning Chicken Broth 382-383
    Chicken Broth Tips 380
    Chicken Pot Pie in a Jar 410

Chicken (cont.)
    Dehydrating Food Temp Chart 61
    Freezing Meat 98
    Freezer Space Chart 99
    Meat Pressure Canning Chart Bone-in 376
    Meat Pressure Canning Chart Boneless 377
    Non-Acidic Foods to Pressure Can, Chart 32
    Preserving Chart - Poultry 386

Corn
    Dehydrating 69
    Freezing 89
    Preserving Chart - Freezing Tutorial - Sweet 200
    Pressure Can Corn 201
    Seasonal Harvest Chart 25

Cranberry
    Dehydrating 69
    Freezing 89
    Fruit pH and Pectin Level Chart Cranberry 279
    Cranberry Jelly 316
    Cranberry Juice Canning 283
    Cranberry Preserving Chart 314
    Cranberry Sauce 315
    Cranberry Sauce Fermented 317
    Seasonal Harvest Chart 25

Cucumber
    Bread and Butter Refrigerator Pickle 210
    Brine Percentage Chart 107
    Cucumber Preserving Chart 202
    Fermented Pickles 203
    Garlic Dill Pickles 206
    How to Make Pickles 204
    Jardiniere Recipe 198
    Mustard Pickle Relish 208
    Pickling 44-46
    Seasonal Harvest Chart 24

Currant
    Currant Preserving Chart and Canning 318
    Dehydrating 70
    Freezing 89
    Fruit pH and Pectin Level Chart Cranberry 279
    Pectin Source 272-273
    Raspberry Red Currant Jelly 361
    Seasonal Harvest Chart 25

Dewberry
    Dehydrating 70
    Dewberry Preserving Chart and Canning 319
    Freezing 90

Eggplant
    Dehydrating 65
    Eggplant Preserving Chart 211

Eggplant (cont.)
    Freezing 82
    Seasonal Harvest Chart 24

Fig
    Dehydrating 70
    Fig Preserving Chart and Canning 320
    Freezing 90
    Fruit pH and Pectin Level Chart 279
    Seasonal Harvest Chart 25

Fish
    Canning Fish - Blue Mackerel, Salmon, Steelhead Trout 397
    Canning Smoked Salmon 398
    Canning Tuna 400
    Dehdyrating Temperature Chart 61
    Fish Preserving Chart 395
    Pressure Canning Chart - Fish 378

Garlic
    Bruschetta in a Jar 262
    Cooking Leather Britches 183
    Curtido 192
    Dehydrating 65
    Dilly Beans 179
    Fermented Carrots 195
    Fermented Cucumber Pickles 203
    Fermented Garlic 213
    Fermented Garlic Beans 180
    Fermented Salsa 264
    Fermented Sugar Snap Peas 225
    Fermenting Brine Percentage Solution Chart 107
    Fresh Summer Salsa 260
    Garlic Dill Pickles 206
    Leekchi 216
    Long-Term Storage Varieties 123
    Peach Salsa 347
    Pickled Asparagus 171
    Pickled Beets 188
    Pickled Garlic 214
    Preserving Chart Garlic 211
    Pulled Pork in a Jar 393
    Red Pepper Garlic Jelly 230
    Root Cellar Curing Chart 121-122
    Root Cellar Storage Chart 127
    Root Cellar Success Tips 137
    Sauerkraut 191
    Sweet and Spicy Plum Sauce 358
    Quick and Fast Larder Chili 419

Gooseberry
    Dehydrating Chart 70
    Freezing 90
    Fruit pH and Pectin Level Chart 279

Index | 427

Gooseberry (cont.)
    Preserving Chart and Canning 321

Grape
    Dehydrating Chart 70
    Dehydrating Grapes (Raisins) 324
    Freezing 90
    Fruit Juice Processing Chart 283
    Fruit pH and Pectin Level Chart 279
    Grape Juice 277
    How to Can Grape Juice 326
    Jar Size Use Chart 15
    Low-Sugar Vanilla Grape Jelly 325
    Preserving Chart Canning Grapes Whole 323
    White Crystals with Grape Products 54

Grapefruit
    Dehydrating Chart 70
    Freezing 91
    Fruit pH and Pectin Level Chart 279
    Root Cellar Storage Chart 128
    Preserving Chart - Canning Grapefruit 327
    Seasonal Harvest Chart 24

Greens
    Dehydrating 65
    Freezing/Blanching Chart 82
    Pressure Canning Chart 163
    Pressure Canning Spinach and
        Leafy Greens 244
    Preserving Chart and Canning - Kale 215
    Preserving Chart and Canning Spinach and
        Leafy Greens 243

Honeyberry
    Preserving Chart 327

Kale
    Dehydrating 65
    Preserving Chart and Canning - Kale 215
    Root Cellar Options 119
    Seasonal Harvest Chart 24-25

Kiwi
    Dehydrating Chart 71
    Freezing Chart 91
    Fruit pH and Pectin Level Chart 279
    Preserving Chart 329

Kumquat
    Dehydrating Chart 71
    Freezing Chart 91
    Fruit pH and Pectin Level Chart 279
    Preserving Chart 329

Leeks
    Leekchi Recipe 216
    Preserving Chart 215

Leeks (cont.)
    Root Cellar Storage Chart 128
    Seasonal Harvest Chart 25

Lemon
    Acid Amounts Per Jar Tomatoes 252
    Browning Preventative Chart 269
    Dehydrating 71
    Dehydrated Lemon Slices 332
    Fermented Lemons 333
    Flavor Options Sauerkraut 191
    Freezing Chart 92
    Fruit pH and Pectin Level Chart 279
    How to Can Tomato Sauce 258
    Jam and Jelly Master Recipe 272-273
    Lemon Marmalade 334
    Preserving Chart 331
    Pressure Can Clams/Crab 402-403
    Pretreating Fruit 68
    Raw Pack Tomatoes 253
    Seasonal Harvest Chart 24
    Tomatoes Packed in Water 254

Lettuce
    Preserving Chart 217
    Seasonal Harvest Guide 24

Lime
    Blubarb Jam 303
    Dehydrating 71
    Fermented Salsa 264
    Freezing Chart 92
    Fresh Summer Salsa 260
    Fruit pH and Pectin Level Chart 279
    Jam and Jelly Master Recipe 272-273
    Low-Sugar Blueberry Jam Without Pectin 302
    Preserving Chart 335
    Seasonal Harvest Chart 24

Loganberry
    Dehydrating 71
    Freezing Chart 92
    Fruit pH and Pectin Level Chart 280
    Preserving Chart 335

Melon
    Dehydrating 71
    Freezing Chart 92
    Root Cellar Storage Chart 129
    Preserving Chart 336

Mulberry
    Freezing Chart 92
    Fruit pH and Pectin Level Chart 280
    Preserving Chart 336

Nectarine
    Dehydrating Chart 71

Nectarine (cont.)
    Freezing Chart 93
    Fruit pH and Pectin Level Chart 280
    Preserving Chart 337

Okra
    Dehydrating Chart 65
    Freezing Chart 83
    Preservation Method Chart 217
    Pressure Canning,
        Processing Time Chart 163 165
    Pressure Can Okra 218
    Seasonal Harvest Chart 24

Onions
    Chicken Pot Pie in a Jar 410
    Chili Con Carne 417
    Dehydrating Chart 66
    Fermented Radish and Onion Pickles 241
    Fermented Salsa 264
    Freezing, Boiling 83
    Hearty Beef Stew 413
    Larder Stew 415
    Long-Term Storage
        Curing Process 121-122, 137-138
    Mustard Pickle Relish 208
    Preservation Method Chart 219
    Root Cellar Storage Chart 129
    Seasonal Harvest Chart 24-25
    Tomatoes and Zucchini 245
    Vegetable Soup Recipe 409

Orange
    Cranberry Sauce 315
    Dehydrating Chart 72
    Dehydrated (Orange) Slices 332
    Freezing Chart 93
    Fruit pH and Pectin Level Chart 280
    Mandarin Oranges 340
    Orange Leather 341
    Orange Marmalade 342
    Preservation Method Chart 339
    Rhubarb Strawberry Pie Filling 365
    Seasonal Harvest Chart 24

Papaya
    Dehydrating Chart 72
    Freezing Chart 93
    Fruit pH and Pectin Level Chart 280
    Preservation Method Chart 339
    Seasonal Harvest Chart 24

Parsnip
    Preservation Method Chart 219
    Pressure Can Parsnip Chart 219-220
    Root Cellaring 130
    Seasonal Harvest Chart 24-25

Pea
    Field 221
    Sugar Snap 223

Peach
    Dehydrating Chart 72
    Freezing Chart 94
    Fruit pH and Pectin Level Chart 280
    Jam and Jelly Master Recipe 272
    Peach Salsa 347
    Peach Jam, No Store-Bought Pectin 348
    Preservation Method Chart 345
    Seasonal Harvest Chart 24

Pear
    Dehydrating Chart 63
    Drying Time in a Dehydrator 72
    Jam and Jelly Master Recipe 273
    Pectin Level Chart 280
    Preventing Discoloration 87
    Preserving Method Chart 350-352
    Seasonal Harvest Chart 25
    Type of Pack 94

Peppers
    Hot
    Fermenting Brine Percentage 107
    Pressure Canning
        Processing Time Chart 163-165
    Preservation Methods Chart 227

    Sweet
    Freezing, Boiling, Blanching Chart 83
    Preservation Methods Chart 229
    Red Pepper Garlic Jelly 215

Pineapple
    Drying Time in Dehydrator 72
    Flavoring Options Sauerkraut 191
    How to Flash Freeze 87
    Pectin Level 280
    Preserving Method Chart 354
    Seasonal Harvest Chart 24
    Type of Pack 94

Plum
    Drying Time in Dehydrator 72
    How to Can Fruit Butters 277
    Jam and Jelly Master Recipe 272
    Pectin Level 280
    Plum Recipes 355-358
    Seasonal Harvest Chart 24
    Syrup Pack 94
    Vegetable Dehydrating Chart 63

Pork
    Canning Ground Meat 388

Pork (cont.)
- For Meat Strips, Cubes, or Chunks 390
- Freezing, Whole Pig, Half Pig Chart 99
- Home-Canned Pork and Beans,
  Molasses Style 175
- Non-Acidic Foods to Pressure Can Chart 32
- Preservation Method Chart 391
- Pressure Canning Processing Time Chart 377
- Pulled Pork in a Jar 393

Potatoes
- Chicken Pot Pie in a Jar 410
- Curing tips 123-124
- Dehydrating Chart 66
- Fermenting Brine Percentage Chart 107
- Freezing, Boiling, Blanching Chart 83-84
- Freezer Hash Browns 234
- Hearty Beef Stew 413
- Potatoes Root Cellaring Chart 131
- Pressure Can Potatoes 233
- Pressure Canning Chart
  Process Time Chart 164-166
- Preservation Chart 232
- Root Cellaring Tips 137-138
- Sweet Potatoes — Preservation Chart 248
- Pressure Can Sweet Potatoes 249
- Seasonal Harvest Chart 24-25
- Sweet Potatoes Root Cellaring Chart 133
- Vegetable Soup Recipe 409

Poultry
- Broth Storage Options 379
- Non-Acidic Foods to Pressure Can Chart 32
- Preservation Method Chart 386

Pumpkin
- Freezing, Boiling, Blanching 84
- How to Can Fruit Bitters 277
- How to Prepare Vegetables 237-238
- Pressure Canning Processing Times 164, 166
- Pumpkin Puree 240
- Reprocessing When a Jar Doesn't Seal 54
- Root Cellar Storage 131
- Seasonal Harvest Chart 25
- Squash Winter 246
- The Do-NOT-Can-at-Home List 34

Radish
- Fermenting Brine Percentage 107
- Fermented Radish and Onion Pickles 241
- Preservation Method Chart 241
- Seasonal Harvest Chart 24

Raspberry
- Dehydrating Chart 73
- Freezing Chart 95

Raspberry (cont.)
- Jam and Jelly Master Recipe 273
- Fruit pH and Pectin Level Chart 281
- Raspberry Red Currant Jelly 318, 360-361

Rhubarb
- Blurbarb Jam 303
- Dehydrating Chart 73
- Freezing 95
- Fruit pH and Pectin Level Chart 281
- No Pectin Strawberry Rhubarb Jam 369
- Preservation Method Chart 362
- Rhubarb BBQ Sauce 363
- Rhubarb Strawberry Pie Filling 365
- Seasonal Harvest Chart 24
- Strawberry Rhubarb Fruit Leather 372
- Strawberry Rhubarb Jam using
  Powdered Pectin 368

Rutabaga
- Freezing, Boiling, Blanching Chart 83
- Preservation Method Chart 242
- Root Cellaring 132
- Seasonal Harvest Chart 24-25

Salmon
- How to Preserve Fish 397
- Smoked Salmon 398

Squash

  Acorn
  - Root Cellaring Chart 132

  Summer
  - Dehydrating Chart 63
  - Freezing, Boiling, Blanching 84
  - Preservation Method Chart 245
  - Seasonal Harvest Chart 25

  Winter
  - Dehydrating Chart 63
  - Freezing, Boiling, Blanching 84
  - Root Cellaring Chart 133
  - Pressure Canning
    Processing Time Chart 164, 166
  - Preservation Method Chart 246

Strawberry
- Dehydrating Chart 73
- Freezing Chart 95
- Jam and Jelly Master Recipe 272
- Fruit pH and Pectin Level Chart 281
- Low-Sugar No Pectin Strawberry Jam 371
- No Pectin Strawberry Rhubarb Jam 369
- Preservation Method Chart 367
- Rhubarb Strawberry Pie Filling 365
- Strawberry Rhubarb Fruit Leather 372

Strawberry (cont.)
    Strawberry Rhubarb Jam
        Using Powdered Pectin 368

Sweet potatoes
    Curing Chart 123
    Freezing, Boiling, Blanching 83-84
    Preservation Method Chart 248
    Pressure Can Sweet Potatoes 249
    Root Cellar Storage Chart 133
    Root Cellar Tips 137
    Season Harvest Chart 25

Tomatoes
    Bruschetta in a Jar Using a Steam Canner 263
    Chili Con Carne 417
    Dehydrating Chart 66
    Fermented Salsa 265
    Fermenting Brine Percentage Chart 107
    Freezing, Boiling, Blanching 84
    Fresh Summer Salsa Recipe 261
    Home Canning Tomatoes 251
    How to Can Tomato Sauce 258
    How to Make Tomato Sauce 256-257
    Jar Size and Headspace for Canning Chart 35
    Preservation Method Chart 250
    Raw-Packed Tomatoes Without Liquid 253
    Seasonal Harvest Chart 24-25
    Tomatoes Packed in Water 254
    Vegetable Soup Recipe 409

Turnips
    Freezing Chart 84
    Fermenting Chart 107
    Preservation Method Chart 265
    Root Cellaring 133
    Seasonal Harvest Chart 24-25
    Store Separate from Celery
        When Root Cellaring Chart 127

Watermelon
    Best to Flash Freeze 87
    Dehydrating Chart 73
    Freezing Instructions Chart 95
    Preservation Methods 373
    Strawberry Pie Filling — See Rhubarb
        Watermelon 373

Zucchini
    Freezing, Boiling, Blanching 84
    Preservation Method Chart 245
    Root Cellar Storage 134
    Seasonal Harvest Chart 24
    Tomatoes Zucchini Recipe 245
    Zucchini Noodles, Dehydrate 20

Resources

The Made from Scratch Life

Ball Complete Book of Home Preserving

The New Ball Book of Canning and Preserving

The Ultimate Dehydrator Cookbook
by Tammy Gangloff

Root Cellaring: Natural Cold Storage of Fruits & Vegetables
by Mike and Nancy Bubel

The Complete Root Cellar Book
by Steve Maxwell and Jennifer MacKenzie

Notes

1 | Barbara H. Ingham, "Elderberries: beautiful to look at, not for canning," June 5, 2020, https://fyi.extension.wisc.edu/safefood/2020/06/05/elderberries-beautiful-to-look-at-not-for-canning/

2 | Pomona's Universal Pectin, "Developing or Converting Recipes for Cooked Jam or Jelly Using Pomona's Pectin," https://pomonapectin.com/developing-your-own-recipes-for-cooked-jam-or-jelly-using-pomonas/

3 | P. Kendall and J. Sofos, "Drying Fruits Colorado State University Fact Sheet," 8/94, revised 6/12, https://foodsafety.ces.ncsu.edu/wp-content/uploads/2017/06/Drying-Fruits-CSU-fact-sheet.pdf?fwd=no

4 | Patricia A. DiPersio, Patricia A. Kendall, Mehmet Calicioglu, John N Sofos, "Inactivation of *Salmonella* during drying and storage of apple slices treated with acidic or sodium metabisulfite solutions," December 2003, https://pubmed.ncbi.nlm.nih.gov/14672220/

5 | Patricia A. DiPersioa, Patricia A. Kendalla, John N. Sofosb, Inactivation of *Listeria monocytogenes* during drying and storage of peach slices treated with acidic or sodium metabisulfite solutions," Food Microbiology Volume 21, Issue 6, December 2004, pages 641-648, https://www.sciencedirect.com/science/article/abs/pii/S0740002004000528#!

6 | Charlotte P. Brennand, "Conditioning or Curing of Dried Fruits and Vegetables," Utah State University, https://extension.usu.edu/preserve-the-harvest/research/drying-conditioning-curing-fruits-vegetables

7 | Nora Olson, 2009 Potato Dormancy, University of Idaho, https://www.uidaho.edu/-/media/UIdaho-Responsive/Files/cals/programs/potatoes/Storage/Dormancy-overview-2009.pdf

8 | SP 50-694, revised February 2015, Oregon State University Extension Service, https://extension.oregonstate.edu/sites/default/files/documents/8836/sp50694preservingasianpears.pdf

About the Author

Melissa K. Norris helps almost a million people each month live a healthier and homemade life with simple modern homesteading through her website, popular Pioneering Today Podcast, the Pioneering Today Academy, and her books.

Melissa lives with her husband and two kids in the foothills of the North Cascade Mountains. When she's not chasing chickens or playing with plants, you can find her stuffing food in Mason jars (after washing her hands, of course), or creating something delicious in a cast-iron skillet and sharing it with others.

To make sure you're one of the people she's sharing it with along with other resources, subscribe to her free e-mail newsletter by visiting **MelissaKNorris.com**.